Law & Reality

The daring publisher, Universal Law Publishing Company, among the foremost in the law publishing field and progressive in venturing to bring out rare legal literature of avant garde *character has rightly enriched the* corpus juris *of India*

Justice V R Krishna Iyer
Random Reflections, page 14

Law & Reality

Justice Devi Prasad Singh
Judge, Allahabad High Court, Lucknow Bench

Universal
Law Publishing Co. Pvt. Ltd.
NEW DELHI - INDIA

2014 Edition

ISBN: 978-93-5035-391-2

Published by

Universal
Law Publishing Co. Pvt. Ltd.
NEW DELHI - INDIA

A-58, G.T. Karnal Road Industrial Area,
(Near Azadpur Metro Station), Delhi-110033
Tel. : 011-47082254, 27458529, 27215334 Fax : 011-27458529
e-mail: unilaw@vsnl.com

- Showroom : C-27, Connaught Place, New Delhi-110001
- Sales : sales@unilawbooks.com
- Editorial : edit@unilawbooks.com
- Website : **www.unilawbooks.com**

Join us on Facebook
www.facebook.com/unilawbooks

Recommended citation: Justice Devi Prasad Singh, *Law & Reality* (New Delhi: Universal Law Publishing Co. Pvt. Ltd., 2014)

Computer Typeset at Aesthetic and *Printed* at Glorious Printers, Delhi.

Preface

Every lecture or speech given on an occasion or article written for souvenir or journals involve application of mind and consume time. Ordinarily the thought flowing from such lectures or articles disappear from people's mind or forgotten in due course of time being spread over multiple forum. Sometime an idea or a thought expressed may be valuable asset to society. I have committed myself to deliver number of addresses and written articles, as the Member of Bar as well as while holding the August Office of High Court Judge. The views expressed in a judgment and order passed may be binding subject to finality by Supreme Court but opinion expressed at other forum are persuasive and thought-provoking.

"Democracy must also be seen in terms of the capacity to enrich reasoned engagement through enhancing informational availability and the feasibility of interactive discussions. Democracy has to be judged not just by the institutions that formally exist (judiciary, bureaucracy or legislature) but by the extent to which different voices from diverse sections of the people can actually be heard".[1]

The process of gradual change is the life of law not only constitutional but statutory provisions are also organic body subject to judicial legislation.[2]

'Philosophy of Life-Random Thought' is a book containing compilation of speeches and articles where I have dealt with human life broadly on philosophy laying down the foundation of social life.[3]

---

1. The idea of justice, Amartya Sen, page xiii.
2. *Vishwanath Chaturvedi* v. *Union of India,* 2011 (29) LCD 454.
3. Published by Rapid Book Service, Lucknow in 2011.

'Morality in law', another book authored by me canvass for unification of law, morality and education.[1]

Instant book is the another compilation of my articles published in different journals and souvenir or lectures given at different forum. Some of the lectures deal with the burning subject and included in the compilation expecting that the views expressed may meet with universal or general agreement or become a subject-matter of debate to serve public interest. They may not likely be thrown in the wind but are fruit of mature consideration based on years of experience and suit of the cognate subjects.

'Sovereignty, judicial review and separation of power' deals with the subject with different angles than the colonial one keeping in view the actualities of life.[2]

Lecture on "Right to Information Act" defends the Act with opinion that burden to check its abuse rest on the shoulder of Information Commissioner. Mere abuse should not be ground to curtail the right flowing from the Act. "Sexual abuse of child" and "female foeticide" are the two lectures which I have given at different forum shows the alarming situation which India is facing in the matter of child abuse and female foeticide. The corruption has crept into the blood and whole country is facing its heat at different level in different form. The article on "corruption" may be thought-provoking to awake the socially conscious citizens and the country to feel the alarming situation and failure on the part of governance. "Quest for good governance" is an article read at a forum ignite the mind to give a second look to our governance system. Lecture given in a seminar organized by UNICEF on "State's Focus on water conservation, safe drinking water and sanitation programme" calls for immediate steps and to take remedial measure for conservation of water. The article on "Time frame for sanction to prosecution" question the legislature's

1. Morality in Law (2012) Edition.

2. *Delhi Transport Corporation* v. *D.T.C. Mazdoor Congress,* AIR 1991 SC 101; *Uttar Pradesh Shaskiya Adhivakta Kalyan Samiti* v. *State of Uttar Pradesh,* 2012 (30) LCD 1066.

and executive right to keep the matter pending with regard to sanction for prosecution in corruption cases under section 19 of the Anti-Corruption Act for unreasonable period. We are celebrating 150th Jayanti of Swami Vivekanand. On the very occasion speech given by me at Ram Krishan Matt in Lucknow is published under the title "Swami Vivekanand – the Soul of India" is a tribute to great son of mother India. Views expressed in "sovereignty, judicial review and separation of power" and "time frame for sanction to prosecution" has been expressed in my judgments. The other lectures/articles are based on personal view and different opinion may be formed on judicial side.

Speeches have been edited to some extent to suit the book and make them up-to-date. Every topic deals with the social problem *vis-a-vis* law, keeping in view the ground realities of life and social order.

I hope and trust that different issues dealt with in the present book shall be beneficial to lawyers, judges, bureaucrats, legislatures and public at large while dealing with subjects at appropriate level. I solicit advice or suggestions from every person across the society on the topics discussed in the present book.

Justice Devi Prasad Singh
31-B, Laxmanpuri Colony,
Faizabad Road, Lucknow,
U.P., India

October 2013

Contents

Table of Cases

A

B

C

N

O

P

R

S

T

U

Sovereignty, Judicial Review and Separation of Power

"The ideally best form of government is that in which the sovereignty, or supreme controlling power in the last resort, is vested in the entire aggregate of the community."[1]

Section 24 of Cr PC was amended by the State of Uttar Pradesh and State Government claimed privilege that with regard to appointment of District Government Councils, the opinion of District Judge, is not a condition precedent in view of separation of power among the three parts of the Government. The findings recorded and observations made while deciding a case of District Government Council[2] dealing with separation of power on judicial side, is revisited in the present article.

Sovereign function includes legislation, administration and dispensation of justice. All the three functions were vested in the King in the Monarchical system of the government. In democratic polity, three powers have been assigned to three parts of the government, *i.e.* legislative, executive and judiciary. Under the Constitution of United States of America or under the unwritten Constitution of

1. Concerning Representative Government, in On Liberty and Other Essays, (Oxford UP, 1991), 244-by J. Mill.
2. *Sadhna Sharma* v. *State of Uttar Pradesh,* W.P. No. 7825 (M/B) of 2011 with *Sadhna Sharma* v. *State of Uttar Pradesh,* W.P. No. 4097 (M/B) of 2011 [decided by the Division Bench comprising of Hon'ble Mr. Justice Devi Prasad Singh and Honble Dr. Justice Satish Chandra by the judgment and order dated 11-1-2012].

England, there is strict separation of power. But under the Indian Constitution, the separation of power is not in strict sense. There is overlapping.

The word, "sovereignty" is derived from the Latin word "super"(above) means the authority which controls the actions of every individual, member of the community. The power of Government to make itself obeyed is called sovereignty, and the person or persons who have this power are called the sovereign.

According to Harold J. Laski, sovereignty is the supreme coercive power and it is by possession of sovereignty that the State is distinguished from all other forms of human association (The State in Theory & Practice by Harold J. Laski).

In Constitutional Law, sovereignty is termed as the supreme power of Legislation and Governance. However, Aristotle, a great Greek legal philosopher said that in democratic States, people are sovereign. The supreme power of legislation and governance rests in the people. The Parliamentary sovereignty is subsequent evolution.

The original concept of sovereignty is of popular sovereignty and even the King or the monarch was to obey the wishes of the people.

The Words and Phrases, Permanent Edition, Vol. 39B, defines the sovereignty as under:

> "The "sovereign powers" of a government include all the powers necessary to accomplish its legitimate ends and purposes. Such powers must exist in all practical governments. They are the incidents of sovereignty, of which a state cannot divest itself". – *Boggs* v. *Merced Mining Co.,* 14 Cal. 279, dismissed 70 U.S. 304, 3 Wall. 304, 18 L. Ed. 245.

Accordingly in broader context, the Legislative, Executive and Judiciary jointly constitute sovereign powers with the division of work amongst them under the constitutional framework. Since, India is governed by written Constitution; the sovereign function of the State should be looked into keeping in view the spirit of written Constitution. However, the proposition that the sovereign function includes the function discharged by Legislature, Executive and Judiciary seems to be correct approach than splitting the sovereign power and making them alien to each other. The Western jurist ordinarily rely upon most celebrated treatise of Montesquieu, *viz.*, Espirit des Lois: Spirit of Laws, published in 1748. Montesquieu discussed and propagated federalism in democratic polity and opined for strict separation of power among legislature, executive and judiciary. Though the larger Benches of Supreme Court of India had continuously ruled that in Indian context and keeping in view the constitutional scheme, there is no strict separation of power and there is overlapping but it appears that in some of the judgments decided by the Bench of lesser number of Judges, Montesquieu has been relied upon as a ground not to interfere with the State action even if it causes public harm.

With profound respect, it appears that Montesquieu's treatise 'Spirit of Laws' has not been read as a whole by Hon'ble Judges who followed Montesquieu blindly. The wholesole and overall reading and understanding of the treatise, "Spirit of Laws" written by Montesquieu reveals that the separation of power among three wings of the government is theoretical and may be made applicable in an "ideal State" means where persons holding offices in all three wings of the government, *i.e.* legislature, judiciary and executive are honest, fair and learned. In case there are allegations of corruption, casteism, nepotism or abuse of power against the members discharging sovereign function, then the Montesquieu's doctrine shall not only be impractical but may result with the serious consequence in due course of time.

Montesquieu himself has said, to quote:—

> "Law in general is human reason, inasmuch as it governs all the inhabitants of the earth; the political and civil laws of each nation ought to be only the particular cases in which human reason is applied.

> They should be adapted in such a manner to the people for whom they are framed that it should be a great chance if those of one nation suit another.
>
> They should be in relation to the nature and principle of each government; whether they support it, as in the case of civil institutions.
>
> They should be in relation to the nature and principle of each government; whether they form it, as may be said of politic laws; or whether they support it, as in the case of civil institutions.
>
> They should be in relation to the climate of each country, to the quality of its soil, to its situation and extent, to the principal occupation of the natives, whether husbandmen, huntsmen, or shepherds; they should have relation to the degree of liberty which the constitution will bear; to the religion of the inhabitants, to their inclinations, riches, numbers, commerce, manner, and customs. In fine, they have relations to each other, as also to their origin, to the intent of the legislator, and to the order of things on which they are established; in all of which different lights they ought to be considered.[1]"

It means strict separation of power shall depend upon each country's histrological, social and cultural matrix. It was Chief Justice Marshall who took initiative in *Marbury* v. *Madison*, 5 US 137 (1803) and while introducing the concept of judicial review under the American constitutional jurisprudence asserted power of higher judiciary to review the statutory enactments, in case, it offends the constitutional provision. It appears to be first case where doctrine of separation of power as propounded by Montesquieu was not adhered to.

In a celebrated book, "Religion, Caste & Politics in India", Christophe Jaffrelot who is a Research Director at Centre National de la Recherche Scientifique (in short, CNRS), author of several books on Indian society and political

---

1. Spirit of Law by Montesquieu, page 11, (from INTERNET).

system had considered corruption and criminalisation of politics. Learned author noted that corruption has become all-pervasive phenomenon in contemporary India (page 621). He further took note of the fact that the criminalisation of politics started long back in the country including Uttar Pradesh. The criminals or mafias developed direct nexus with the politician of the State and helped them to be elected. Initially, the politicians availed the help of criminals in electoral matters but later on, criminals entered into politics and get themselves elected in the Assemblies and Parliament. It shall be appropriate to reproduce a portion from the book (supra) with regard to criminalisation of politics in the State of Uttar Pradesh and other States of the country. To quote:—

> "The 1996 Legislative Assembly in Uttar Pradesh did not reverse but may have increased the 1993 trend. Not only did the BJP, the BSP, and the SP give tickets to dozens of candidates against whom legal proceedings had been instituted (33, 18, and 22 respectively), but a certain number of BJP, BSP, and Congress MLAs amongst them became ministers when the BJP formed the government, first jointly with the BSP, then alone, from October, 1997. This was achieved by recruiting dozens of MLAs from the BSP and the Congress (and offering up to a few hundred thousand rupees per MLA), with a ministerial post for each. Thus, the Uttar Pradesh cabinet comprised 92 members. The BJP Chief Minister, Kalyan Singh, tried to project himself as clean and set-up a Special Task Force (STF) in 1998 to capture or liquidate criminals. However, public enemy number one, then, was Shri Prakash Shukla, who appeared to have colluded with at least eight ministers of Kalyan Singh's government; they protected him, making the task of the STF more complicated (Mishra 1998 : 52).
>
> Uttar Pradesh is not the only State where the entry of the mafia into politics has accelerated in the

> last few years. Bihar is certainly as seriously affected as Uttar Pradesh. In 2000, 31 Legislative Assembly candidates had cases registered against them for crimes ranging from murder to dacoity. Most of them contested as 'Independents', but there were BJP, Congress, RJD, and Samata candidates as well. Maharashtra is also suffering from the same disease. During the municipal elections in 1997, 150, 72, and 50 candidates with past or present difficulties with the law (Godbole 1997) were fielded from Mumbai, Nagpur, and Pune respectively. Andhra Pradesh is not lagging behind, since in 1999 an NGO called Lok Satta Election Watch released a list of 46 candidates contesting elections to the Lok Sabha or the Legislative Assembly with, allegedly, some criminal background (The Hindu, 3 September, 1999 : 5).
>
> Delhi is also new in this circle of most criminalized states. In fact, Delhi is gradually taking over from Mumbai as the crime capital of India. This city-state tops the list of number of crimes per head, with 527 in 1996 (against 121 in Bihar) and, in terms of percentage change, with +55 per cent. change in 1996 over the quinquennial average of 1991 : 5 (Swami 1998: 17). Out of 815 Legislative Assembly candidates in 1998, 120 had more than two criminal cases registered against them, and out of 69 MLAs, 33 had criminal cases against them (The Hindustan Times, 26 October, 1998; The Hindu, 23 November, 1998)."

It shall be unwise to think or infer that the politicians having criminal antecedent do not affect the decision-making process, or the governance. Whether in such a situation, in case the argument of the propagators with regard to strict separation of power is accepted, it is easy to understand that the country may see doom's day in due course of time.

While considering the anarchy and autocratic rule prevailing in some of the countries of the world because of committed bureaucracy and judiciary and the trouble, pain and agony faced by the peoples of respective country, Bertrand Russell critically expressed his views as under:

> "Stalin could neither understand nor respect the point of view which led Churchill to allow himself to be peaceably dispossessed as a result of a popular-vote. I am a firm believer in democratic representative government as the best form for those who have the tolerance and self-restraint that is required to make it workable. But its advocates make a mistake if they suppose that it can be at once introduced into countries where the average citizen has hitherto lacked all training in the give-and-take that it requires. In a Balcan country, not so many years ago, a party which had been beaten by a narrow margin in a general election retrieved its fortunes by shooting a sufficient number of the representatives of the other side to give it a majority. People in the West thought this characteristic of the Balkans, forgetting that Cromwel and Roberpierre had acted likewise. (UE)[1]"

Russell also took note of American legislators and Nazis under the democratic form of government. To quote:

> "The American legislators who made the immigration laws consider the Nordics superior to Slavs or Latins or any other white men. But the Nazis, under the stress of war, were led to the conclusion that there are hardly any true Nordics outside Germany; the Norwegians, except Quisling and his few followers, had been corrupted by intermixture with Finns and Lapps and such. Thus politics are a clue to descent. The biologically pure Nordics love Hitler, and if you did not love Hitler, that was proof of tainted blood. (UE)[2]"

Framers of Indian Constitution were wise enough to take care of such situation. With foresightedness while

1. Page 91 from Bertrand Russell's Best Special Indian Edition.
2. Page 91-92 from Bertrand Russell's Best Special Indian Edition.

considering the process of judicial review under article 226 of the Constitution of India, they used the words, "for other purposes" and gave ample power to High Courts and Supreme Court to interfere under article 32 in the event of violation of fundamental right of the citizens straightway. Conferment of such power to the High Courts and Supreme Court by the constitutional framers belies the argument with regard to strict separation of power. Needless to say that in the event of judicial overstepping or arbitrariness, legislators have got ample power to legislate law to dilute the effect of judgments of courts subject to constitutional limitations.

In such a situation, remedy is to "check and balance" which has been provided in the Indian Constitution and affirmed by the Supreme Court from time to time holding that the separation of power is not applied under Indian Constitutional Scheme in strict sense.

Under article 143 of the Constitution of India, the President of India, has been conferred power to seek opinion from Supreme Court. Article 144 provides that all civil and judicial authority shall act in aid of Supreme Court in discharge of its obligations. All matters of inter-state disputes with regard to land and water, are adjudicated by the Tribunal constituted for the purpose. Thus, the Constitution does not envisage strict separation of power.

In a case,[1] a seven Judges Special Bench of Supreme Court, has considered the doctrine of separation of power and ruled that strictly speaking, it has no place in the system of governance in India nor at the present day under her own Constitution or which she had during the British rule. Unlike the American and Australian Constitutions, the Indian Constitution does not expressly vest the different sets of powers in the different organs of the State. Under article 53(1), the executive power is indeed vested in the President, but there is no similar vesting provision regarding the legislative and the judicial powers. Our

1. *In re: Constitution of India and Delhi Law Act, 1912*, AIR 1951 SC 332: 1951 SCJ 527: 1951 SCR 747.

Constitution, though federal in its structure, is modeled on the British Parliamentary system, the essential feature of which is the responsibility of the executive to the legislature. The President, as the head of the executive, is to act on the advice of the Council of Ministers, and this Council of Ministers, like the British Cabinet is a "hyphen which joins—a buckle which fastens—the legislative part of the State to the executive part."

Again, a Constitution Bench[1] of Supreme Court ruled that the Indian Constitution has not indeed recognized the doctrine of separation of powers in its absolute rigidity but the functions of the different parts or branch of the Government have been sufficiently differentiated and consequently it can very well be said that our Constitution does not contemplate assumption, by one organ or part of the State, of functions that essentially belong to another. The executive can exercise the powers of departmental or subordinate legislation when such powers are delegated to it by the legislature.

The aforesaid proposition has been reiterated by Supreme Court in various cases.[2]

A Constitution Bench[3] of Supreme Court of India, opined that doctrine of separation of power is carried into effect in countries like America, Australia. In India, separation of powers is in a broader sense and not like America and Australia where it is in strict sense. The constituent power is independent of the doctrine of separation of powers. The constituent power is sovereign. It is the power which creates the organs and distributes the powers. The rigid

1. *Rai Sahib Ram Jawaya Kapur* v. *State of Punjab*, AIR 1955 SC 549: 1955 SCJ 504: (1955) 2 SCR 225.
2. *Jayantilal Amratlal Shodhan* v. *F.N. Rana*, AIR 1964 SC 648: (1964) 2 SCA 284: (1964) 5 SCR 294; *Chandra Mohan* v. *State of Uttar Pradesh*, AIR 1966 SC 1987: 1967 (2) SCJ 717: (1967) 1 SCR 77; *Udai Ram Sharma* v. *Union of India*, AIR 1968 SC 1138: (1968) 2 SCA 277: (1968) 3 SCR 41; *Associated Cement Companies Limited* v. *P.N. Sharma*, AIR 1965 SC 1595: 1966 (1) SCJ 786: (1965) 2 SCR 366; *Keshvananda Bharati* v. *State of Kerala*, (1973) 4 SCC 225: AIR 1973 SC 1461.
3. *Indira Nehru Gandhi* v. *Raj Narain*, 1975 Supp SCC 1: AIR 1975 SC 2299: (1976) 2 SCR 347.

separation of power as in American or Australian Constitution, does not apply to India. Though the legislature is entitled to change with retrospective effect the law which forms the basis of judicial decision, it is not permissible to legislature to declare judgment of Court to be void or not binding. The Indian Constitution does not recognise the rigid separation of power. The reason is that the concentration of powers in any one organ may, by upsetting that fine balance between the three organs, destroy the fundamental premises of a democratic government to which we are pledged. In a federal system which distributes powers between three co-ordinate branches of government, though not rigidly, disputes regarding the limits of Constitutional power have to be resolved by courts and therefore, as observed by Paton, "the distinction between judicial and other powers may be vital to the maintenance of the Constitution itself". No Constitution can survive without a conscious adherence to its fine checks and balances. The principle of separation of powers is a principle of restraint which "has in it the precept, innate in the prudence of self-preservation that discretion is the better part of valour"

In a case,[1] Supreme Court held that independence of judiciary is the basic feature of the Constitution. The concept of independence of the judiciary is a noble concept which inspires the constitutional scheme and constitutes the foundation on which rests the edifice of our democratic polity. If there is one principle which runs through the entire fabric of the Constitution, it is the principle of the rule of law and under the Constitution, it is the judiciary which is entrusted with the task of keeping every organ of the State within the limits of the law and thereby making the rule of law meaningful and effective. The concept of independence of the judiciary is not limited only to independence from executive pressure or influence but it is a much wider concept which takes within its sweep

1. *S.P. Gupta* v. *President of India,* AIR 1982 SC 149: 1982 Rajdhani LR 389: 1981 Supp SCC 87.

independence from many other pressures and prejudices. It has many dimensions, namely fearlessness of other power centers, economic or political, and freedom from prejudices acquired and nourished by the class to which the Judges belong. Judges should be of stern stuff and tough fibre, unbending before power, economic or political, and they must uphold the core principle of the rule of law which says, "Be you ever so high, the law is above you." This is the principle of independence of the judiciary which is vital for the establishment of real participatory democracy, maintenance of the rule of law as a dynamic concept and delivery of social justice to the vulnerable sections of the community.

Justice Fazal Ali (supra), while considering the independence of judiciary, opined that it comprises two fundamental and indispensable elements, *i.e.,* (1) independence of judiciary as an organ and as one of the three functionaries of the State, and secondly, the independence of the individual Judge. Their lordships ruled that Constitution of India did not fully envisage complete separation of powers. The power of judicial review has been conferred as a safeguard not only to ensure the independence of judiciary but also to prevent Judge from vagaries of executive. Their Lordship held that judiciary has to be inspired by the values enshrined in our Constitution. If rule of law is to run akin to rule of life and a feudal society is to be transformed into an egalitarian society by the rule of law, an introduction of the element of reflection of 'popular will' so as to make judicial system more viable and effective as an instrument of change is inevitable and total aloofness of judiciary is inconceivable.

In a case,[1] Supreme Court observed that although, the doctrine of separation of powers has not been recognized under the Constitution in its absolute rigidity but the Constitution-makers have meticulously defined the functions of various organs of the State. Legislature,

1. *Asif Hameed* v. *State of Jammu and Kashmir,* 1989 Supp (2) SCC 364: AIR 1989 SC 1899: JT 1989 (2) 548.

executive and judiciary have to function within their own spheres demarcated under the Constitution. No organ may usurp the functions assigned to another. Legislature and executive, the two facets of people's will, have all the powers including that of finance. Judiciary has no power over sword or the purse; nonetheless it has power to ensure that the aforesaid two main organs of State function within the constitutional limits and if it is not so that Court must strike down the action. It is the sentinel of democracy. Judicial review is a powerful weapon to restrain unconstitutional exercise of power by the legislature and executive. The expanding horizon of judicial review has taken in its fold the concept of social and economic justice. While exercise of powers by the legislature and executive is subject to judicial restrain, the only check on court's own exercise of power is the self-imposed discipline of judicial restrain. While exercising power of judicial review of administrative action, the court is not an appellate authority. The Constitution does not permit the court to direct or advise the executive in matters of policy or to sermonize *qua* any matter which under the Constitution lies within the sphere of legislature or executive, provided these authorities do not transgress their constitutional limits or statutory powers. The principle of 'broad separation of power' under the Constitution, has been reiterated in the case of *Swamy Shraddananda*.[1] In another case,[2] a Constitution Bench of Supreme Court while upholding the right of higher judiciary with regard to enforcement of fundamental rights and direction to CBI to hold inquiry in a given case, has not found it to be a encroachment over other's jurisdiction. Supreme Court held that there is no strict separation of power under Indian Constitution. Being the protectors of civil liberties of the citizens, the Supreme Court and the High Courts have not only the power and jurisdiction but also an obligation to protect the

1. *Swamy Shraddananda* v. *State of Karnataka,* AIR 2007 SC 2531: 2007 AIR SCW 4513: (2007) 8 SCALE 1.
2. *State of West Bengal* v. *Committee for Protection of Democratic Rights,* AIR 2010 SC 1476: 2010 AIR SCW 1829: (2010) 3 SCC 571.

fundamental rights, guaranteed by Part III in general and under article 21 of the Constitution in particular, zealously and vigilantly. In a federal constitution, the distribution of legislative powers between Parliament and the State Legislature involves limitation on legislative powers and, therefore, this requires an authority other than Parliament to ascertain whether such limitations are transgressed. Judicial review acts as the final arbiter not only to give effect to the distribution of legislative powers between Parliament and the State Legislatures, it is also necessary to show any transgression by each entity. Therefore, to borrow the words of Lord Steyn, judicial review is justified by combination of "the principles of separation of powers, rule of law, the principle of constitutionality and the reach of judicial review." If the federal structure is violated by any legislative action, the Constitution takes care to protect the federal structure by ensuring that courts act as guardians and interpreters of the Constitution and provide remedy under articles 32 and 226, whenever there is an attempted violation.

A Constitution Bench[1] of Supreme Court, after considering the cases[2] ruled that in modern governance, the strict separation of power is neither possible nor desirable. The Indian Constitution does not prohibit overlap of functions, but in fact provides for some overlap as a parliamentary democracy. But what it prohibits is such exercise of function of the other branch which results in wresting away of the regime of constitutional accountability. This is the test for violation of separation of powers. The constitutional principle of separation of powers will only be violated if an essential function of one branch is taken over by another branch, leading to a removal of 'checks and balances'. Till the principle of accountability is preserved, there is no violation of separation of powers. Accordingly, the MPLAD Scheme is not a violation of the

1. *Bhim Singh* v. *Union of India,* (2010) 5 SCC 538.
2. *Keshvananda Bharati* v. *State of Kerala,* (1973) 4 SCC 225: AIR 1973 SC 1461 and in *Indira Nehru Gandhi* case, (1976) 3 SCC 321.

concept of separation of powers. However, the Constitution Bench seems to have not taken into account the observation made by larger Bench of seven Judges in the case of Delhi Law Act, 1912 (supra) whereby, the article 53(1) has been interpreted canvassing with regard to vetting of executive powers in the President. Whether executive functioning may be discharged by elected representative, is a crucial question which has not been considered in the light of the observation of larger Bench of Supreme Court of India? In a case,[1] their Lordships of Supreme Court had considered the principle of separation of power in Indian context and held that the power is overlapping. In appropriate case the higher judiciary may pass appropriate order to secure public interest, to quote relevant portion of paras 35 and 36 of the judgment of GVK Industries Limited (supra), as under:

> "**35.** Our Constitution charges the various organs of the State with affirmative responsibilities of protecting the interests of the welfare of and the security of the nation. Legislative powers are granted to enable the accomplishment of the goals of the nation. The powers of judicial review are granted in order to ensure that legislative and executive powers are used within the bounds specified in the Constitution. Consequently, it is imperative that the powers so granted to various organs of the State are not restricted impermissibly by judicial fiat such that it leads to inabilities of the organs of the State in discharging their constitutional responsibilities.
>
> **36.** Powers that have been granted, and implied by, and borne by the Constitutional text have to be perforce admitted. Nevertheless, the very essence of constitutionalism is also that no organ of the State may arrogate to itself powers beyond what is specified in the Constitution. Walking on that razor's edge is the duty of the judiciary. Judicial restraint is necessary in dealing with the powers of another

1. *G.V.K. Industries Limited* v. *Income Tax Officer,* (2011) 4 SCC 36: 2011 AIR SCW 2047.

coordinate branch of the government; but restraint cannot imply abdication of the responsibility of walking on that edge."

Their Lordships have further proceeded to consider the constitutional philosophy in terms of Indian Constitution and ruled that prime concern of the courts are to maintain rule of law and secure the public interest, to quote relevant portion of paras 113, 114 and 115 as under:—

> "**113.** The path to modern constitutionalism, with notions of divided and checked powers, fundamental rights and affirmative duties of the State to protect and enhance the interests of, welfare of, and security of the people, and a realization that "comity amongst nations" and international peace were *sine qua non* for the welfare of the people was neither straight forward, nor inevitable. It took much suffering, bloodshed, toil, tears and exploitation of the people by their own governments and by foreign governments, both in times of peace and in times of war, before humanity began to arrive at the conclusion that unchecked power would sooner, rather than later, turn tyrannical against the very people who have granted such power, and also harmful to the peaceful existence of other people in other territories. Imperial expansion, as a result of thirst for markets and resources that the underlying economy demanded, with colonial exploitation as the inevitable result of that competition, and two horrific world wars are but some of the more prominent markers along that pathway.
>
> **114.** The most tendentious use of the word sovereignty, wherein the principles of self-determination were accepted within a nation-state but not deemed to be available to others, was the rhetorical question raised by Adolf Hitler at the time of annexation of Austria in 1938: "What can words like 'independence' or 'sovereignty' mean for a state of only six million?"

> **115.** We must recognize the fact that history is replete with instances of sovereigns who, while exercising authority on behalf of even those people who claimed to be masters of their own realm, contradictorily claimed the authority to exercise *suzerain* rights over another territory, its people and its resources, inviting ultimately the ruin of large swaths of humanity and also the very people such sovereigns, whether a despot or a representative organ, claimed to represent."

It has been consistent view of Supreme Court of India that the Indian Constitution does not envisage for strict separation of power and in appropriate case, the higher judiciary may interfere and correct the error committed by other two wings of the government to secure public interest and there may be overlapping function to secure public good.

In view of above, it is evident, why the principle of strict separation of power has not been accepted by Supreme Court in Indian context.

An industrialist of the country, Azim Premji, who was the part of a group wrote a letter to the Prime Minister showing deep concern to mal-administration in the country, remarked, "The biggest concern now are governance issues and the complete absence of decision-making in the government, in the bureaucracy". Even if there is little truth in the allegation whether in such a situation, as canvassed by the State or a section of society, strict separation of power should be enforced leaving peoples in the state of uncertainty?

Jeffrey Goldsworthy, working in Faculty of Law at Monash University in Melbourne, Australia, in his book, *"Parliamentary Sovereignty"*, has considered this aspect of the matter. According to Goldsworthy, to quote:—

> "The once popular idea of legislative sovereignty has been in decline throughout the world for some time. 'From France to South Africa to Israel, Parliamentary sovereignty has faded away.' A

> dwindling number of political and constitutional theorists continue to resist the 'rights revolution' that is sweeping the globe, by refusing to accept that judicial enforcement of a constitutionally entrenched Bill of Rights is necessarily desirable....
>
> For what it is worth, my opinion is that constitutional entrenchment might be highly desirable, or even essential, for the preservation of democracy, the rule of law and human rights in some countries, but not in others. In much of the world, a culture of entrenched corruption, populism, authoritarianism, or bitter religious, ethnic or class conflicts, may make judicially enforceable bills of rights desirable. Much depends on culture, social structure and political organization."

What explains the loss of faith in the old democratic ideal? I am aware of possible 'agency problems': failures of elected representatives faithfully to represent the interests of their constituents. In many countries this is a major problem. But I suspect that in countries such as Britain, Canada, Australia and New Zealand, the real reason for this loss of faith lies elsewhere. There, a substantial number of influential members of the highly educated, professional, upper-middle class have lost faith in the ability of their fellow citizens to form opinions about important matters of public policy in a sufficiently intelligent, well-informed, dispassionate, impartial and carefully reasoned manner. Even though the upper-middle class dominates the political process, in any event, the force of public opinion still makes itself felt through the ballot box, and cannot be ignored by elected politicians no matter how enlightened and progressive they might be.

Learned author while considering the judicial encroachment of constitutional right in some of the countries, opined that shifting power to Judges, amounts to return of mixed government in the political process to check the ignorance, prejudice and passion of the mob. Learned author proceeded to observe as under, to quote:—

> "If I am right, the main attraction of judicial enforcement of constitutional rights in these countries is that it shifts power to people (judges) who are representative members of the highly educated, professional, upper-middle class, and whose superior education, intelligence, habits of thought, and professional ethos are thought more likely to produce enlightened decisions. I think it is reasonable to describe this as a return to the ancient principle of 'mixed government', by reinserting an 'aristocratic' element into the political process to check the ignorance, prejudice and passion of the 'mob'. By 'aristocratic', I mean an element supposedly distinguished by superior education, intellectual refinement, thoughtfulness and reasonability, rather than by heredity or inherited wealth."

Author opined that, recent challenges in judicial innovation, may require new theories and may constitute a challenge to doctrine of parliamentary sovereignty. But they cast very little light on the nature of Parliamentary authority in the past. Author proceeded to observe that defenders of Parliamentary sovereignty cannot ignore constitutional change. Constitutional arrangements and understandings today are in many respects very different from those of the past. But the doctrine of Parliamentary sovereignty has survived centuries of change, and has the capacity to survive many more. The recent constitutional developments discussed by its critics are compatible with the doctrine. The author noted a passage from 'Constitutional and Administrative Law in New Zealand,[1] to quote as under:—

> "Throughout English Constitutional history, Parliament and the courts have exercised coordinate, constitutive authority... Theirs is a symbiotic relationship founded in political realities. Parliament and the political executive must look to the Courts for

1. Constitutional and Administrative Law in New Zealand (3rd Edn.) (543-5).

judicial recognition of legislative power, and the Courts must look to Parliament and the political executive for recognition of judicial independence."

In a journal, "The American Journal of Comparative Law", while writing an article, Prof. Jiunn-Rong Yeh, College of Law. National Taiwan University, and Associate Prof. Wen-Chen Chang, National Taiwan University, have considered the extensive interference by South Korean and Taiwan Constitutional Court, to quote:—

> "South Korea underwent successful democratization in 1987, culminating in an extensively revised Constitution and a new Constitutional Court. In the two decades since, government power has shifted to the opposition and back, swinging among various political parties. Most impressive has been the performance of the South Korean Constitutional Court. In its decisions involving the constitutionality of statutes or government actions, it has ruled against the government about one-third of the time.
>
> Similarly, Taiwan also began an incremental democratization process in the late 1980s. Since then, the 1947 Constitution, that was originally adopted in mainland China, has been amended seven times. Governmental power was peacefully passed to the long-term opposition party in 2000 and then swung back again to the former ruling party in 2008. The Constitutional Court of Taiwan, despite being an old institution established in 1948, began exhibiting greater vibrancy since the 1990s and produced a record in which about thirty to forty per cent of challenged legislative or administrative acts were ruled unconstitutional."

How adversely affected system of Governance, caused mental pain, agony and persecution of peoples of various countries, may be seen from agitation in different parts of the world. Fatima Bhutto in her most celebrated book,

"Songs of Blood and Sword", discussed fallacy if it in the trial of Bhutto, to reproduce relevant extracts as under:—

> "After reviewing the case files and documents pertaining to Bhutto's trial at the hands of the military regime the jurists issued a statement that would be released to the international press. They agreed that Bhutto's trial clearly failed to meet several necessary standards of justice in 'at least' the six following ways; maintaining a distinct bias in regard to the trial judges and lawyers, the failure of the junta to hold an open trial, the failure of the courts to maintain an accurate record of Bhutto's trial, the failure to institute a proper trial structure, and the court's decision in moving ahead with clear evidentiary improprieties and insufficiencies. Lastly, the jurists noted that Bhutto's physical maltreatment at the hands of the state was ominous and a cause for international concern." (Page 168)

Anatol Lieven, a journalist, who had worked in Pakistan and conducted extensive research and also visited India, had written a book, "Pakistan, a Hard Country". While writing the book, learned author noted how the South Asia particularly, Pakistan and India are likely to suffer a lot because of blindly following the British legacy in dispensation of justice. In Pakistan, how extra-constitutional pockets and extra-constitutional nucleus power has been created affecting dispensation of justice is eye opener. This happens since higher judiciary could not evolve new principle of law to match the political evils. Now after sixty years, Chief Justice of Pakistan is striving to regenerate the democracy to establish rule of law but now seems to be too late. Learned author Anatol Lieven observed, to quote:—

> "A visit to the Mohmand Tribal Agency in September 2008 (described further in Chapter 11) summed up for me the attitudes of most ordinary Pakistanis to the official judicial system, and how the Pakistani Taleban have been able to exploit this to their advantage. As Tazmir Khan, a farmer, told me,

to the approval of the other local men sitting with him,

Taliban justice is better than that of the Pakistani state. If you have any problem, you can go to the Taliban and they will solve it without you having to pay anything —not like the courts and police, who will take your money and do nothing."

The author further proceeded to observe as under:—

"...Even clearer was the entire local population's absolute loathing for the state judicial system; and this was an attitude which I found among ordinary people across Pakistan.

However, it would be wrong to see the Pakistani population simply as innocent victims of a vicious judicial system run from above for the benefit of the elites. Rather, justice in Pakistan is an extension of politics by other means, and everyone with the slightest power to do so tries to corrupt and twist the judicial system to their advantage in every way possible.

Thus cases brought before the state judicial system are key weapons in the hands of individuals and groups fighting for national and local power; and in both the state and the traditional systems of justice, outcomes are determined largely by political considerations. That means kinship, wealth, influence and armed force, but also sometimes and to some extent the ability to win over public opinion in general. The means to do this have changed over time, with the modern media now playing an important role in some cases."

The author (supra) further in very strong words, proceeded to observe, to quote:—

"It would be quite wrong, however, to see the Pakistan masses faced with the state justice system as simply the passive, sheep-like victims of predatory lawyers, judges, policemen and political elites. This is

> true, but it is also true that the vast majority of Pakistanis (and Indians) with even the most limited power to do so have contributed to the wreckage of the state judicial system by their constant efforts to twist it to their own individual or group purposes. One reason for this is the continual struggles for power which permeate Pakistani society—struggles in which politics and property are often inextricably mixed. In turn, these struggles generate and are generated by the lack of mutual trust that permeates Pakistani society, between but also within kinship groups."

In the aforesaid book, the author has cited several instances of Pakistan, how gradually the judiciary lost its significance, how the judiciary has become weaker and weaker day-by-day making people dischanted with the system. Judiciary has become an instrument to persecute the weaker in the hands of mighty people in politics.

Poverty, illiteracy, lack of basic amenities, poor governance, are the prime concern not only for the citizens of the State of Uttar Pradesh, but for whole of India. According to Human Development Report, 2011, prepared by the "Institute of Applied Manpower Research Planning Commission, Government of India", published by Oxford University Press, though per capita income has grown but still, it is lower than several other States, to quote:

> "Over the years, the gap between the per capita income of the state and the national average has grown considerably. In 1950-1, the per capita income of Uttar Pradesh was 7 per cent lower than the national average. This difference had grown to 40 per cent in 2000-1 (Uttar Pradesh Human Development Report 2003). In recent years (2002-3 to 2007-8), the average annual growth rate of NSDP was 5.6 per cent as against the national average of 7.9 per cent, while the growth rate of the per capita SDP was 3.6 per cent compared to the national average of 6.4 per cent."

In the field of health also, the State of Uttar Pradesh, is worse than the national average, to quote:—

> "In terms of health indicators, the state's performance was worse than the national average (Figures 3, 4 and 5). The proportion of women with BMI<18.5, underweight children and the U5MR are higher in the state as compared to the national average. The SCs and STs are worse off compared to the state average and their community's respective national averages for all the health indicators.
>
> Although the state made significant efforts in building healthcare infrastructure, it has failed to keep pace with the increasing demand. The state's performance in providing health infrastructure was lower than the national average. The shortage of medical personnel and their absenteeism, particularly in the rural areas, the shortage of medicines, and lack of accountability in the public health system have seriously affected the healthcare system. There was a vast network of private health providers, who were expensive and often beyond the reach of the poor. The State Human Development Report further noted that the state had one of the lowest health expenditures in India by both Indian and international standards. Despite that, the bulk of the expenditure was allocated for the payment of salaries."

With regard to literacy rate, again Uttar Pradesh is lower than the national average, to quote:—

> "The literacy rate in Uttar Pradesh was lower than the national average. According to latest estimates of Census (2011), Uttar Pradesh has a literacy rate of 70 per cent as compared to the 74 per cent national literacy rate in 2011. As per NSS (2007-8), all the social groups including SCs and STs have a literacy rate lower than the state average and also lower than the literacy rate of their communities at the national level. Among the various programmes undertaken, Uttar

Pradesh Basic Education Project (UPBEP 1 and 2) initiated in select districts of the state in 1993 and 2000, respectively, and DPEP (Centrally-sponsored) resulted in a notable improvement in enrolment and a decline in dropout rates in the districts where these programmes were implemented. During the period 1996-7 to 1999-2000, enrolment in UPBEP districts increased by 68 per cent as against 37 per cent in non-UPBEP districts (*Uttar Pradesh Human Development Report, 2003*). Poor infrastructure along with inadequate financial allocation were the major hindrances in achieving higher educational targets. The state allocation on education increased from 0.5 per cent of the SDP in 1950-1 to 3.2 per cent in 2007-8, but it is still very low compared to the demand."

With regard to Basic household amenities again, Uttar Pradesh is marginally below the national average in terms of improved drinking water facilities to quote:—

"In terms of basic household amenities, the performance of the state is marginally below the national average in terms of improved drinking water facilities. However, it is one of the rare states where the average for the SC and ST households was better than the state average and also than the national average for their respective communities in terms of access to improved sources of drinking water. In the case of sanitation, the state average is slightly better than the all India average. However, only 16 per cent of SC households have access to toilet facilities *vis-a-vis* 35 per cent of SC households at the all India level."

Several other States of India are in tune with Uttar Pradesh sofaras socio-economic development is concern.

In such a situation, it is not easy for the citizens to avail justice from the Government. There shall always be disparity in public dealing and peoples may suffer for one or the other cause because of poor governance system."

Mahatma Gandhi Ji compared the governance system of European countries and India and expressed his views, to quote from *"Mahatma Gandhi Essays & Reflections"*[1]:—

> "In my humble opinion the ordinary method of agitating by way of petitions, deputations, and the like is no remedy for moving to repentance a Government so hopelessly indifferent to the welfare of its charge as the Government of India has proved to be. In European countries, condemnation of such grievous wrongs as the Khilafat and the Punjab would have resulted in a bloody revolution by the people. They would have resisted, at all cost, national emasculation. Half of India is too weak to offer violent resistance, and the other half is unwilling to do so. I have therefore ventured to suggest the remedy of non-co-operation, which enables those who wish to dissociate themselves from Government, and which, if unattended by violence and undertaken in an ordered manner, must compel it to retrace its steps and undo the wrongs committed; but whilst I pursue the policy of non-co-operation, insofar as I can carry the people with me, I shall not lose hope that you will yet see your way to do justice.
>
> While he maintains that British rule in its present form has made India "poorer in wealth, in manliness, in godliness and in her sons' power to defend themselves."

He was firmed that no improvement in Indian situation was possible so long as the British adopted an unnatural attitudes of patronage and superiority. Things not changed, even after independence, men in power are stashing Indian currency to foreign countries. Be the bureaucracy or the people's representatives, the malpractices, mal-administration, misappropriation of Government fund, or discriminatory treatments, in all parts of Indian governance system continues and it has become part of life with full of scams. In such a situation, strict separation of power shall

1. By Sarvepalli Radhakrishnan (pp. 18-19).

neither be feasible nor appropriate for India in its national and social interest.

It may be noted that according to the report,[1] amongst 395 members of the legislative assembly of the State of Uttar Pradesh against 138 members (34%), criminal cases are pending. Out of 138, against 72 members of the Legislative Assembly (18%), cases with regard to heinous crime like murder, kidnapping, robbery, dacoity, extortion, rape and sale of minors etc., are pending.

The 16th Legislative Assembly of the State of Uttar Pradesh constituted in pursuance of General Election, 2012, consists more representatives having criminal antecedents. According to Report,[2] 189 elected candidates possess criminal antecedents in comparison to 2007 Election, 140 MLAs were having criminal antecedents. Out of 189, 98 MLAs are named in serious pending criminal cases whereas, in 2007 only against 78 MLAs, serious criminal cases were pending. Against one MLA, 36 criminal cases have been registered and out of which 14 cases relate to murder. Thus, there appears to be no room of doubt that Legislature has failed to check the infiltration of persons having criminal antecedents in the Legislative Assembly.

According to an article,[3] the record of 15th Lok Sabha is also not encouraging; rather it is a matter of deep concern for the civilized society. In 15th Lok Sabha, as many as 153 (162 according to author) MPs have criminal records, out of which, 74 of them are charged with serious offences like murder, abduction, misappropriation of public fund etc.

Christophe Jaffrelot,[4] in an article had narrated the magnitude of corruption in India. Learned author also consider the criminalisation of Indian politics to quote:—

1. (Hindustan Times, dated 9-8-2011).
2. Times of India, Lucknow Edn., dated 12-3-2012 [page 2].
3. Published in "Times of India", dated September 2, 2011, written by Dipankar Gupta.
4. Senior research fellow at CERI-Sciences Po/CNRS (Paris), Professor of Indian Politics and Sociology at King's India Institute, London, and non-resident scholar at the Carnegie Endowment for International Peace and Milan Vaishnav associate with the South Asia programme at the Carnegie Endowment in Washington, DC.

> "Besides grand corruption, however, the criminalisation of politics has also put down roots in India's democracy. Criminalisation is a distinct but related concept from corruption: politicians with criminal associations exploit the vacuum presented by the corrupt state, but they also reinforce its pathologies. The data that candidates at the state and national levels now must disclose to the EC, and which one of us has (Vaishnav) extensively analysed, enables us to measure this phenomenon in many different ways. As many have reported, the data show that out of 543 sitting MPs, 163 (or 30 per cent) face some type of criminal charge. Naturally, one needs to disaggregate criminal charges to separate minor violations from potentially serious ones. To separate "serious" crimes, we discard minor charges, such as those that might be related to elections, campaigning, opinion, lifestyle, speech or assembly — or those plausibly related to a politician's vocation. We are left with charges of a serious nature (a subset of "serious" charges can be called "heinous," which is even narrower in scope). For instance, assault to deter a public servant from discharging his duty is a "serious" charge, while murder and attempted murder qualify for the "heinous" category. Among sitting MPs, 103 (roughly 19 per cent) are accused of serious charges and 74 (about 13.5 per cent) of heinous charges."

The criminalisation of politics affects political parties of all stripes, but with interesting differences of degree. In percentage terms, Shiv Sena tops the list with nine of its 11 MPs (82 per cent) facing criminal charges. Two parties sharing a similar battle field (geographically as well as sociologically), the SP and the JD(U) also share a similar profile insofar as criminalisation is concerned, with roughly 40 per cent of MPs under criminal scrutiny. The BSP lags behind with "only" 29 per cent of its MPs facing such a dubious distinction.

But the two large, national parties are, for obvious reasons, the most interesting ones to examine. While the BJP claims that it is "a party with a difference", 44 of its 116 MPs (38 per cent) stand accused of criminal charges when "only" 22 per cent of the 206 Congress MPs are in this uncomfortable position. The differences remain even when one disaggregates criminal charges: 24 per cent of BJP MPs and 14 per cent of Congress MPs are accused of serious crimes, while 16.5 per cent and 6 per cent respectively are accused of heinous crimes.

In which states are these national parties the most badly affected? Surprisingly, if we go by the clean image of Gujarat after 12 years of a government that has brandished its credentials for tackling corruption and crime, the BJP in Narendra Modi's State is not very different than in Uttar Pradesh and Bihar, with respectively 40, 30 and 50 per cent of its MPs facing serious charges. The situation is better at the MLA level, however, since "only" 12 per cent. of Gujarat MLAs are carrying heinous charges (2012 data comes from ADR). The situation is much more precarious in Bihar, where the corresponding figure for the BJP is 32 per cent.

By and large, out of 1200 BJP MLAs (elected before 2010) for which we have collected data, 15 per cent stand accused of serious charges and 10 per cent of heinous charges. The Congress does slightly better with 8 per cent and 6 per cent, respectively, accused of these two kinds of charges out of 1515 MLAs.[1]

In the election of Karnataka Legislative Assembly out of 218 elected MLAs, 203 MLAs are crorepati. Average asset is Rs. 30.15 crores which is an increase from Rs. 17.53 crores in 2008. 34 per cent or 74 of the 218 MLAs have declared criminal cases against them. Out of which 39 elected Members of Legislative Assembly are charged with criminal cases like attempt to murder, kidnapping and dacoity. In such scenario it may not be ruled out that elections are influenced by money and muscle power.[2]

1. Indian Express, dated 9-5-2013.
2. Hindustan Times, May 11, 2013.

Thus, the peoples' representatives seem to have failed to check infiltration of persons having criminal record in the legislative bodies.

According to statistics compiled by the Lok Sabha Secretariat, 1,157 hours of sittings had taken place until the 12th session of the 15th Lok Sabha, which has been functional since 2009. Among Houses that completed five-year terms, the least productive so far was the 14th Lok Sabha, which clocked just 1,737 hours of sittings. But even that could prove beyond the present House, which will have to manage almost 600 hours of sittings in less than a year if it is to overtake its immediate predecessor. Some Houses, like the 9th, 11th and 12th Lok Sabhas, did end up with fewer than 1,737 hours. But none of them completed their full terms., While the 9th Lok Sabha clocked 754 hours, it has a life of barely two years (1989-91). The 11th Lok Sabha clocked 814 hours in 1996-1997 and the 12th 575 hours in 1998-1999.[1]

Almost 64 years ago during the Constituent Assembly debate, Dr. Rajendra Prasad articulated the path ahead for the people's representatives. He said, to quote *"To all we give the assurance that it will be our endeavour to end poverty and squalor and its companions, hunger and diseases; to abolish distinction and exploitation and to ensure decent conditions of living.[2]"*

It is unfortunate that the opinion expressed by Former President of India in the Constituent Assembly seems to be over sighted. Planning Commission decide poverty line keeping in view the expenditure of Rs. 32 per day. The farmers of the country belongs to grower of foodgrains, but they seems to robbed, who robbed them? The poverty and lack of sustainable alternative flora robbed them. The time spent in the Parliament or in the State Legislatures by the people's representatives indicative of their sincerity, in such situation whether higher judiciary should be moot spectator?[1]

1. Times of India, 29 April, 2013.
2. Constituent Assembly debate.

Coming to second limb of governance, the bureaucracy, where also things are not too good. It is of common knowledge that substantial number of bureaucrats succumb to political pressure and do not tender correct advice to the government resulting in loss of revenue, misappropriation of public fund and abuse of power. Shri Bhaskar Ghose, an IAS officer who served for 36 years in the cadre has shown his deep concern with regard to falling standards among the bureaucracy. He has written his autobiography in the name and title, "SERVICE OF THE STATE, THE IAS RECONSIDERED." Learned author observed as under:

> "A number of IAS officers have been charged with, even arrested for, corruption; and many, many more have taken to ways that are not, strictly speaking, illegal but are repellent nonetheless-the ways of nepotism, of intrigue, of lobbying and cultivating the politically powerful to worm their way up the administrative ladder. Krishnan and Somanathan have reported wryly on a 'formulation' to which another officer, K. Ashok Vardhan Shetty, has, according to the two, made a contribution. I cannot resist reproducing it in full:
>
> In a sense, the IAS can be divided into three groups – the 'vives' (those who are attached to one party), the 'nuns' (officers who remain unattached to any party), and the 'prostitutes' (who attach themselves to whichever party is in power and switch when there is a change of government). The authors have been at pains to clarify that these terms are used metaphorically, to make an analytical point and should not be misconstrued or misquoted, out of context.
>
> Point taken, and the quotation is very much in context and has not been misconstrued; in case anyone has any doubts the metaphorical nature of the terms is emphasized; after all, whoever heard of an IAS officer actually being a prostitute?

> But this study, and others like it, have made the enquiry into the service and its relevance in the twenty-first century not just relevant, but urgent. If India is to take its place in the world as an economic superpower it cannot be burdened with an administrative system that is controlled by one group of officers, some of whom have been exposed as corrupt and many more known to be courtiers and arch intriguers and lobbyists."

Learned author while concluding the book had placed on record his opinion with pain and sorrow. To quote:

> "It is true that there are a number of corrupt officers in the IAS, more than one would like to see, and it makes me – and I'm sure many, many other IAS officers – ashamed and disgusted. One hopes they will be punished and driven out of the service. Apart from corruption, there are others who openly practice nepotism, who manoeuvre to get themselves coveted postings, who cultivate people who they think will be useful to them in some way at some time."

Another IAS Officer Shri Radhey Shyam Agarwal while writing his autobiography, titled "Inside Story of....Bureaucracy" has given glimpse of state of affairs of bureaucracy in Uttar Pradesh, in the following words:

> "As a matter of fact the new Minister wanted to shift the responsibilities on to me and would not like to be bothered by others. I had a lot of difficulty in dealing with the union leaders who always had been putting forth their demands of promotion and transfer. Whenever they went to meet the director, he always referred them to me. The actual fact was rather different. He would say something to me and would do something otherwise."

Learned author (supra) while in-capsuling his experience suggested to adopt remedial measures to maintain the intellectual integrity of political bosses as well as that of the bureaucracy in the following words:

> "This is high time that one should give serious thoughts on how to maintain the intellectual integrity of political bosses as well as that of the bureaucracy. It is for the political parties in the interest of the country, not to create a vicious circle by exploiting the bureaucracy in their own interest. Let the bureaucracy work with impartial mind and if anybody amongst them is found corrupt or having a partisan attitude such a bureaucrat must be given punishment. At the same time the members of the Legislative Assembly and Members of the Parliament should not be allowed to interfere in the affairs of transfers and postings and day-to-day administration. Since we have not been able to implement the policies of government in the true sense, nor have we developed a proper work culture, there is an adjustment gap which needs to be filled in a reasonable way."

Shri Vinod Rai, Comptroller and Auditor-General of India while giving a lecture[1] had shown his deep concern to the succumbing bureaucracy indulged in corruption in different forms of mal-practices giving way to political system to be more corrupt and whimsical. It shall be appropriate to quote relevant portion of the opinion expressed by Shri Vinod Rai, Comptroller and Auditor-General of India as published in the newspaper[2]:—

> "That governance is at its lowest ebb. That the morale of the civil servants is low. That credibility of the government is at its lowest. That decision-making has become a casualty. *Second*: That this situation is deleterious for the nation. That too much is at stake for toomany in such a situation. *Third*: On you and officers of the All India Services, among others, rests the *onus* to remedy the situation.................................

1. On 11th October, 2011 at Sardar Vallabhbhai Patel National Police Academy in Hyderabad.
2. Newspaper, "Hindu" of 13th October, 2011.

Today, we are facing a testing time in the history of our nation. The quality of governance is below par. There has been an erosion of people's faith in government. Their confidence in public institutions has declined. National trust in the bureaucracy, including the police force has collapsed. The integrity and professionalism of civil servants are being questioned. This has brought the credibility of the government to the lowest since Independence.

...........Most of us would not be able to convince ourselves that we are capable of being part of a legacy which provided this nation the foundations on which the edifice of good governance stood. And that is where the greatest challenge to the police force lies today, when the moral fabric of the nation seems to be tearing apart in the absence of an optimal governance system, characterised by a near total absence of accountability; where loyalty takes precedence over the sense of one's duty, and where national interests are often, and with impunity, subjugated to individual gains."

While discussing the fall of political system and bureaucracy, the Times of India, Lucknow dated 17-10-2011 remarked, "The steel framework is cracking – bending under the weight of people's expectations and being pulled down by the political class. The IAS and IPS officers themselves are caught in a debilitating dilemma as governance, in the words of Vinod Rai, "touches a new low".

After considering number of instances with regard to evil or persecuted bureaucracy, the reporter (supra) considering the plight of certain honest upright officers observed, to quote:—

"It's an evil throughout the country. Ruling parties do post people arbitrarily, without merit. It's done to subjugate the bureaucracy into toeing a certain line: says T.S.R. Subramanian, former cabinet secretary of India. But, says Subramanian, the bureaucrats should voice their concerns within the bounds of service rules.

"Done in that manner, the service rules protect you and provide immense immunity."

But others blame bureaucrats themselves for their plight as they have not learnt to say "no" to their political masters. "The message should be loud and clear that reshufflings would not help matters," says a Maharashtra cadre IPS officer, giving the example of a fiercely independent cadre-mate, then Nasik IG, B.D. Mishra, who had to be reinstated because of public pressure after he was shunted out for acting against some local heavyweights."

The reporter while considering the plight of honest officers quoted the comments of some bureaucrats and remarked, to quote:

"While an officer may lower his own expectations, he may not always have the luxury of ignoring people's expectations. Nor can he afford to antagonize the political class. To maintain that difficult balance, while some seek central deputation, others go on unending sabbaticals. Yet others, like a 1985-batch Bihar-cadre IPS officer, plead to the government that instead of all the harassment they just be declared insane.[1]"

Keeping in view the present scenario and creeping paralysis of moral will, which has substantially corrupted the governance causing mental pain and agony and set back of socio-economic development of the countries, strict separation of power is neither feasible nor possesses constitutional mandate. The Government (executive and legislature) cannot claim immunity of their actions which suffer from violation of constitutional mandate and the Rule of law under the realm of separation of power.

---

1. (Extract from The Times of India, Lucknow, Monday, October 17, 2011).

Democracy restores to man a consciousness of his value, teaches him by the removal of authority and oppression to listen only to the dictates of reason, gives him confidence to treat all other men as his fellow beings, and induces him to regard them no longer as enemies against whom to be upon his guard, but as brethren whom it becomes him to assist.[1]

In democracy there is no unfettered discretion to any wing of government. Each one have to balance (check and balance) the other for a successful democracy.

---

1. Political Justice by Godwin, 268-269.

Time Frame for Sanction to Prosecution

"All that means is that there is nothing in the constitution forbidding the Legislature to do insane things. One would not expect to find such a provision there. The Constitution of every free civilized community if based on the assumption that the body to which it commits the power of making its laws may be trusted to bring to the exercise of that power a reasonable degree of sanity. If at any time that trust should prove to be misplaced, then the State would be in very evil case, and would be hard put to it to find a way of escaping disaster.[1]"

In post-independent India, crime and corruption (indispensable part of crime) possesses rising graph because of loss of morality with the passage of time[2]. Ineffective law is one of the main cause of the manifold increase of crime in India.[3]

The spurt in the crime, is because of various reasons like paid laws as observed by Arvind Shivaramkrishnan in an article "Paid Laws, American Style"[4], the Institutionalization of Corruption at different strata of Governance, loss of morality. Unfettered discretion to deal with the mercy

1. Observation by J. Ferguson, (1930) 31 SR (NSW) 183 (202, 208).
2. Morality in Law, Published by Eastern Book Co. Ltd., 2012 Edn., by the author of this Article.
3. Hindustan Times, October 11, 2012.
4. Hindu, May 28, 2012.

petitions by the Government (article 72 of the Constitution) and unfair discretion exercised by the Government in granting sanction under section 19 of the Prevention of Corruption Act, 1988 (in short the Act) are other reasons for the increase of crimes. Section 19 of the Act provides that in case of a person, who is employed in connection with the affairs of the Union or the State Government, is removable from his or her office except by the sanction of the Central Government or the State Government, the previous-sanction shall be necessary for prosecution. The power conferred on the State and the Central Government under section 19 of the Act, ordinarily, is not exercised in a time frame. Sometimes, matters are kept pending for decades to come. Non-exercise of discretion by the Government expeditiously, extend wrong message, to the Government servants and gives them unfettered liberty to abuse their office or misappropriate public funds, sometimes in collusion with political masters. Courts sometimes are helpless. Repeated judgments of Supreme Court to decide the application for sanction within three months or so, right from the *Vineet Narain's* case,[1] remains unattended. The result is, corruption has been institutionalized in India. Scams after scams, eroded the people's faith not only in the governance, which include legislature and bureaucracy but also in the administration of justice. While enacting Prevention of Corruption Act, 1947, under the aims and object, the Parliament observed, to quote:—

> "The scope for bribery and corruption of public servants had been enormously increased by war conditions and though the war is now over, opportunities for corrupt practices will remain for considerable time to come. Contracts are being terminated; large amounts of Government surplus stores are being disposed of; there will be years of shortage of various kinds requiring imposition of controls, and extensive schemes of post-war

---

1. *Vineet Narain* v. *Union of India,* AIR 1996 SC 3386: 1996 AIR SCW 2835: (1996) 2 SCC 199 (Para 58).

> reconstruction, involving the disbursement of very large sums of Government money. All these activities offer wide scope of corrupt practices and seriousness of the evil and possibility of its continuance or extension in future are such as to justify immediate and drastic action to stamps it out."
>
> "The existing law has proved inadequate for dealing with the problem which has arisen in recent years and the Bill is intended to render the criminal law more effective in dealing with cases of bribery and corruption of public servants."[1]

Seriousness of evils still persists and corruption continues with more vigour digesting substantial portion of public fund.

While adjudicating a controversy under the Public Interest Litigation in the High Court (Lucknow Bench) Uttar Pradesh, it came to light that food grains meant for poor and down trodden classes (BPL card-holders and others), were sent not only outside the State of Uttar Pradesh but exported outside the country.[2] The question cropped-up, how section 19 should be interpreted and whether courts have power under article 226 of the Constitution or article 32 or article 136, to provide a time frame commanding the Government to decide all sanction matters within specified time frame? Though, the statement, object and reason ordinarily may not be admissible for the construction of statute but in case statutory provisions are vague, extend uncontrolled, unguided, unbridled power to Government causing miscarriage of justice or public loss and misappropriation of public fund, then aims and object of an statute may be taken into account while interpreting statutory provisions.[3] Accordingly, courts are entitled to

1. (Gazette of India dated November 23, 1946, Part V, page 374).
2. W.P. No. 10503 (M/B) of 2009; *Vishwanath Chaturvedi S/O M.P. Chaturvedi* v. *Union of India,* 2011 (2) LCD 454.
3. *Emperor* v. *Benoari Lal,* 1913 PC 36; *M.K. Ranganathan* v. *Government of Madras,* AIR 1955 SC 604: 1955 SCJ 515: (1955) 2 SCR 374; *Express Newspaper Pvt. Limited* v. *Union of India,* AIR 1958 SC 578: 1958 SCJ

Contd. on next page

ascertain the legislative intent and remove the ambiguity by construing the statutory provisions as a whole keeping in view, the mischief which the legislation sought to remove is aimed at.

The purpose of section 19 is to save the public servants from false prosecution. In case the allegation against the Government servants is false or based on unfounded fact or FIR has been lodged to persecute such Government servants, then in such a situation, a quick decision shall be more warranting than keeping the matter pending giving opportunity to people to raise finger over the conduct of the Government and cause public resentment. It was for this reason that Supreme Court from time to time held that sanction is not intended to be nor is an automatic formality but sanction should be observed with complete strictness and with due application of mind.[1] It is solemn and sacrosanct act and should not be construed in a pedantic manner.[2]

Section 19 of the Act does not provide any time frame for the Government to decide an application for grant of

---

Contd. from previous page

1113: 1959 SCR 12; *S.C. Prashar* v. *Vasantsen Dwarkadas,* AIR 1963 SC 1356: 1963 (1) SCJ 687: (1964) 1 SCR 29; *State of West Bengal* v. *Union of India,* AIR 1963 SC 1241: (1963) 2 SCA 448: (1964) 1 SCR 371; *A.C. Sharma* v. *Delhi Administration,* AIR 1973 SC 913: (1973) 1 SCC 726: 1973 Cr LJ 902; *Kameshwar Singh* v. *IV Additional District Judge, Lucknow,* AIR 1987 SC 138: (1986) 4 SCC 661: 1986 (4) Supreme 236; *R.S. Nayak* v. *A.R. Antulay,* (1984) 2 SCC 183: AIR 1984 SC 684: 1984 Cr LJ 613; *Girdhari Lal & Sons* v. *Balbir Nath Mathur,* AIR 1957 SC 29: (1986) 2 SCC 237: 1986 (2) Supreme 69; *State* v. *Govindan Thampi Bhaskaran Thampi,* AIR 1957 Travancore-Cochin 29; *Kunwar Murli Manohar* v. *State of Uttar Pradesh,* AIR 1957 All 159, on a reference made by Ravinandan Sahai, Sessions Judge, Patna.

1. *Afzalur Rahman* v. *Emperor,* ILR 22 Pat 349: 44 Cr LJ 466: AIR 1943 FC 18 (21); *R.R. Chari* v. *State of Uttar Pradesh,* AIR 1962 SC 1573 (1581): (1962) 2 Cr LJ 510: (1963) 1 SCR 121; *H.H.B. Gill* v. *The King,* AIR 1948 PC 128: (1948) 49 Cr LJ 503: 75 IA 41; *Albert West Meads* v. *The King,* AIR 1948 PC 156: 75 IA 185: 49 Cr LJ 660; *Ronald Wood Mathams* v. *State of West Bengal,* AIR 1954 SC 455: 1954 Cr LJ 1161: (1954) 1 SCR 216.
2. *Jaswant Singh* v. *State of Punjab,* AIR 1958 SC 124 (126): 1958 Cr LJ 265: 1958 SCR 762; *Mohammad Iqbal Ahmed* v. *State of Andhra Pradesh,* AIR 1979 SC 677: 1979 Cr LJ 633: (1979) 2 SCR 1007; *State of Karnataka* v. *Ameer Jan,* AIR 2008 SC 108: 2008 Cr LJ 347: (2007) 11 SCC 273.

sanction. It is because of this reason that the Government does not proceed within reasonable time frame to decide an application. Often employees are retired, evidence collected by the prosecution become ineffective or witness die, giving no option to courts but to acquit the accused at the end of the day when the sanction is granted at belated stage. In any case, in such a situation, to secure public good, it shall be appropriate to supply *causus omissus* to section 19 of the Act. On account of the absence of time frame, it deserves absurdity, anomaly and loss of injury to public exchequer. It was in *Viluswami Thevar's* case[1] in which Supreme Court held that a construction which gives rise to anomalies should be avoided.

In *Tirath Singh's* case[2] Supreme Court held that where the language of a statute, in its ordinary meaning and grammatical construction, leads to a manifest contradiction of the apparent purpose of the enactment, or to some inconvenience or absurdity, hardship or injustice, presumably not intended, a construction may be put upon it which modifies the meaning of the words, and even the structure of the sentence. The ratio of the *Tirath Singh's* case has been affirmed.[3]

In *R.S. Nayak's* case,[4] Supreme Court observed as under:—

1. *N.T. Veluswami Thevar* v. *G. Raja Nainar,* AIR 1959 SC 422 (427, 428): 1959 SCJ 751: 1959 SCR Supp (1) 623.
2. *Tirath Singh* v. *Bachittar Singh,* AIR 1955 SC 830 (833): (1955) 2 SCR 457: 1955 SCC 77.
3. *State of Madhya Pradesh* v. *Azad Bharat Finance Co.,* AIR 1967 SC 276 (278): 1967 Cr LJ 285: 1966 Supp SCR 473; *Union of India* v. *Sankalchand Himatlal Sheth,* 1978 (7) SCJ 265: (1978) 1 SCR 423: AIR 1977 SC 2328 (2337, 2358, 2373); *Commissioner of Income-Tax* v. *National Taj Traders,* AIR 1980 SC 485 (490): (1980) 1 SCC 370: (1980) 2 SCR 268; *R. Rudraiah* v. *State of Karnataka,* AIR 1998 SC 1070: (1998) 3 SCC 23: (1998) 1 SCR 553; *Molar Mal* v. *Kay Iron Works (P) Limited,* AIR 2000 SC 1261: (2000) 4 SCC 285: (2000) 2 SCALE 334; *Padmasundara Rao* v. *State of Tamil Nadu,* AIR 2002 SC 1334 (1340, 1341): (2002) 3 SCC 533: (2002) 2 SCALE 580 and *Modern School* v. *Union of India,* AIR 2004 SC 2236 (2257): 2004 AIR SCW 2698: (2004) 5 SCALE 170.
4. *R.S. Nayak* v. *A.R. Antulay,* (1984) 2 SCC 183: AIR 1984 SC 684: 1984 Cr LJ 613.

"34..............Even apart from precedents the basic purpose underlying all canons of construction is the ascertainment with reasonable certainty of the intention of Parliament in enacting the legislation........................In this connection, it would be advantageous to refer to a passage from Crawford on Statutory Construction (page 388). It reads as under:

"The judicial opinion on this point is certainly not quite uniform and there are American decisions to the effect that the general history of a statute and the various amendments or modifications of the original bill and reports of Legislative Committees can be looked at for ascertaining the intention of the Legislature where it is in doubt; but they held definitely that the legislative history is inadmissible when there is no obscurity in the meaning of the Statute." In *United States* v. *St. Paul, M.M. Rly. Co.*, (1917) 62 L Ed 1130 (1134), it is observed that 'the reports of a Committee, including the bill as introduced, changes made in the frame of the bill in the course of its passage and the statement made by the Committee Chairman in-charge of it, stand upon a different footing, and may be resorted to under proper qualifications". The objection therefore of Mr. Singhvi to our looking into the history of the evolution of the section with all its clauses, the Reports of Mudiman Committee and K. Santhanam Committee and such other external aids to construction must be overruled."

The principle of reading down or supply of *causus omissus* has been applied by the Supreme Court in number of cases from time to time to fill-up the vacuum.[1]

1. *Central India Spinning, Weaving and Manufacturing Company Limited, Empress Mills, Nagpur* v. *Municipal Committee, Wardha*, AIR 1958 SC 341 (346): 1958 SCJ 604: 1958 SCR 1102; *Rakesh Wadhawan* v. *Jagadamba Industrial Corporation*, AIR 2002 SC 2004: (2002) 5 SCC 440: (2002) 4 SCALE 134; *A.A. Hajee Muniuddian* v. *Indian Railways*, AIR 1993 SC 361: (1992) 4 SCC 736: (1992) 3 SCR 72; *I.R.C.* v. *Mutual Investment*

Contd. on next page

In the case of *Mutual Investment Co.*[1] while affirming the construction on the basis of absurdity, it has been observed that in case of ambiguity, that construction which better serves the ends of fairness and justice will be accepted, but otherwise it is for the Legislature in forming its policy to consider these elements.

It was Lord Denning, L.J. in his of quoted judgment, in *Seaford Court Estates Limited* v. *Asher,*[2] had given the landmark verdict with regard to principle of reading down or supply of *causus omissus*. Denning L.J. opined:

> "When a defect appears a judge cannot simply fold his hands and blame the draftsman. He must set to work on the constructive task of finding the intention of Parliament and then he must supplement the written words so as to give 'force and life' to the intention of the Legislature. A judge should ask himself the question how, if the makers of the Act had themselves come across this rock in the texture of it, they would have straightened it out? He must then do as they would have done. A judge must not alter the material of which the Act is woven, but he can and should iron out the creases."

Lord Denning, L.J., in the case of *Magor,*[3] observed, to quote, "We sit here to find out the intention of Parliament and of ministers and carry it out, and we do this better by

---

Contd. from previous page

Co., (1966) 3 All ER 265 (268) (PC); *Seaford Court Estates Limited* v. *Asher,* (1949) 2 All ER 155 (164) (CA); *Magor & St. Mellons Rural District Council* v. *Newport Corporation,* (1950) 2 All ER 1226 (1236); *Bangalore Water Supply* v. *A. Rajappa,* (1978) 2 SCC 213: AIR 1978 SC 548: 1978 Lab IC 467; *Bengal Immunity Co. Limited* v. *State of Bihar,* AIR 1955 SC 661: 1955 SCJ 672: (1955) 2 SCR 603; *Padmasundara Rao* v. *State of Tamil Nadu,* AIR 2002 SC 1334 (1340): (2002) 3 SCC 533: (2002) 2 SCALE 580; *Pratap Singh* v. *State of Jharkhand,* (2005) 3 SCC 551: AIR 2005 SC 2731: 2005 AIR SCW 3088; *ISPAT Industries Limited* v. *Commissioner of Customs,* (2006) 12 SCC 583: JT 2006 (12) SC 379.

1. *I.R.C.* v. *Mutual Investment Co.,* (1966) 3 All ER 265 (268) (PC).
2. 65 TLR 379: (1949) 2 KB 481: (1949) 2 All ER 155 (164) (CA).
3. *Magor & St. Mellons Rural District Council* v. *Newport Corporation,* (1950) 2 All ER 1226 (1236).

filling-in the gaps and making sense of the enactment than by opening it up to destructive analysis".

Justice Krishna Iyer in the case of *Carew and Company Limited,*[1] observed, to quote:—

> "20. The law is not 'a brooding omnipotence in the sky' but a pragmatic instrument of social order. It is an operational art controlling economic life, and interpretative effort must be imbued with the statutory purpose. No doubt, grammar is a good guide to meaning but a bad master to dictate. Notwithstanding the traditional view that grammatical construction is the golden rule, Justice Frank further used words of practical wisdom when he observed" (*Massachusetts B. & Insurance. Co.* v. *United State,* (1956) 352 US 128 (138): 1 Law Ed 2d 189).

Lord Denning in his famous treatise, "Discipline of Law" has observed that the Judges should not be mute spectator to ground realities and may proceed with ideas to remedy the mischief. The observation of Lord Denning in the "Discipline of Law" is reproduced as under:

> "Whenever a statute comes up for consideration it must be remembered that it is not within human powers to foresee the manifold sets of facts which may arise, and, even if it were, it is not possible to provide for them in terms free from all ambiguity. The English language is not an instrument of mathematical precision. Our literature would be much the poorer if it were. This is where the draftsmen of Acts of Parliament have often been unfairly criticized. A Judge, believing himself to be fettered by the supposed rule that he must look to the language and nothing else, laments that the draftsmen have not provided for this or that, or have been guilty of some or other ambiguity. It would certainly save the judges' trouble if Acts of Parliament were drafted

---

1. *Carew and Company Limited* v. *Union of India,* AIR 1975 SC 2260: (1975) 2 SCC 791: (1976) 1 SCR 379.

with divine prescience and perfect clarity. In the absence of it, when a defect appears a judge cannot simply fold his hands and blame the draftsmen. He must set to work on the constructive task of finding the intention of Parliament."

"15. And it is clear that when one has to look to the intention of the Legislature, one has to look to the circumstances under which the law was enacted. The Preamble of the law, the mischief which was intended to be remedied by the enactment of the statute and in this context, Lord Denning, in the same book at Page No. 10, observed as under:

"At one time the Judges used to limit themselves to the bare reading of the Statute itself – to go simply by the words, giving them their grammatical meaning and that was all. That view was prevalent in the 19th century and still has some supporters today. But it is wrong in principle. The Statute as it appears to those who have to obey it – and to those who have to advise them what to do about it; in short, to lawyers like yourselves. Now the eccentrics cut off from all that is happening around them. The Statute comes to them as men of affairs – who have their own feeling for the meaning of the words and know the reason why the Act was passed – just as if it had been fully set out in a Preamble. So it has been held very rightly that you can enquire into the mischief which gave rise to the Statute-to see what was the evil which it was sought to remedy."

The aforesaid observation of Lord Denning has been reiterated and reproduced by Supreme Court of India in the case of *Uttar Pradesh Bhoodan Yagna Samiti, Uttar Pradesh* v. *Braj Kishore,*[1]

In the case of *Dadi Jagannadham,*[2] Supreme Court of India held that Courts should strongly lean against any

1. AIR 1988 SC 2239: JT 1988 (3) SC 640.
2. *Dadi Jagannadham* v. *Jammulu Ramulu,* AIR 2001 SC 2699: (2001) 7 SCC 71: 2001 AIR SCW 3051.

construction which tends to reduce a Statute to a futility (para 49).

In appropriate cases, Courts must supply purposive interpretation while ascertaining the intention of legislature.[1]

Apart from the principle of reading down or supply of *causus omissus*, there is one other trend, applied by the western courts that is, presumptive construction.

According to Bennion on Statutory Interpretation to quote, "The interpretative presumptions are not distinct from rules and principles of law, but are to a large extent drawn from them. At the same time they recognise the essential nature of legislation, and look in particular to its effective working..................

The literal meaning is one arrived at from the wording of the enactment alone, without consideration of other interpretative criteria. When account is taken of such other criteria (for the purpose of arriving at the legal meaning of the enactment), it may be found necessary to depart from the literal meaning and adopt a strained construction."

Learned author (supra) further observed that according to recent trend, the courts while construing the statutory provisions and to remove absurdity, apply the "presumptive construction", to quote:—

> "The modern attitude is indicated by a dictum of Mustill J. that 'a statute.....cannot be interpreted according to its literal meaning without testing that meaning against the practical outcome of giving effect to it. Some modern judges have gone so far as to suggest that the correct course is to start by considering which result would be desirable, and then see if the law permits it. Thus Lord Radcliffe said:

---

1. *M. Rathinaswami* v. *State of Tamil Nadu,* (2009) 5 SCC 625: 2009 AIR SCW 3930: 2009 Lab IC 2900; *N. Kannadasan* v. *Ajoy Khose,* (2009) 7 SCC 1.

> '...............it sometimes helps to assess the merits of a decision, if one starts by noticing its results and only after doing that allots to it the legal principles upon which it is said to depend'."

Lord Radcliffe went on to say that in the instant case he had begun by considering the consequences of the apparent meaning of the enactment, and found these disquieting. He went on: I start then with the assumption that something must have gone wrong in the application of legal principles that produce such a result.

Prima facie, as we have seen, the ordinary meaning of the words is to be followed. If the consequences are adverse, this presumption may be displaced. As Donaldson M.R. put it:

> "Our task, as I see it, is to construe [the Act], and in so doing the *prima facie* rule is that words, have their ordinary meaning. But that is subject to the qualification that if, giving words their ordinary meaning, we are faced with extraordinary results which cannot have been intended by Parliament, we then have to move on to a second stage in which we re-examine the words...."

The '*prima facie* rule' referred to in the above dictum of Donaldson M.R. was called by Viscount Simon the 'golden rule'. He said: 'The golden rule is that the words of a statute must *prima facie* be given their ordinary meaning'. However, the terms golden rule is more usually applied to the precept Lord Blackburn described as 'what Lord Wensleydale used to call the golden rule. Lord Blackburn went on to express this so-called rule as:

> '...........that we are to take the whole statute together, and construe it all together giving the words their ordinary signification, unless when so applied they produce an inconsistency, or an absurdity or inconvenience so great as to convince the Court that the intention could not have been to use them in their ordinary signification.'

> This was an attempt by Lord Blackburn to provide in a few words an all-embracing single prescription for the task of statutory interpretation."

Learned author (supra) noted that by passage of time, the intention of the originator of the statute loses its effectiveness and become irrelevant but even then the statutory provisions continue to operate. With the change of social condition and keeping in view the fact that the Constitution is living organism, an "Act" may also be treated as "living statute" and may be constructed in such a manner which may remove the absurdity. The old enactments should be read in the light of the dynamic processing received over the years with such modification of current meaning of its language as will now give effective legislative intention. Learned author observed that updating principle may be applied in mind while interpreting the statutory provisions after passage of time.

It shall be appropriate to reproduce relevant portion from the Bennion on Statutory Interpretation (supra):

> "With the updating principle in mind, the competent drafter frames the language in terms suitable for continuing operation into the unforeseeable future. The drafter does not conspicuously compose the Act as at the date of the draft. Rather the aim is to employ a continuous present tense, using the word 'shall', as enjoined, as 'an imperative only, and not as a future'. Yet, since language (like human society) is continually in flux, the formula expressed in the words of one age may not feel comfortable as current law to its subjects in another. It might even fill them with the consciousness of governance from the grave: an always absurd, and sometimes intolerable, infliction. Where the words have changed their meaning, an interpreter may find it impracticable to apply the original sense. Imagination and historical awareness are here required."

Each generation lives under the law it inherits. Constant formal updating is not practicable, so an Act takes on a life of its own. What the original framers intended sinks gradually into history. While their language may endure as law, its current subjects are likely to find that law more and more ill fitting. The intention of the originators, collected from an Act's legislative history, necessarily becomes less relevant as time rolls by. Yet their words remain law. Viewed like this, the ongoing Act resembles a vessel launched on some one-way voyage from the old world to the new. The vessel is not going to return; nor are its passengers. Having only what they set out with, they cope as best they can. On arrival in the present, they deploy their native endowments under conditions originally unguessed at.

In construing an ongoing Act, the interpreter is to presume that Parliament intended the Act to be applied at any future time in such a way as to give effect to the true original intention. Accordingly, the interpreter is to make allowances for any relevant changes that have occurred, since the Act's passing, in law, social conditions, technology, the meaning of words, and other matters. Just as the United States Constitution is regarded as 'a living Constitution', so an ongoing British Act is regarded as 'a living Act'. The today's construction involves the supposition that Parliament was catering long ago for a state of affairs that did not then exist is no argument against that construction. Parliament, in the wording of an enactment, is expected to anticipate temporal developments. The drafter will try to foresee the future, and allow for it in the wording.

On one view of the definition of 'superior court' in the Contempt of Court Act, 1981 section 19, it applied to a type of court that did not yet exist in 1981. Lord Diplock said:

> "I should......have reached the same conclusion on the construction of the definition of "superior court"

> in section 19, even if it were impossible to point to any existing court which complied with the description and one were driven to the conclusion that the draftsman was making anticipatory provision for possible new courts that might be subsequently created with the status of superior courts of record.
>
> An enactment of former days is thus to be read today, in the light of dynamic processing received over the years, with such modification of the current meaning of its language as will now give effect to the original legislative intention. The reality and effect of dynamic processing provides the gradual adjustment. It is constituted by judicial interpretation, year in and year out. It also comprises processing by executive officials."

Learned author (supra) further observed that if the original terminology referred to has been allotted a different meaning, the court will look at the substance behind the wording. The fact that the term referred to by the enactment is still in use does not mean the enactment will apply if the current use gives the term an essentially different meaning.

Accordingly, whether it is purposive interpretation or presumptive construction, the Courts have got ample power to provide the time frame for disposal of an application with regard to grant of sanction under section 19 of the Act. The Government cannot keep an application pending with regard to sanction for prosecution by the agencies for indefinite period. Neither it can be presumed nor it shall be just and fair that the Parliament has conferred power with unfettered discretion to keep an application for grant of sanction under section 19 of the Act, pending for indefinite period or decline to take a decision for any reason whatsoever. Such uncontrolled and unguided power shall be hit by article 14 of the Constitution.

A quick decision in the matter of sanction is necessary for one another reason *i.e.,* peoples may have chance to approach higher judiciary for judicial review of the State action.

Benjamin N. Cardozo, while appreciating works of Roscoe Pound observed to quote:

> "My present purpose will be attained if I arouse in you a sense of the bond between law and its philosophy. In the analysis of ends, the most fruitful generalizations yet reached, at least in Anglo-American law, are those of Roscoe Pound. Certain branches of the law call in conspicuous measure for certainty and order, for an administration of justice that is strict and in a sense mechanical."

Justice Cardozo was of the view that the purpose of law is not only to secure present but also future interest of the society, to quote:—

> "Psychologically, law is a science of prediction *par excellence*. It concerns primarily our future interest; people do not study cases for pleasure, but generally with a view to anticipating what the courts will do when future cases arise."

In *Vineet Narain's* case (supra) Supreme Court of India provided three months to decide an application for sanction. While deciding the case of *Vishwanath Chaturvedi* (supra) by applying presumptive constructions, the author while following *Vineet Narain's* case (supra) held that in case sanction is not granted within three months, there shall be 'deemed sanction' and court may proceed with trial. The abuse of power conferred by section 19 of the Act is so extensive that unless the higher judiciary applies the presumptive or purposive construction and provide a time frame for grant of sanction by the Government, the purpose of the Act (Prevention of Corruption Act, 1988) shall be frustrated.

Sometimes courts are hesitant to supply *causus omisus* or the principle of reading down, while construing statutory provisions because of the principle of separation of power. Such thought seems to be based on misconceived notions.

It is well-settled principles of law that higher judiciary of the country also discharges sovereign function and there is broader separation of power and not the strict one.[1] In the case of *K.B. Nagar*[2] the Supreme Court of India ruled that where no specific time-limit is prescribed, the concept of reasonable time shall hold the field for completing such an action. The Courts in the process of interpretation can supply the lacuna, which would help to achieve the object of the Act and the legislative intent and make the provisions effective and operative.

Again, in the case of *Subramaniam Swamy,*[3] Supreme Court has shown its deep concern to the delay caused in considering the request for sanction. By delaying the request for sanction, the sanctioning authority stultifies judicial scrutiny and determination of the allegation against corrupt official and thus the legitimacy of the judicial institutions is eroded. Delay in grant of sanction also deprives the citizen of its legitimate and fundamental right to get justice by setting the criminal law in motion and thereby, frustrate his right to assess the judicial remedy which is constitutionally protected right. The corruption devalues human rights, chokes development and undermines justice, liberty, equality, fraternity which are the core value in our Preambular vision. Supreme Court ruled that it shall be obligatory for the State to consider the request for sanction within three months.

Judgment and order of Supreme Court is binding under article 141 of the Constitution. In case not complied with, it shall be contempt of Supreme Court and accordingly punishable. Other consequence may be deemed sanction with option to the Trial Court to proceed with the trial after lapse of three months.

In legislative enactment, deemed provisions are made creating fiction of law assuming certain things to be

1. "Sovereignty Separation of Power", Article by the author published in (2012) 7 SCC Page J-1, Journal Section.
2. *K.B. Nagar* v. *Union of India,* (2012) 4 SCC 483.
3. *Subramanian Swamy* v. *Manmohan Singh*, (2012) 1 SCC 1041: AIR 2012 SC 1185: 2012 Cr LJ 1519.

happened. Now, fiction of law is a well-settled principle of statutory construction affirmed by the Supreme Court of India in catena of judgments.[1]

Accordingly, in case within the period of three months stipulated by Supreme Court in Vineet Narain's case (supra) followed by *Subramanium Swami's* case (supra), State does not accord or reject sanction in response to application moved for, then there may be deemed sanction and courts may have option to proceed with the trial of the cases to its logical end.

The Supreme Court further ruled that public administration is responsible for effective implication of the rule of law and constitutional commands which effectuates fairly the objective standard set for executive and administrative decisions. Wherefore, the courts must come forward.[2]

While showing deep concern with regard to spreading of corruption in the country, Supreme Court observed that it should be deep paramountly borne in mind that corruption at any level does not deserve either sympathy or leniency.[3]

---

1. *Shah Bhojraj Kuverji Oil Mills and Ginning Factory* v. *Subbash Chandra Yograj Sinha,* 1962 (2) SCR 159: 1962 (1) SCJ 377: (1962) 2 SCR 159; *State of Tamil Nadu* v. *Arooran Sugars Limited,* (1997) 1 SCC 326: AIR 1997 SC 1815: 1997 AIR SCW 1188; *Bengal Immunity Co. Limited* v. *State of Bihar,* AIR 1955 SC 661: 1955 SCJ 672: (1955) 2 SCR 603; *Commissioner of Income-Tax* v. *S. Teja Singh,* AIR 1959 SC 352: 1959 SCR Supp (1) 394: ILR 1959 Punj 573; *Commissioner of Income-Tax* v. *Shakuntala,* AIR 1966 SC 719: (1962) 2 SCR 871: 1963 (1) SCJ 283; *Boucher Pierre Andre* v. *Supdt. Central Jail,* AIR 1975 SC 164: 1975 Cr LJ 182: (1975) 1 SCC 192; *State of Maharashtra* v. *Narayan Rao Sham Rao Deshmukh,* (1985) 2 SCC 321: AIR 1985 SC 716: 1985 Mah LR 540; *Harish Tandon* v. *A.D.M.,* (1995) 1 SCC 537: AIR 1995 SC 676: 1995 AIR SCW 453; *Gajraj Singh* v. *State Transport Appellate Tribunal,* 1996 AIR SCW 3793: (1997) 1 SCC 650; *Lokmat Newspapers (P) Ltd.* v. *Shankarprasad,* (1999) 6 SCC 275: AIR 1999 SC 2423: 1999 AIR SCW 2565; *Ex parte Walten, In Re Levy,* (1881) 17 CHD 746; *East and Dwellings Co. Ltd.* v. *Finsbury Borough Council,* (1951) 2 All ER 587: (1951) 2 TLR 485: (1952) AC 109 (HL).
2. *Ravi Yashwant Bhoir* v. *District Collector*: (2012) 4 SCC 407: AIR 2012 SC 1339: 2012 AIR SCW 1877.
3. *Narendra Champaklal Trivedi* v. *State of Gujarat,* (2012) 7 SCC 80: AIR 2012 SC 2263: 2012 Cr LJ 3025.

It is because of misuse or abuse of provisions with regard to sanction in India coupled with delay in disposal of case, the corruption has been institutionalized. The period of three months or alike time frame, is necessary for the State Government to decide an application with regard to sanction, and in case no decision is taken within the time frame, it should be presumed that sanction has been granted and courts may proceed with trial without awaiting a response from the Government.

Corruption

"In a republic, where a private citizen has obtained an exorbitant power, the abuse of this power is much greater, because the laws foresaw it not, and consequently made no provision against it."[1]

Corruption means depravity, perversion, or taint; an impairment of integrity, virtue, or moral principle; esp., the impairment of a public official's duties by bribery.[2]

Corrupt also means changed from a sound to a putrid state, dishonest, open to bribery, not genuine, full of errors.[3]

Misuse of power or position in pursuit of a private satisfaction may amount to corruption.[4] The word "corruption" has a wide connotation and embraces almost all the spheres of our day to day life the world over. In a limited sense it connotes allowing decisions and actions of a person to be influenced not by rights or wrongs of a cause, but by the prospects of monetary gains or other selfish considerations.[5] However, irregularity committed on *bona fide* and lawful considerations may not be corruption because the juxtaposition of the word corrupt means and impliedly, include "dishonest intention".

A judgment delivered or order passed with corrupt intent may make out a case of retrial or rehearing. "Corrupt

1. The Spirit of Law by Montesquieu.
2. Black's Law Dictionary, Ninth Edition, page 397.
3. The New Lexicon Webster's Dictionary, page 219.
4. *Jaipur Development Authority* v. *Daulat Mal Jain,* (1997) 1 SCC 35.
5. *State of Andhra Pradesh* v. *V. Vasudeva Rao,* (2004) 9 SCC 319: AIR 2004 SC 960: 2003 AIR SCW 6555.

intent" as necessary for conviction for misconduct in office, may be established where there is intentional or purposeful misbehaviour or wrongful conduct pertaining to the requirement and duties of office by an officer. The corrupt intent requires to constitute usury, is intent to take or receive more than law permits for forbearance of money, regardless of whether taker knows that he is violating usury law.[1] A Judge who attempt to induce witness to withhold testimony require his removal from office being involving in corruption.[2]

It is generally a ground for a new trial that, for the evident purpose of influencing the verdict, members of jury or the court were entertained or treated just before or during the trail by the successful party or by his or her attorney, agent, or by a friend or relative of the party, on the party's behalf.[3]

In order to warrant a new trial, in case of such entertainment or treating, it need not be shown that the offending person understood the impropriety of his or her act or that any juror was actually influenced thereby.[3]

The order passed or judgment delivered, influenced by corrupt practice may be set aside requiring to pass fresh order or judgment at the behest of affected party subject to specific plea raised for the purpose (emphasis supplied). The principle has its significance in the present atmosphere where fingers are raised not only against bureaucracy and legislature but also against the persons working in administration of justice.

Every Indian citizen is deeply concerned with the report of Transparency International which put India at number 84 in the seriatim of corrupt countries. Even China is at number 80. All the three wings of the Government are facing allegations with regard to corrupt practices. It is the question of degree as to which one is more corrupt than

1. Word and phrases (permanent edition), Vol. 9B, page 510.
2. Word and phrases (permanent edition), Vol. 9B, page 511.
3. *Corpus Juris Secundum*, Volume 66, page 85.

other. Fact remains that people are raising voice being affected with corruption in our governance. Millions of rupees are subject-matter of discussion in this poor country which according to reports has been stashed abroad or misappropriated within the country for personal use.

The sixty-five years of independent India suffered multiple scams where billions of public fund has been misappropriated. According to report,[1] the various scams which the country suffered keeping in view the index value of 2011 may be summarized as under:—

(i) the Jeep Scandal (1948) Rs. 80 lakh, (Rs. 36.52 crore);

(ii) the Mundra Scandal (1958) Rs. 1.20 crore (Rs. 47.73 crore);

(iii) the Dharma Teja loans Rs. 22 crore (Rs. 785.32 crore).

The Total Indexed value in 2011 would be Rs. 869.57 crore;

(iv) the Nagarwala Scandal (1971) Rs. 60 lakh, (Rs. 11.10 crore);

(v) the Kuo Oil Scandal (1976) Rs. 2.2 crore (Rs. 24.80 crore);

(vi) the Cement Scam: Donations for the Indira Pratishthan Trust collected by Antulay Rs. 30 crore (Rs. 208.80 crore);

The Total Indexed value would be Rs. 244.70 crore;

(vii) The Bofors Scandal of Rs. 64 crore in 1987 (Rs. 313.72 crore);

(viii) the Lakhubhai Pathak Pickles Scam (1984) $1,30,000 equivalent at the then conversion rate to Rs. 22.75 lakh (Rs. 7.79 crore);

(ix) the Sugar Import Scam (1994) Rs. 650 crore (Rs. 1627.99 crore);

(x) the Sukhram Telecom Scandal (1996) Rs. 3.6 crore (Rs. 12.33 crore);

1. Published in the newspaper "The Hindu", dated 31-11-2012.

(xi) the C.R Bhansali Scam (1998) Rs. 1,100 crore (Rs. 2,438.60 crore);

(xii) the Fertilizer Scam (1996) Rs. 133 crore, (Rs. 294.85 crore). The total indexed value of these scams comes to Rs. 4,381.56 crore;

(xiii) the Kargil Coffin Scandal (1995) $1.87 lakh equivalent at the then conversion rate to Rs. 80.64 lakh (Rs. 1.87 crore);

(xiv) the Barak Missile Scandal $80.64 lakh equivalent at the then conversion rate to Rs. 36.29 crore (Rs. 66.13 crore). The total indexed value would be approximately Rs. 68 crore.

(xv) the Scorpene Submarine Deal (2006) Rs. 500 crore (Rs. 685.80 crore);

(xvi) the Cash-for-votes Scandal Rs. 50 crore (Rs. 59.95 crore);

(xvii) the 2G Spectrum (2010) Rs. 1,76,000 crore (Rs. 1,89,200 crore);

(xviii) the Commonwealth Games Scam Rs. 8,000 crore (Rs. 8,599.99 crore). The total indexed value of corruption so far is Rs. 1,98,546 crore.

The latest one is Augasta West Land (Italy) Helicopter scam involving 3500 crores of rupees with the allegation of Kickbacks to the tune of Rs. 350 crores or more and Railgate scam.

The Railgate scam (Lucarative Posting Scam) exposes the underhand dealing to fill-up higher posts of the governance. Allegation is that an amount of Rs. 10-12 crores was settled with the nephew of Rail Minister for fixing appointment on lucrative posts for making a person member of Railway Board and thereafter provide him a lucrative jurisdiction (or office). CBI trapped and registered a case and is investigating the matter.[1]

---

1. Hindustan Times.
2. The Hindu, Sunday, November 18, 2012.

These figures do not include black money stashed away in numbered accounts outside India.[2] All these scandals directly or indirectly involved Cabinet Ministers of the then Prime Ministers.

Supreme Court of India while hearing Coalgate scam, while indicting the CBI to share the investigating report with the government observed, to quote:—

> "CBI has become a caged parrot, speaking in its masters' voice. It is a sordid saga that it is one parrot with many masters.[1]"

Pratap Bhanu Mehta,[2] in an article while taking note of the observation made by the Supreme Court shown his deep concern to the distributing features in the matter of governance and investigation. Learned author said,[3] *In court, the same sordid drama unfolded;* scandal after scandal, made even more egregious by initial attempts to cover them up, then to brazen it out and then, in the final gambit, to insulate the highest authorities from any responsibility.

Shri Mehta further observed that, the republic is now at a delicate crossroads. The Government may brazen it out. But in doing so, it is creating a crisis of institutions not seen since the Emergency days, when an executive took on the judiciary on the dubious grounds that it had a mandate.

One of the main reason for the perpetuation of scams in India seems to be absence of independent agency. Political interference with the investigation of a case seems to be common. In 'Coal Scam' CBI filed an affidavit in the Supreme Court of India that report prepared by it was shared by the Law Minister and the Prime Minister's Office. CBI Director Shri Ranjit Sinha while filing affidavit in Supreme Court stated that the contents of final report was not shared with the Government but fact remains that original report was shared by the Government. Unless India possess an independent investigation agency, it shall not be

1. The Indian Express, May, 9, 2013.
2. The writer is President, Centre for Policy Research, Delhi and a contributing editor for "The Indian Express".
3. *Ibid.*

possible to stop the country suffer from billions of rupees on account of scam after scam.[1]

A noted laureate Brahma Chellaney, Geostrategist, showing his deep concern to the existing states of affairs in India while dealing with corruption in defence, wrote, to quote:—

> "Make no mistake: The biggest threat India faces is not terrorism or China; it is institutionalized corruption, which undermines national security and threatens to eviscerate the republic. Those who take or engineer bribes on defence deals, in effect, are waging war on the country. They are worse than the Afzal Gurus because of the wider and corrosive impact of their actions. Yet as the history of scams attests, they customarily go scot-free.
>
> One way to start cleaning-up the augean stables is to impose at least a three-year moratorium on new defence contracts. This will put out of business the proliferating arms agents and cut-off the Kickbacks fattening India's political nobility, the new rajas and ranis. Such a moratorium, far from having an adverse impact on national security, will actually save the tax-payers billions of dollars annually while facilitating the overhaul of defence procurement, initiation of a domestic arms-production base, and expansion of non conventional deterrent capabilities.
>
> Yet entrenched interests have such a huge stake in the present system that the prospect of stanching India's bleeding without drastic reforms seems bleak. A reminder of how a corrupt India formulates a policy, only to undermine its objectives, was the 2008 move to help build a domestic arms base by requiring foreign arms sellers to plough about 30 per cent of deal value into Indian military firms. It took just three years for the Government to overturn the intent of that policy by issuing revised guidelines.[2]"

1. Hindustan Times, April 27, 2013.
2. India Today, March 4, 2013 edition, page 8.

According to survey, 55.4% persons of India feels that governance is bad because of corruption.[1] There is lots of despair among the people which may result disastrous consequence in due course of time. The loss of faith of the majority of people in the politician is of serious concern.

It pricks to the mind of the men of common prudence as to why India has become a country of scams, in spite of the fact that it possessed brilliant persons in its administrative services who may block the infiltration of public fund. Reason may be in two-fold. *Firstly;* Substantial number of bureaucracy is indulged into corrupt practices and having in queue with the elective representative a-mass wealth. *Second* reason may be the post retiral appointments. According to report[2] dated 12 March, 2013, 15 civil servants, police officers and army men were appointed on the post of Governor. Out of which, four are Ex-IAS Officers and eight are former IPS Officers and one is Army Chief. Needless to say that gubernatorial position occupied by civil servants, police officers or army personnels are based on political judgments. Ordinarily such appointment may not be made by politicians unless these officers have serve them while in office. This section of bureaucracy gives an easy passage to misappropriate public fund by the persons in office.

Amartya Sen[3] had shown his deep concern to decline of public institution in India. According to noble laureate, corruption is the other face of the decline of public services. It dis-empowers the citizen, and reflects a weakening of the rule of law, and most dangerously the intertwining of business and politics (and crime).[4]

In a recent Book, "The Rediscovery of India" by Meghnad Desai, the learned author observed as under:

---

1. Hindustan Times, dated 15-11-2012.
2. Published in The Hindu newspaper, dated March 12, 2013.
3. While delivering a lecture on 5-12-2012 S. Guhan Memorial Lecture in Chennai.
4. The Hindu, Saturday, December 29, 2012.

> "What the explorers were looking for was India, and wherever they made a landfall they described the natives as Indians. On the western shores of the Atlantic the Spanish found America, rich in land and natural resources and relatively sparsely populated—before the disease the Europeans brought decimated the locals. They destroyed urban settlements that they found—of the Inca and the Aztec cultures—and proceeded to extract as much gold and silver as they could by dragooning the native population to work in mines and, when necessary, supplementing this with slaves shipped from their African outposts. This land became, over the next half-a-millennium, Latin America; only the fact that the islands to the north had been named the 'West Indies' and the term used for the native peoples was 'Indians', are signs that remind us that the original quest had been for India."

The learned author (supra) further noted, the finding of Angus Maddison with regard to wealth, taken away from India between 1500 and 1780 AD. To reproduce relevant portion from "Rediscovery of India", as under:

> "Angus Maddison estimates that between 1500 and 1700, Spain and Portugal shipped 308 metric tons of gold and 33,668 tons of silver. In the next century, which does not impact on India, 1400 tons of gold and 39,157 tons of silver. The British and Dutch East India Companies between them shipped 10,045 tons of gold and silver in equivalent terms between 1600 and 1780. Maddison does not say how much Portuguese silver came to India during its trading heyday from 1500 to 1650. This would be a rough measure of the export surplus the sought Indian regional economies enjoyed."

During colonial rule how the country was robbed has been noted by Mushirul Hasan.[1] According to author, *Dadabhai Naoroji* and Romesh Chunder Dutt, whose lives

1. Faith and Freedom, Gandhi in History by Mushirul Hasan.

overlapped with many public figures of their time, wrote on the continuing impoverishment and exhaustion, and a ruinously heavy tribute. In fact, 'no civil servant of Dutt's generation was so agitated by the conditions of the Bengal peasants, whose improvement became his life-long crusade." The economic issues on which he confronted the rulers relentlessly—unfair taxation, neglect of irrigation, destruction of a thriving handloom industry, draining the country's wealth to fight wars on other soils, etc., were the results of his grass-roots experience as an administrator.[1] When Gandhi read Dutt's Economic History of India, he wept. He responded to that particular strand of his closely knit narrative which describes the decline of Indian handloom through unfair competition with machine-made cloth imported from Manchester.[2]

The Dutt-Naoroji combine calculated the drain in 1882 amounting to Rs. 1,355 million (at 1946-47), over 4 per cent of the national income that year. Later, they and others established that India paid approximately 40 million pounds (equivalent to a normal year's revenue) to meet the cost of the 1857 revolt. Public debt, which had arisen from nearly 34 million pounds in 1857 to 97 million pounds in 1862,[3] increased further owing to the redemption of the EIC's stock in 1874, by wars in Afghanistan and Burma, and by the famines of 1874-77 and 1896-1900."

Relying upon the magazine 'Avadh Punch' and other material learned author noted that exploitation and servitude was not because of poverty but because of mal-administration. Learned Author says "Exploitation and servitude went hand-in-hand. Poverty wasn't due to the poor person's natural inferiority or the inscrutable laws of God, but because others picked their pockets. Through this

1. Mukherjee, An Indian For All Seasons, 6 (307).
2. *Ibid*, p. 194.
3. John McGuire, "The World Economy, the Colonial State, and the Establishment of the Indian National Congress", in Mike Shepperdson and Colin simmons (eds), The Indian National Congress and the Political Economy of India, 1885-1985 (Aldershot, n.d.), p. 48.

process nearly a million people died of starvation and consequent disease in Orissa in 1865. Excessive rents, land taxes, and the usury affected Awadh, an area of 37,169 sq. m., and a population of nearly 12.5 million. An Avadh Punch cartoon depicts a "native" lady holding John Bull, a symbol of enslavement, by the arm and pointing out to him half-starved men, women, and children. They stand behind her appealing for relief.[1]"

The learned author (supra) while condemning the colonial rule referred the material published in 'Avadh Punch' and says "*painting an* unflattering picture of the district officer's temper and manners in general. Avadh Punch looked up to them matter-of-factly as negligent, selfish, and corrupt. As miniature despots, they lacked imagination, insight, and sympathy."

The agony of Indians under colonial rule was not only because of foreign rule but also because of rampant corruption in the governance. Mushirul Hasan referred the popular poem which become so popular within the students and others used to form processions and went round singing it from street to street with the demonstrators being trailed everywhere by the police. Enchanting poem written by Josh depicts some of the ugly features of British rule, to quote,

> "Do you recall the story of your limitless oppression?
>
> Do you recall the Company's age of crime?
>
> When in caravan upon caravan the wealth of India
>
> Was circulating unprotected, you went round looting it.
>
> You went round cutting off the weavers' thumbs
>
> You filled their weaving pits with their lifeless corpses.
>
> Death overtook the handicrafts of India.

---

1. 25 June 1891, Selections, p. 443.

What death was that?—The death brought by your hand.[1]

Devaluation of moral values also seems to reflect from the fact that 146 MPs *i.e.* 104 from the Lok Sabha and 42 from the Rajya Sabha have appointed 191 relatives in their personal staff drawing salary of 30,000 per month from public exchequer. Out of these, 60 sons, 36 wives, 27 daughters, seven brothers, seven daughters-in-law, four husbands and 10 cousins.[2]

Stashing abroad the public fund by the Indian rulers still continues. It is known fact that billions of rupees belonging to public exchequer has been stashed away in post-independent India by the members of different governments from time to time. Corruption seems to become way of life in ruling class.

In a recent survey[3], being fed up with rampant corruption in India, 52.1% youth shown inclination towards dictatorship being dischanted with democracy, 67.8% opined that almost all politicians are corrupt, 76,7% said that any person with criminal records should not be permitted to contest election, 79.5% opined for minimum qualification for politicians and 70.6% stated that there should be age of retirement for them.

An another survey reveals that 60% transfer of officers are not done to meet out the exigency of service, 33% bureaucrats admit that they are under constant pressure, 43% bureaucrats stated that they are compelled to do illegal works, 40% of Indian bureaucrats state that because of political interference in their lawful discharge of duty, they want to leave the Government office. In last 10 years, 190 IAS have resigned being fed up with political interference in their discharge of duty.[4] Young mind seems to ignited

1. Translated from Urdu and introduced by Christopher Shackle, Nijhawan (ed.), Nationalism in the Vernacular, p. 199.
2. Indian Express, 15-5-2013.
3. Hindustan Times, 6-8-2013.
4. Amar Ujala, 12-8-2013.

across the board and gradually loosing patience from democratic set up as it exists today.

It is a matter of deep concern that an impression has been generated across the country that upright and honest bureaucracy is persecuted by their political masters. Public perception has become worse after suspension of an IAS officer Smt. Durga Shakti Nagpal. It should be understood that honest and upright officers are not personal vessels of politicians. The question is of protective and preserving the constitutional democracy of India whose lynchpin is the permanent executive working in tandem with political executive and the former is not expected to be subservient to the latter much less carry out its illegal orders. In the Constitutional Assembly debate, the constitutional framers have rejected the "spoiled system" which seems to indirectly creeping in the governance of our country. What cannot be done directly, it may not be done indirectly. Our system is a mixture of upright, honest as well as dishonest and weak stretchered officers. The former should be encouraged and the latter should be deprecated.

The recent exposure of massive corruption in governance is the good sign for healthy democracy. The national mood is sullen, cynical and despondent. Delhi gang rape has shown the way to enlighten the government and the administration to come out from the cocoon and purify the falling system of governance. Law-making is still being held hostage to the colonial mindset of command and control and known for their complexity, obtuseness and ambiguity. Half hearted making of law or its interpretation to solve current problems created gallery to all sort of crime including corruption. It is time to give a second look to old paper based administration leading to opaqueness in the governmental functioning.

'Corrupts' are thick skinned. Now "public perception" as well as "public interest" is sidelined by the 'corrupts' while discharging their statutory or constitutional obligations.

Being conscious with the situation Supreme Court had rejected the principle of "high authority".[1]

Supreme Court emphasize to be conscious with the actualities of life. While dealing with the matter of corruption the court should circumspect, pragmatic and realistic to the actualities of life.[2] Presumption of fairness on the part of higher authorities had also been rejected by Supreme Court being unrealistic,[3] though, it is expected that authorities including the constitutional functionaries shall discharge their obligations in a just and fair manner keeping in view the constitutional spirit and law.

The situation is alarming. It is unfortunate, people are not coming forward to raise voice against corrupt practices with iron hand and firm voice leaving burden on judiciary, which has its own limitations.

In a recent published book edited by Adam Graycar and Russell G. Smith titled, "Handbook of Global Research and Practice in Corruption",[4] learned authors opined that the whole of the world is suffering from menace of corruption which varies among the countries but it affect the poorest and most vulnerable in any society. Its pervasiveness has weakened economic growth and undermines the rule of law for every nation and invariably deters investment. In developed countries or rich countries, the corruption pushes taxes to higher levels than they need to be and services are of lesser quality than they might be. In case corruption is minimized, the affect will be reduction of tax around 20%.

Learned authors observed:—

> "Corruption manifests itself in many ways and at different levels corrupt behaviour causes outrage to victims and those who value civil society, it impedes

1. *Shivajirao Nilangekar Patil* v. *Dr. Mahesh Madhav Gosavi,* (1987) 1 SCC 227: AIR 1987 SC 294: 1987 (2) Supreme 97; *S. Pratap Singh* v. *State of Punjab,* AIR 1964 SC 72: (1965) 1 SCA 259: (1964) 4 SCR 733; *Delhi Transport Corporation* v. *D.T.C. Mazdoor Congress,* AIR 1991 SC 101: JT 1990 (3) SC 725.
2. *Ibid.*
3. *Ibid.*
4. Published by Edward Elgar Publishing Ltd., 2012 U.K.

> good government and administrative practice. In 2008 the World Economic Forum (2008) estimated that corruption accounts for about 5 per cent of global GDP (about US $2.6 trillion) and furthermore it is estimated that every year around $ 1 trillion is paid in bribes and $40 billion is looted by corrupt political leaders.
>
> Corruption poses threats to principles of democracy, justice and the economy. It affects all countries regardless of their level of development. Nevertheless, some countries experience corruption more than others, and of course some places have more corruption than others. There is a widespread but still non-random distribution of corruption in societies."

Things are going to be worst in due course of time, and likely to create chaos across the nations. Our civilization survives with fine records because of its ancient tenets but now causing pain and agony on account of loss of its civilizational qualities.

The four-fold order collectively constituted the ancient Indian society. There had been 5th fold (not order) that was known 'Rakshasa'. The leaders of 5th fold or class, also possessed knowledge, practice, religion and bestowed with power but they were expansionist, and tried to persecute and subvert the 'civilized' society governed by the four-fold order. The commission of major offences like dacoity, robbery, murder, terrorism, rape and interference with religious practices of the civilized society governed by four-fold order, was routine feature of Rakshasas' lives. There has been consistent fight between the civilized society governed by the four-fold order on the one hand and the Rakshasas on the other hand. In spite of all knowledge, spiritual power and scientific temperament born in first-fold order, Ravana was a Rakshasa because of his conduct.

The Indian civilization survived because of collective work and concerted efforts of the people. From time to time, according to Indian mythology there has been consistent conflict between the civilized society and the 5th fold or class. There has been situation when civilized society was overpowered by the 5th fold or class but in due course of time, the civilized society regained the power. The mythological stories with regard to 5th fold order, are nothing but warning the humanity to beware, generate power to fight collectively against evil forces. The 5th fold in this context, include the terrorists, rapists, murderers, dacoits and corrupt peoples engaged to establish the empire of bad men with the vested interest.

According to ancient *Indian* mythology, the stories of "Devasur, Sangram" reveals how the civilized society fought against the Rakshasa from time to time.

Writers Dominique Lapierre and Larry Collins in their most celebrated book, "Freedom at Midnight"[1] from their research work, opined that *Dalits* or *Shudras* when become knowledgeable person, and expert of a field, they were also entitled to be kept under the first fold order *i.e., Brahmin* and similarly, a Brahmin's son becomes *Shudra* in case he or she does not acquire knowledge. Position would have been the same for others *i.e., Kshatriya* & *Vaish*. The example is Sage Valmiki who commanded utmost respect because of knowledge and magnanimity. There are several other alike personalities. Later on, the system of four-fold order gradually disappeared. The destruction of four-fold order and its conversion based on birth has caused injury to the Indian society. The competitive mind and the motivation to acquire knowledge lost its fervour resulting in a society divided on basis of castes, creed and religion.

One of the folly lies in the administration of justice is reliance placed on colonial jurisprudence. Right from Montesquieu, the western jurists professed for pure theory of law and strict separation of power. The implementation of these principles gradually causing irreparable injuries to western countries.[2] I have discussed the *pros* and *cons* of

1. *Azadi Adhi Rat Ko,* Page 43.

2. Sovereignty, Judicial Review and Separation of Power by the author— 2012 Vol. 7 (September 7, 2012) Part 5 SCC.

pure theory of law precisely in my book, "Morality in Law" (published by Eastern Book Co.). Virtually, the strict separation of power is based on, theoretical principle, which suits to a society where all the three wings of the government are learned, honest and dedicated to their duty. A society or a system of governance where there is corruption, there is ethnic violence and corruption among the rulers, this principle may not be applied. Our whole education system is making the young boys and girls employment (service) dependent. In case they are employed, after end of academic life, their education may be fruitful, otherwise as a jobless person, the majority of young generation leads impatient life. Instead of making independent with capacity to avail self-employment, they are being dependent on the government's whimsical approach. Except some of the colleges in private sector, young generation is deprived to learn morality. In consequence thereof, there is rise of "animal instinct" in human resource which shall be fatal in due course of time.

According to a report[1] there is falling rate of conviction in criminal cases. According to one other report, in Delhi, 67% children are suffering from child abuse from their own near and dears. According to another report (Hindustan Times dated 15-11-2012), 55% peoples of India blame the corruption as the root cause of pain and agony to common Indians. 30% girls married underage in India. Percentage is more higher in State of Uttar Pradesh *i.e.* 54.9%. Public fund is amassed abroad collectively by bureaucrats and politicians and judiciary seems to be ineffective to punish them.

Supreme Court of India in a recent judgment of Niranjan Hemchandra Sashittal[2] shown its deep concern to the epidemic corruption prevailing in India. Supreme Court held to quote:—

> "It can be stated without any fear of contradiction that corruption is not to be judged by degree, for

1. Newspaper Hindu, dated 22-10-2012.
2. Passed in Writ Petition (Cri) No. 50 of 2012, decided on 15-3-2013.

> corruption mothers disorder, destroys societal will to progress, accelerates undeserved ambitions, kills the conscience, jettisons the glory of the institutions, paralyses the economic health of a country, corrodes the sense of civility and mars the marrows of governance. It is worth noting that immoral acquisition of wealth destroys the energy of the people believing in honesty, and history records with agony how they have suffered. The only redeeming fact is that collective sensibility respects such suffering as it is in consonance with the constitutional morality.[1]"

Supreme Court further emphasis that a tendency has been developed to abuse the official position resulting in epidemic corruption in the governance, to quote:—

> "It can be stated with absolute assurance that the tendency to abuse the official position has spread like an epidemic and has shown its propensity making the collective to believe that unless bribe is given, the work may not be done. To put it differently, giving bribe, whether in cash or in kind, may become the "mantra" of the people.[2]"

These observations are based on the basis of several judgments and orders of High Court, Apex Court of the country and newspaper reports. The position is same with several other countries of the world.

One immediate change required in administration of justice is 'multi-member' courts for trial and decision of appeals. Not only bureaucracy and legislatures but there are allegations against the members of judicial fraternity with regard to indulgence in corrupt practices. People's faith is eroding day by day. Trial by single man court sometime creates multiple problem. Every year different High Courts dismiss or compulsory retire the presiding officers on account of misconduct or corrupt practices. Even High

---

1. Passed in Writ Petition (CRL) No. 50 of 2012, decided on 15-3-2013.
2. *Ibid.*

Court Judges are facing trial. Fingers also raised on Apex Court Judges. Though comparatively judiciary is still good so far as honesty integrity is concerned but time has come to take preventive steps. The first out of others should be that every case relating to corrupt practices or seriousness misconduct should be decided by minimum two or three-member Benches consisting session Judges or in High Court by High Court Judges. It shall strengthen the people confidence in administration of justice.

The misappropriation of public fund in a routine manner has worsened the situation. Young mind is ignited. Without referring to any country, it may be noticed across the nation all over the world. It is time to innovate new rules or law which may suit the society. Curbing corruption to stop the misappropriation of public fund, should be prime concern. Young generation should be taught how to meet the challenges of life and save public fund and work for future generation in true spirit of 'Geeta'. It is said that in case humanity does not correct itself and keep on going with all kind of abuses, the nations may collapse. It shall be appropriate to quote a hymn of Rigveda:

> "We all have various hopes and plans
> and many are the ways of men:
> The craftsman seeks for jobs to do,
> the priest his fold, the healer the sick.
> Flow, Indu, flow for Indra's sake;
> The arrow-smith with hard dry reeds
> and feathers from the birds of air,
> bronze for the tips, and glowing coals,
> seeks out the man who'll pay him best.
> Flow, Indu, flow for Indra's sake:
> A bard am I, my father's a healer,
> and mother grinds corn on the quern,
> striving for wealth, with varied plans,
> we follow our desires like kine.
> Flow, Indu, flow for Indra's sake."

Exploitation, major disparity in income and living status, accumulation of wealth from unfair means, mis-appropriation of public fund by the persons at the helms of affairs, make a country prone to social revolution in due course of time. In case the system does not correct itself, then nature corrects in one or the other way, which we may be noticed from the present state of affairs of various countries. Every person born in a country, have right over its natural resources to avail food, cloth and shelter for a "human living". Apart from the food, cloth and shelter, for a quality of life, education and peaceful atmosphere (law and order) are equally necessary in a civilized society. Education ordinarily, should be based on morality and humanitarian approach. It is time for introspection and time for cultivation of new order in the society to make us more civilized.

We should be conscious to "Arab Spring" where people come to street on account of inaction and corruption in the ruling class. Let us pray Almighty, India may not become "Tahrir square".

During recent election in Pakistan, a survey was made. Astonishingly, fed up with political corruption, 79% of youth expressed their views against democracy and shown their loyalty to Madarsas and Army. It is open secret that in substantial portion of Pakistan, justice to the citizen is dispensed by "Jigra Panchayat". Because of political corruption having hand in gloves with bureaucracy and sometimes uncared by judiciary, people become dischanted with democratic process and divert to Madarsa and Army. The failure of democratic institution for any reason whatsoever, may lead to doomsday.

Corruption perpetuate and increase mani-fold because of political corruption. Politicians should be role model while discharging their obligation as constitutional functionaries or holding high offices but things appear to be otherwise. Generally Politics is the organized dispute about power and its use, involving choice among competing values, ideas, persons, interests, demands.

Political power means the capacity to regulate national life through genuinely elected national representatives. Political corruption is caused by the misuse of political power by the national representatives. Political power is the best means to attain the political as well as the social ends. In addition to that, our politicians tainted towards this power gain their own economic benefits. They are using this as the more profitable and easiest route to attain wealth and rich. In the corruptive institution the political power is subordinated for the political value in order to achieve the economic ends. That means fundamental principle of politics is not an act to attain the publics aims but only for the promotion of the selfish ends. Thereby Gandhi said, "Corruption and hypocrisy ought not to be inevitable products of democracy, as they undoubtedly are today." This implies the meaning of our system of government: the democratic government is basically good but our politicians by losing morality, they are liable to corruption. The moral empowerment of the politician is necessary factor to act as the genuine representative of the people. It only can promote their mental maturity in the proper manner that lead them to proper policy-making and implementation. Gandhi had rightly said I have derived my politics from ethics... It is because I swear by ethics that I find myself in politics.[1] Similarly along with Gandhi, Rousseau said that the operating principle of the community is moral and a man in his moral pursuit works in the interest of fellow citizens. It is a fact that the political power is always liable to corruption.

According to Rousseau there is fundamental difference in the sovereignty of each nation. If the people could not administer their own laws properly in a democracy, neither could their magistrates, monarchical or aristocratic alike, rule in their stead. The threat of government's abuse of powers belonging only to the people was filet as fiercely by Rousseau as by Locke before him, and it is most

1. *M.K. Gandhi, Harijan,* 3-10-1936.

characteristically that all too frequent tendency of a government's substitution of its particular Will for the general Will of the sovereign which he regards as despotism.[1] While writing a letter to Voltaire in 1756 Rousseau observed "Providence has made us free so that we may choose the good and refuse the evil. Its making us capable of choice excludes its choosing for us. When we abuse our faculties and commit evil, we perform not God's work but ours.[2]"

According to Mahatma Gandhi, "Corruption will go when the larger numbers of persons given to the unworthy practice realize that the nation does not exist for them, but that they do for the nation. It requires a high code of morals, extreme vigilance on the part of those who are free from the corrupt practice and also have influence over corrupt servants. Indifference in such matters is criminal.[3]" Further Mahatma Gandhi says, "the best and the only right course would be for the public to prevent actual corruption from taking place by maintaining a sleepless vigilance, and for the servant to keep the public on the *qui vive*.[4]"

Commercialization of politics seems to be root cause of corruption. Now politics is no more for 'public service' but ordinarily it is to serve own family, friends and relatives. Lack of public vigil, protest, weak bureaucracy and overburden administration of justice has made the thing worst.

The corrupt-less society may be Utopian thought but society with minimum corruption at tolerable level and effort to root out corruption is practically possible. That may be done by unification of morality with law and education, electing honest, fair and learned legislatures and appointing alike person on constitutional and higher posts to govern the country or dispense justice. Beginning today

1. Rousseau, A very short introduction by Robert Workler page 90.
2. *Ibid,* page 110.
3. *M.K. Gandhi, Harijan,* 1-2-1948.
4. *Collected Works of Mahatma Gandhi,* p. 312.

shall take at least a quarter century to have a generation in practice (action), who may be fair, honest and committed to cause of country.

Abraham Lincoln, the 16th President of the United States of America, said:

You can fool all the people some of the time, and some of the people all the time, but you cannot fool all the people all the time."

Sexual Abuse of Child

"Mama may have, papa may have But God bless the child that's got his own Then that's got shall get Them that's not shall lose So the Bible said and it still is news Mama may have, papa may have But God bless the child that's got his own That's got his own Yes, the strong gets more While the weak ones fade Empty pockets don't ever make the grade Mama may have, papa may have But God bless the child that's got his own That's got his own.[1]"

Child sex abuse was not known to ancient Indian civilization. It seems to commercially surfaced in 19th or 20th century during industrialization of Western countries or medieval Europe. Millions of children worldwide, suffer with commercially sexual exploitation. It is a phenomenon as I have said, was not known to ancient India where, family units were managed in such a way leaving no scope for exploitation of children sexually or otherwise. Though prostitution was very well there but that too, was in a dignified form.

The reason behind was the code of self-control and regulated life. Under Indian civilization, Kama (satisfaction of sensual needs) was regarded as one of the four desirable goals of human life along with Dharma, Artha and Moksha. Simultaneously, it was also considered as the first among shadripus (six enemies) which human beings should overcome through self-restraint *i.e.,* Kama (when satisfaction of sensual needs becomes lust), Krodha (anger),

1. "God Bless the Child" a song with Arthur Herzog Jr. (1941) by Billie Holiday, an American Singer.

Lobha (greed), Mada (self-ego), Moha (attachment) and Matsara (covetousness).

Mahatma Gandhi was of the view that it is easy to conquer the entire world than to subdue the enemies in our body. The man who subdues in this conquest, shall overcome all enemies. In ancient India, all these evils were prime objects and the subject-matter of curriculum of the child to inculcate knowledge for self-control. However, we have to look into the problem under the present set-up and context.

Under our constitutional set-up, every citizen is obliged to abide by the Constitution and respect its ideals and institutions.[1] The justice, liberty, equality and fraternity including social, economic and political justice, are the golden goals set up in the Preamble of the Constitution, are to be achieved by the Legislature and Bureaucracy.[2] The Preamble reflects the high purpose and noble objective of the Constitution-makers.[3]

Article 23 of the Constitution, prohibits human trafficking and forced labour whereas, article 24 of the Constitution prohibits employment of children in factories. Under the Directive Principles of State Policy provided under the Constitution, the State is obliged to secure a social order for the promotion of welfare of the people (article 38). Social order means an atmosphere preserving and promoting the rights for a dignified and quality of life. Right to live with dignity or quality of life are the fundamental rights protected by article 21 of the Constitution. The State is also obliged under article 45 of the Constitution for early childhood care and education to children. It is obligatory to raise the level of nutrition, standard of living and improve public health (article 47).

---

1. *Official Liquidator* v. *Dayanand,* (2008) 10 SCC 1: AIR 2008 SC (Supp) 1177.
2. *P.A. Inamdar.* v. *State of Maharashtra,* (2005) 6 SCC 537: AIR 2005 SC 3226: 2005 AIR SCW 3923.
3. *Pradeep Jain* v. *Union of India,* AIR 1984 SC 1420: 1984 3 SCC 654: 1984 Ed Cas 237.

Right to life protected by article 21 of the Constitution, includes the "finer grace of human civilisation"[1], and it includes right to live with human dignity.[2] The right to healthy environment,[3] right to equality of life and so many other which rights are necessary for civilised society.[4] A child is also entitled to secure all these rights, right from womb. The child offenders are liable for speedy trial.[5]

Under Part IVA of the Constitution, certain fundamental duties have been imposed by the Constitution framers on the citizen which include to be abide by the Constitution and respect its ideals and institutions, to value and preserve the rich heritage of our composite culture, to develop the scientific temper, humanism and the spirit of inquiry and reforms and to strive towards excellence in all spheres of individual and parents or guardians, to provide opportunity for education to child and wards between 6-14 years. In spite of all these constitutional safeguards and duties, country is suffering with menace of child sexual abuse.

Apart from the constitutional provisions, the United Nations Convention on the Rights of the Child (UNCRC), came into existence in 1992, requires the Signatory States to ensure and protect the rights of children with regard to their survival, protection, development and participation. India is the signatory of UNCRC (1992). Being the signatory of UNCRC, Indian Parliament and the Government is obliged to implement the resolution passed in the Convention.[6]

---

1. *P. Nalla Thampy Terah* v. *Union of India,* AIR 1985 SC 1133.
2. *Francis Coralie Mullin* v. *Administrator, Union Territory of Delhi,* AIR 1981 SC 746: 1981 Cr LJ 306: (1981) 1 SCC 608.
3. *M.C. Mehta* v. *Union of India,* AIR 1987 SC 1086: (1987) 1 SCC 395: 1987 1 Supreme 65.
4. *Kapila Hingorani* v. *State of Bihar,* (2003) 6 SCC 1: JT 2003 (5) SC 1.
5. *Sheela Barse* v. *Union of India,* AIR 1986 SC 1773: 1986 Cr LJ 1736: (1986) 3 SCC 596.
6. *Madhu Kishwar* v. *State of Bihar,* AIR 1996 SC 1864: JT 1996 (4) SC 379: (1996) 5 SCC 125; *D.K. Basu* v. *State of West Bengal,* AIR 1997 SC 610: 1997 AIR SCW 233: 1997 Cr LJ 743; *Vishaka* v. *State of Rajasthan,*

Contd. on next page

As per article 34 of the UNCRC, the State Parties will undertake to protect the child from all forms of sexual exploitation and sexual abuse. For these purposes, the State parties shall in particular take all appropriate national, bilateral and multilateral measures to prevent:

(a) The inducement or coercion of a child to engage in any unlawful sexual activity;

(b) The exploitative use of children in prostitution or other unlawful sexual practices;

(c) The exploitative use of children in pornographic performances and materials.

Since the Government of India is signatory, it is obliged to implement the resolution in letter and spirit.

Bill No. XIVC of 2011 namely The Protection of Children from Sexual Offences Bill, 2012 was introduced and passed by the Parliament enacting "The Protection of Children from Sexual Offences Act, 2012 (in short hereinafter referred as Act). Indian Parliament had passed the bill at belated stage in pursuance to UN Resolution dated 11-12-1992 (supra) when much damage has already been caused to the Indian society. Better late than never.

Section 2 of the Act defines the children means person below the age of 18 years. The penetrative sexual assault is punishable for minimum seven years which may be extended up to life imprisonment under section 4 of the Act. The punishment has become more serious under section 5 when the offence is committed by public servant. Sexual assault has been defined under section 7 of the Act which is punishable for minimum punishment under section 3. For convenience section 7 is reproduced as under:—

> "7. Whoever, with sexual intent touches the vagina, penis, anus or breast of the child or makes the

---

Contd. from previous page

(1997) 6 SCC 241: AIR 1997 SC 3011: 1997 AIR SCW 3043; *People's Union for Civil Liberties (PUCL)* v. *Union of India,* (1997) 1 SCC 301: AIR 1997 SC 568: 1997 AIR SCW 113; *Chairman Railway Board* v. *Chandrima Das,* (2000) 2 SCC 465: AIR 2000 SC 988: 2000 AIR SCW 649.

> child touch the vagina, penis, anus or breast of such person or any other person, or does any other act with sexual intent which involves physical contact without penetration is said to commit sexual assault."

The sexual harassment has been defined under section 11 which is punishable under section 12 for imprisonment to three years.

Section 11 is reproduced as under:—

> "11. A person is said to commit sexual harassment upon a child when such person with sexual intent,—
>
> (i) utters any word or makes any sound, or makes any gesture or exhibits any object or part of body with the intention that such word or sound shall be heard, or such gesture or object or part of body shall be seen by the child; or
>
> (ii) makes a child exhibit his body or any part of his body so as it is seen by such person or any other person; or
>
> (iii) shows any object to a child in any form or media for pornographic purposes; or
>
> (iv) repeatedly or constantly follows or watches or contacts a child either directly or through electronic, digital or any other means; or
>
> (v) threatens to use, in any form of media, a real or fabricated depiction through electronic, film or digital or any other mode, or any part of the body of the child or the involvement of the child in a sexual act; or
>
> (vi) entices a child for pornographic purposes or gives gratification therefor.
>
> *Explanation.*—Any question which involves sexual intent shall be a question of fact."

Using a child for pornographic purposes has also been made punishable under section 14 of the Act. The definition has been given under section 13 of the Act, which is reproduced as under:—

"13. Whoever, uses a child in any form of media (including programme or advertisement telecast by television channels or internet or any other electronic form or printed form, whether or not such programme or advertisement is intended for personal use or for distribution), for the purposes of sexual gratification, which includes—

(a) representation of the sexual organs of a child;

(b) usage of a child engaged in real or simulated sexual acts (with or without penetration);

(c) the indecent or obscene representation of a child,

shall be guilty of the offence of using a child for pornographic purposes.

Explanation.—For the purposes of this section, the expression "use a child" shall include involving a child through any medium like print, electronic, computer or any other technology for preparation, production, offering, transmitting, publishing, facilitation and distribution of the pornographic material."

Abetment of and attempt to commit an offence under the Act has also been defined under section 16 of the Act, which is reproduced as under:—

"16. A person abets an offence, who—

First.— Instigates any person to do that offence; or

Secondly.— Engages with one or more other person or persons in any conspiracy for the doing of that offence, if an act or illegal omission takes place in pursuance of that conspiracy, and in order to the doing of that offence; or

Thirdly.— Intentionally aids, by any act or illegal omission, the doing of that offence.

Explanation I.—A person who, by wilful misrepresentation, or by wilful concealment of a material fact, which he is bound to disclose, voluntarily causes or procures, or attempts to cause or procure a thing to be done, is said to instigate the doing of that offence.

> *Explanation II.*—Whoever, either prior to or at the time of commission of an act, does anything in order to facilitate the commission of that act, and thereby facilitates the commission thereof, is said to aid the doing of that act.
>
> *Explanation III.*—Whoever employ, harbours, receives or transports a child, by means of threat or use of force or other forms of coercion, abduction, fraud, deception, abuse of power or of a position, vulnerability or the giving or receiving of payments or benefits to achieve the consent of a person having control over another person, for the purpose of any offence under this Act, is said to aid the doing of that act."

Abatement of and attempt to commit offence has been punishable under section 18 of the Act which may be extended one half of the imprisonment of life as the case may be.

Under section 19, a detailed procedure has been provided with regard to recording of statement of child and trial of the case.

It is the welcome act of the Indian Parliament to safeguard the interest of child. However, mere enactment shall not be sufficient unless time-bound provision is made for the investigation and trial of the offence through Special Court. It shall be appropriate that separate Special Courts (designated) may be created in every district for trial under the Act as well as the cases of female foeticide and other cases related to assault on women. Such courts should not be allocated other cases. Of course, in the absence of any case under the subject in question other cases may be allocated. Unless we develop a 'work culture' in our court campus for time-bound disposal of cases it shall be futile to hope justice by the mere enactment of statutory provisions.

It is unfortunate that in spite of India became the signatory in the year 1992, 53.22% children have been sexually abused in one or the other form.[1]

1. The study conducted by MWCD upon Child Abuse in India, 2007.

According to World Health Organization (WHO), one in every 10 children in India, gets sexually abused.

Apart from above recent enactment, different other statutory enactments, directly or indirectly also deal with sexual abuse, trafficking and sexual exploitation of children. Some of them are:—

1. The Indian Penal Code, 1860.
2. The Immoral Traffic (Prevention) Act, 1956.
3. The Young Persons Harmful Publications Act, 1956.
4. The Indecent Representation of Women (Prohibition) Act, 1986.
5. The Juvenile Justice (Care and Protection of Children) Act, 2000.
6. Child Marriage (Restraint) Act, 1929.
7. Information Technology Act, 2000.

Some other national statutes include:

1. Criminal Procedure Code, 1973.
2. Indian Evidence Act, 1872.
3. Probation of Offenders Act, 1958.
4. Bonded Labour System (Abolition) Act, 1976.
5. Child Labour (Prohibition and Regulation) Act, 1986.
6. Factories Act, 1954.
7. Hindu Adoptions and Maintenance Act, 1956.
8. Hindu Minority and Guardianship Act, 1956.
9. Orphanages and other Charitable Homes (Supervision and Control) Act, 1960.
10. Commission for Protection of the Rights of the Child Act, 2005.
11. The Andhra Pradesh Devadasis (Prevention of Dedication) Act, 1982.
12. The Goa Children's Act, 2003.

These Central and State legislations deal with child sex abuse directly or indirectly but seems to have failed to check the menace.

In a book titled *"Child Sex Abuse and Exploitation in India"*, by S.C. Singh, the problem has been elaborately dealt with. Learned author noted that though all children are at risk of sexual exploitation but girls living in poverty, those who have been abandoned or abused, street children, mentally retarded, physically handicapped, refugees and other children affected by armed conflicts, are more vulnerable. Learned author noted, to quote:—

> "In countries and areas where the military forces are deployed, girls are supplied from rural areas to urban areas or military centres to quench the carnal thirst of the foreign or national soldiers as the case may be. Rural girls are lured with various attractive promises, owing to which they agree to go to the metropolis where they are used by the urban people and foreigners. This is the case of Thailand, Singapore, Saudi Arabia and Philippines, for examples, where tens of thousands of girls are serving as prostitutes.
>
> Child prostitution is rampant in this country and those elsewhere around the world. Children as young as 6-year old have been found on the street selling themselves. In fact, younger the children are, the more money they can ask for, both in selling sex and in making films. Investigations have revealed that child sex is readily available to foreigners, especially to Americans in all parts of the developing countries. The World Congress Against Commercial Sexual Exploitation of Children documented sex tourism in the Philippines, Cambodia, Thailand, other Asian countries, North America connecting to Brazil, the Dominican Republic, Sri Lanka, and Eastern Europe. The tours are advertised in slick promotions that include brochures and organised clubs.

Child prostitution in Asia has caused authorities worried. It is estimated that there are 500,000 child prostitutes, some 16 years old and younger, in South East Asia. It has become so well-known that

> paedophiles come from throughout the world to use their services. Another report, done for the United Nations estimated over 400,000 child prostitutes worldwide."

Child pornography were propagated by an organised group by "pirating" or copying films and magazines. Pictures of the material contained within printed magazines and films were copied and sold or traded as original materials. This is now being done to the extent that it is conceivable that a child porn model could be seen by his or her own children. The paedophile pornographers cater to the perverse desires of the underground, satisfying the sexual fantasies of its members through the medium of pictures. They play on the innocence of the children and lechery of adults. Pictures, magazines, films and video-tapes depicting children in acts of sexual intercourse, sodomy, bondage, bestiality, sadomasochistic act—boy/boy, boy/girl, girl/girl—sold for as little as $7.50 or as much as $50. The sale of the child pornography has been estimated to be in excess of two-and-a-quarter million dollars to one-half a billion dollars annually. The majority to this commercial child pornography is available by mail-order purchase from Europe, yet the material, the photography contained in these publications comes from the individual paedophile and is not commercially produced. The United States is the 'largest single source' of this material. The procedures of this type of pornography are often affluent, mobile, educated and powerful "pillars of 92 the community", however most of the material produced, even that depicting children being mutilated and beaten, is produced by the individual paedophile who works out of his home. Now this material is available through clandestine purchase on the internet."

Learned author while dealing with Indian situation, further recorded to quote:—

> "Street children are more vulnerable to sexual exploitation. It is estimated that there are 314,700

street children in Mumbai, Kolkata, Chennai, Kanpur, Bangalore and Hyderabad combined at about 100,000 in Delhi. Factors which have given rise to the increase in number of street children in India include poverty, family break-ups, armed conflicts, natural and man-made disasters, lack of employment opportunities and the attraction of cities. Street children have received much attention in the media, both national and international in the recent years. The awareness and sensitisation efforts have led to several initiatives involving numerous groups at the local, state and national level."

According to a report[1] the gender-wise percentage of children suffered from child abuse in different States, is as under:—

States	% Boys	% Girls
Andhra Pradesh	54.21	45.79
Assam	53.48	46.52
Bihar	52.96	47.04
Delhi	65.64	34.36
Goa	52.27	47.73
Gujarat	36.59	63.41
Kerala	55.04	44.96
Madhya Pradesh	42.54	57.46
Maharashtra	49.43	50.57
Mizoram	59.96	40.04
Rajasthan	52.50	47.50
Uttar Pradesh	55.73	44.22
West Bengal	43.71	56.29
National overall average [total]	52.94	47.06

1. "Study on Child Abuse: India 2007, Ministry of Women and Child Development, Government of India.

According to same report of the Government of India, 2007 in different states of the country, the percentage of children facing one or more form of sexual abuse is as under:—

State	No.	One Form of Abuse	Two Form of Abuse	Three Form of Abuse	Four Form of Abuse	% of Children Facing One or More Forms of Abuse
Andhra Pradesh	66.13	15.98	10.39	6.59	0.90	33.87
Assam	42.73	20.16	24.67	11.13	1.30	57.27
Bihar	66.73	15.13	8.62	9.02	0.50	33.27
Delhi	59.10	18.09	12.36	9.45	1.01	40.90
Goa	97.62	1.78	0.40	–	0.20	2.38
Gujarat	92.66	4.73	2.01	0.40	0.20	7.34
Kerala	82.30	9.20	3.40	4.10	1.00	17.70
M.P.	90.13	5.58	3.09	1.10	0.10	9.87
Mahar-ashtra	90.21	7.39	1.60	0.80	–	9.79
Mizoram	83.80	13.06	2.30	0.84	–	16.20
Rajasthan	89.18	6.21	2.40	1.20	1.00	10.82
Uttar Pradesh	94.02	2.69	1.10	1.49	0.70	5.98
West Bengal	82.80	8.55	5.33	2.72	0.60	17.20
National overall average [total]	79.10	10.20	6.20	3.91	0.59	20.90

The forms of sexual abuse includes sexual assault, making the child fondle private parts, making the child exhibit or exhibiting private body parts and being photographed in the nude.

In Delhi, 662 rape cases were reported in 2012 out of which, substantial numbers are minor girls, out of which in 202 cases, neighbours are involved and in 189 cases, the friends and relatives are involved. All victims have usually been under-age. The age group of the higher number of victims is 286 between 12-18 years, followed by 167 cases of which group is between 18-25 years.[1]

The data maintained by the National Crime Records Bureau reveals that out of 45,600 people who are in jails across the country on rape charges, more than 80 per cent were known to the victim. Less than half of those in jail have been convicted. The age groups of the victims (in Delhi) may be summarised as under:

Number of victims		Age group
5	—	under 2 years of age.
105	—	between 2 and 12
286	—	between 12 and 18
167	—	between 18 and 25
99	—	over 25
(Total 662)		

Apart from the 202 neighbours indulged into sexual abuse in terms of relationship, 5 are fathers, 7 are step fathers, 2 ex-husbands, 17 brother-in-laws, 4 uncles, 3 cousins, 1 stepson, 2 father-in-law and 189 other relatives and friends.[1] The figure reveals the spoiling system and family unit of our country.

According to recent report[2] in the State of Uttar Pradesh in the year 2012, there were 1533 reported cases of rape which include minors. 1369 cases of eve-teasing and 2983 cases of outraging the modesty were reported. In the State of Uttar Pradesh 13,263 cases of rape are pending in the Sessions Courts.

1. The Indian Express: 31st December, 2012.
2. Amar Ujala, January 3, 2013 [Lucknow Edn.].

Thus, the State of Uttar Pradesh is not far behind Delhi. The study report on child sexual abuse in booklet 'Invisible Crime', published by 'Vatsalya',[1] is horrifying. It shows the enormity of sexual abuse among children.

In Western Uttar Pradesh, according to report, the sexual abuse is comparatively higher to other zones of Uttar Pradesh *i.e.* Eastern, Western and Bundelkhand). Almost 99% school-going boys faced sexual abuse in Bundelkhand, 99.9% girls living in 'institutional care' faced sexual abuse in Central Uttar Pradesh Majority of children did not report the incident to their parents or guardians because of shame and fear. The marriages took place at adolescence age. School-going children and working children were compelled to watch pornographic material in the form of film by their teachers, colleagues, friends etc. One startling feature is that the magnitude of sexual abuse is more rampant in boys and majority of the paedophile are the people who are known to children. However, in the event of hue and cry raised by the affected persons ordinarily, such incidents stops.

The report further reveals only 39% of sexual abused children reported the incident to their adult trustworthy. Among the school-going children, 80.9% have been sexually abused in one or the other form. The percentage is higher in Bundelkhand *i.e.,* 99.1%. According to report, children whether male or female, have been sexually abused at every stage right from home to school and working places. Persons indulged in sexual abuse, psychologically are abnormal, repulsive or obsessive. The trust, power and attraction are the main strategies which are often employed by the abuser under the veil of closer or distant relationships or acquaintances. In India, offence against children have increased three-fold from 10314 in 2001 to 33098 in 2011.

The booklet, *"Invisible Crime"* is not only informative but reveals the rotting family unit as well as the society. The *"Invisible Crime"* booklet shall be useful not only for law-makers but also for the members of judiciary and citizen to

1. A. NGO in State of U.P., Lucknow.

look after their children carefully. I have also noted some instances with regard to child sexual abuse and given certain instances in my book *"Morality in Law"*.[1]

The Law Commission in its 172nd report has suggested drastic change in the Indian Penal Code to combat child sex abuse.

The Central Social Welfare Board (CSWB) organised Workshop on Prostitutes and their Children (28, 29 May 1990), with regard to 6 metropolitan cities of the country, opined that the major contributory factors for the commercial sexual exploitation of women and children are poverty and unemployment or lack of appropriate rehabilitation.

Other reason with regard to sexual exploitation of child seems to be the way of life we possess. Sexual abuse of child were unknown to ancient Indian civilization because of inculcation of moral values from the beginning of life *i.e.*, childhood. The morality was the part of education with different imposed restrictions on both boys and girls. The fabric of social structure was such that a person of easy virtue was not able to outrage the modesty of child, not only because of fear of punishment but social discard. Western jurists propounded the theory of separation of power coupled with pure theory of law. The adverse affect of these principles may be noted from American and European society where a person having gun shoots his own parents and children in school, prostitution and infidelity become way of life.

In Western countries particularly, in Australia, there are number of cases where father and brother molested their own daughters, married to them and given birth to children openly without fear of social indictment. There are number of instances with regard to illicit relationship or marriage between father and daughter in European countries. In Australia, John Earnest Deaves married to his daughter Jennifer Anne Deaves and gave birth to two children, the first of which was born in 2001 and died few days later.

1. Published by Eastern Book Company (2012 Edn.).

Valerie Spruill (60), Ohio having illicit relationship with father, gave birth to three children. The news was published in newspaper on 21st September, 2012. There are so many other cases of similar illicit relationship, details of which are available on the Internet. Paedophiliac scandals are on rise in the western world including churches. It is endemic to the extent that Pope Benedict XVI apologised.[1] In United States of America in 2011, total 11,29,456 children were arrested (according to FBI) as compared to 33,887 children in India (according to National Crime Record Bureau).

On 26-4-2013, twelve dead bodies of girls found in rented room at Mangolpuri, Delhi. Five people including 16 years old girl in Mumbai arrested for alleged gang rape of 13 years old girl at Wakola on 25-4-2013[2] In Varanasi, district of Uttar Pradesh, India twelve years old girl was alleged to rape by her own father. Being disturbed by the incident the minor girl was heading towards railway track in a distraught state to commit suicide but prevented by the villagers. FIR lodged.[3] In Mainpuri district of State of Uttar Pradesh, India another father belonging to Barnahal area raped his own daughter aged about 14 years. An FIR was lodged by the mother against her own husband at Police Station, Barnahal? A minor girl was gang raped within Ramsanehi Ghat District Barabanki, Uttar Pradesh India by two persons. Police declined to register a case but ultimately registered case on interference of the District Magistrate. The FIR was lodged in Ramsanehi Ghat, District Barabanki. In District Gonda, minor girl aged about 12 years was molested and raped by a person.[4]

This is the worst outcome of personal liberty and constitutional protection. India is going the same way. No one knows how to tackle this problem. Wise advises are

1. "Morality in Law", by Justice Devi Prasad Singh, page. 204.
2. Times of India, April 27, 2013.
3. Times of India, April 28, 2013.
4. Amar Ujala, 28 April, 2013.

discarded and ancient Indian preachings are held to be old one. The morality is at its lowest ebbs. Person has become individualistic, avoids to take the issue of others or help others who are in distress.

Recently, one of the eyewitness and sufferer of Delhi Gang Rape, has given statement before the media which reveals the horrible state of mind of the present generation, to quote:[1]—

> "If we are lighting candles to support someone, I feel that we should also help someone who is lying on the road. We were without clothes. We tried to stop people passing by. For about 25 minutes, several auto-rickshaws, cars and bikes slowed down but no one stopped. Then someone called the police. Three PCR vans arrived after 45 minutes, before that no one came to help us..."

The victim further stated, to quote:—

> "We didn't have clothes, we were not able to stand and there were people passing by... They could have taken us to hospital..."

Let us ponder why the hero, who fought with the six accused to save himself and the girl, were lying on road naked, without any public help or response.

A Russian Laureate Pitirim Alaxendrovitch Sorokin (1889-1968), had written a widely acclaimed book, "*Sane Sex Order*", and who happens to be Professor of Harvard University, admired Lord Buddha and Gandhi Ji both, and writes in his book, to quote:—

> "When the disorderly sexual life spreads among a large part of the members of a society, then mental diseases, emotional storms and crises, and paralysis of will begin to mount. Through volitional paralysis, there is a growing inability of the society to control biological and emotional drives; to resist the temptations of flesh and of material wealth and comfort; to curb the lust for power; to discharge

1. The Indian Express, 5th January, 2013, Lucknow Edition.

painful duties and to make necessary sacrifices; and to chart and to follow its own historical course. From a self-determining and self-controlling collectivity, the society deteriorates into passive drifter until it is brought to the brink of an historical Niagara.[1]"

It is of common knowledge that large number of pornographic sites are available on Internet. These sites have spoiled the moral fabric of western countries and now peeped into India. They entered into "classroom to bedroom". Everyone including the teenagers as well as young generation have access to it. These sites create sexual disorder and is one of the reason causing child sex abuse as well as rape and gang-rape.

According to report every second $ 3,075.64 is spent on pornography, 28,258 people are viewing pornography every second, 372 people while using Internet are typing adult search terms in every second. In every 39 minutes, a new pornographic video is created in the United States of America. Until 1999 United States of America video depictions of hardcore material were illegal but later on to remove barrier European Members allowed for free movement. Though child pornography is illegal United States of America with punishment up to ten years but it is available on different sites in abundance.

In India, possession or watching of pornographic materials seems to be not illegal but distribution is prohibited. Pornographic material is easily available. Section 67B of the Information Technology Act make the downloading, publishing child porn criminal offence but Bombay High Court in 2010 ruled that watching porn in private is legal. Virtually there is no strict enforceable law in India to check the video depiction of hardcore materials of pornographic sites or videography. Immediate step requires at the level of government to check pornography.

How the pornography has devastating effect in a man's life and social order, may be noted from a news item

1. The Indian Express, 6th January, 2013, Lucknow Edition.

published in the newspaper.[1] The news item under the heading, "Sex addiction is on the rise across India", reveals how sex addiction is increasing day by day in Indian society. The reporter Shobha John noted that a man Nirmal aged about 38 years, living married life having two children, becomes sex addicts with 922 partners both, male and female. After alcohol and drug addiction, sex addiction is one another problem which country is likely to face. To reproduce relevant portion from the news item:—

> "...growing hordes of sex addicts in a country free and connected like never before, had no where to go for deaddiction. Sex addiction, which can ruin families and lives, is on the rise in India. But there are very few clinics in the country that recognize this condition, treated as the hush-hush disease. Apart from the anxiety of the patients, in a country like India with little security for women (Delhi) recorded a 24% rise in rape cases in 2012, it can also be downright dangerous. It is easy for these addicts to turn into sexual predators.
>
> Steven Pinker, professor of psychology at Harvard, recently told TOI, "Ordinarily, men woo and seduce women. But in unregulated settings, and when men are desperate, it can lead to harassment and rape." In Sex Addicts Anonymous a book published in the United States in 2005, several sex addicts admitted they had committed rape. Experts are unanimous that the time has come to accept that the affliction—also called paraphilia, meaning 'beyond love'—exists in substantial numbers in India, and deal with it. "Sex addiction cases I get have doubled in the last decade," says Dr. Rajan Bhonsle, head of the department of sexual medicine at Seth G.S. Medical College, Mumbai. "I have 25-30 cases every month and they come from all parts of India." Sexologist Dr. Prakash Kothari says he used to get 1-3 patients a month at KEM Hospital earlier. "Now it's 10-12."

1. "Times of India", dated 26-1-2013.

Pornography, indecent audio and video material, vulgarity and alike matters influence the immature mind, create temptation to indulge into immoral activities and increase negativity. It shall be appropriate to reproduce two verses from the Bhagavad Gita, to quote:—

इन्द्रियाणां हि चरतां यन्मनोऽनुविधीयते ।
तदस्य हरति प्रज्ञां वायुर्नावमिवाम्भसि ।। 67।।

67. For, the mind which yields to the roving senses
carried away his knowledge, as the wind
(carried away) a ship on water"[1]

कर्मेन्द्रियाणि संयम य आस्ते मनसा स्मरन्।
इन्द्रियार्थान्विमूढात्मा मिथ्याचारः स उच्यते।। 6 ।।

6. He who, restraining the organs of action, sits thinking
in his mind of the objects of the senses, self-deluded,
he is said to be one of false conduct.[2]

The mind which yields to senses engaged in their respective objects, destroy the morality and self-control like wind carries away ship from intended course of the sailors and drives her astray.

Similarly, a person, who restrain his organ of action but continues in his mind to brood over the object of senses, whose nature is deluded shall be a hypocrite. Control of outward activities without restraining the desire, which impel a person shall be of ill consequence.

Ordinarily a man cannot control the senses in case surrounding posses indecent audio and video visuals or printed matters.

Needless to say, that one of the major factors behind sex addiction or sexual abuse is pornography. It is time to stop pornographic sites on web sites within India. Morality seems to be at lowest ebb to the extent that allegation with regard to wife swapping has been brought on record levelled by a lady who happens to be wife of Navy Officer.[3]

---

1. Chapter II, Verse 67 from The Bhagavad Gita.
2. Chapter III, Verse 6 from The Bhagavad Gita.
3. The Times of India, dated 12-4-2013.

It is a matter of great concern for all men who have concern for Nation and society as to whether we are at the brink of collapse because of sexual disorder. We are not concerned with the abrasions of young life but we are concerned with the 'habitual sexual disorder' where boys and girls are facing sexual abuse, putting scar on their whole life. We require better law as well as stricter enforcement of law coupled with self-corrective measures. In the words of Sorokin, "the initial kingdom of the human animal" should be checked and substituted by more and more ennobled kingdom of man necessary for a civilized society which the ancient India was having.

Time has come to revisit the ancient Indian theories and give a second look to administration of justice. Some of the steps which may be looked into are:—

1. Unification of morality with law, education and judicial pronouncements.
2. Constitution of specialised separate courts not only for juvenile justice but all cases relating to child sex abuse, rape and foeticide in different districts to decide cases within specific period. Penal statutes be amended in appropriate manner to investigate and decide cases in specified period.
3. Law and order should be separated from the investigating agency and in every district, special investigating team may be constituted to investigate the cases with regard to rape and child sex abuse. Investigation must be quick and charge-sheet may be submitted within two months and trial be concluded within four months (total six months). For failure, the officers may be made accountable.
4. Floor discussion should be encouraged to awaken the people and wherever necessary, voice may be raised against child sex abuse and gender discrimination by socially conscious people. It is necessary for a qualitative change of mind-set across the board.
5. Parents or guardians may be taught to realize and discharge their responsibility with regard to their

children. There should be social boycott by the peoples, of the persons who are involved in child sex abuse, rape and other immoral acts.

6. Structure of flats, houses and living style may be given a second look to safeguard the interest of children, girls or ladies of the house in appropriate way.
7. Expert Committees be appointed to consider for reduction in age of majority keeping in view the biological and intellectual maturity attained by children at an early age and accordingly in case experts and sociologist agree, under the Juvenile Justice Act, their age may be reduced to 16 years.
8. Large number of pornographic sites showing blue films, are available on Internet. They must immediately be stopped by the Government of India. These sites are spoiling the entire social fabric and shall result with disastrous consequences in due course of time.

These are some of the suggestions which may be looked into by the social organisations, Government, legislature and bureaucracy along with various reports of Law Commission and different committees to check the menace.

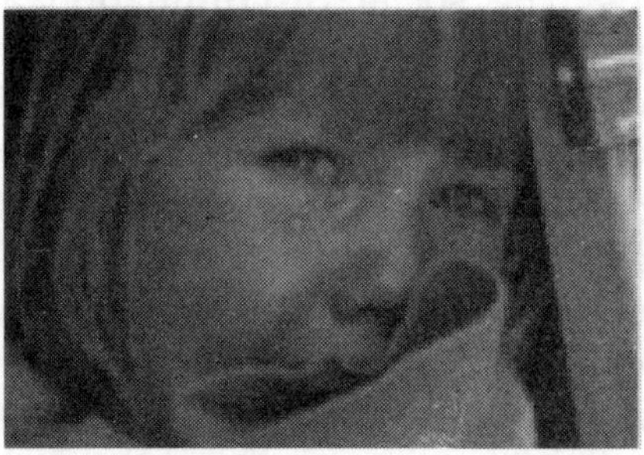

Female Foeticide

Om! In the beginning this was but the absolute self-alone.
There was nothing else whatsoever that winked.
It thought, 'let me create the worlds.'[1]

Feticide or foeticide is an act which causes death of foetus. Female foeticide is an act of aborting a foetus because it is a female. Female foeticide taken monunentum from 1990s with technical development meant for sex determination test. It acquired genocide proportion finally catching up in States of India. Other countries of all over the world, are also facing the problem but magnitude of female feticide in South East Asia, is much more than other countries. It is only tip of demographic and social problem confronting India in coming years. With horrific number of foeticide, the foetal sex determination and sex selecting abortion by unethical medical professionals, according to reports, has grown up into an Industry of more than Rs. 1000 crores. The social discrimination against women has already entrenched Indian society, and spurred on by the technical developments with upto a mobile sex clinic, to drive into in village or neighbourhood unchecked. The most prosperous State in India is the Punjab which is the leader of female feticide as appears from the available reports. The rate of conviction merely with a fine of few hundred or thousand rupees is too low. Female foeticide is also laid to an increase in human trafficking. According to report, in 2011, 15,000 Indian women were brought and sold as brides in the area where feticide has laid to a lack of women. Actor Amir Khan devoted an episode in his serial "Satyamev

1. Aitareya Upanishad, verse 1.

Jayate" to raise the awareness of the issue. On account of low conviction rate and inaction on the part of the State, it has become routine feature of the day. UNICEF has shown its deep concern to a declining sex-ratio in the State of Punjab and some other parts of the country.

Now, it is trite law that right of life and livelihood guaranteed under article 21 of the Constitution, is available to the child in womb and accordingly, higher judiciary in different parts of the world as well as India, has issued guidelines and direction laid down law for the child in the womb. It is a topic which requires discussion at appropriate forum.

The socio-cultural development of Indian society compel to give birth to a male child. The reason behind is, thousands years of mindset to ensure the birth of male child and *secondly*, expenditure involved in marriage of female child in the form of dowry and related problems. In medieval India, the avoidance of female child was also for the reasons that ordinarily, the life of good-looking girls was not secured. On account of cultural conflict and dominance, the girls were first target by the mighty rulers of opposite culture.

However, Vedic India was golden period for the status of women where, the women were at par with men in their social activities. Decisions were taken collectively for the welfare of female child and the nation. It was in later period with the evolution of orthodoxy in the field of religion, the problem arose.

In post-constitutional era, no major effort has been made with regard to protection of child and check the foeticide. Only 0.034% of total Union Budget is allocated for the child development. The plight of child in India as well as foeticide discussed and disclosed in a book namely, Child Sexual Abuse and Exploitation in India, by Sri S.C. Singh (Serials Publications) is not only startling but disturbing. Children are not secured in their own family and according to report, 67% problem faced by the children in Delhi, is from their own family members, friends and relatives.

Flourishing of child prostitution and involvement of girl from lower strata of society in prostitution or as bar girl, reveals the female compulsion because of financial crunch. In case whereby feticide birth is not prevented, then under the financial constraints the young generation indulge into immoral trade. It is because of mal-administration and mal-planning in the country.

In one other book, "Women in India—Trials and Triumphs", edited by Shweta Prasad, different aspects have been dealt with regard to gender discrimination, female feticide and plight of women in India. In my own book, "Morality in Law", published recently,[1] I have discussed certain instances where because of poverty followed by immorality in the governance, how the country may suffer more in coming days.

Only women are not responsible for female foeticide but it is the combined action of husband and wife with the involvement of other female members of a family. Framers of law must look into this aspect of the matter, and shifting the burden only on women, is not justified and is far from ground realities.

The decennial census has always been a much awaited national exercise which comes out with figures of paramount socio-economic significance. One of the areas of great concern has been the sex-ratio which shows the number of females per thousand males. When I did read, that the over-all sex ratio in our country has increased from the level of 933 in 2001 to 940 in 2011; I was enveloped with sense of pride and satisfaction. This was a simple declaration of a true fact that the survival rate of the female population in the country was on the upswing. This gave the impression that the social status of the fair sex was improving. But a real picture emerged after seeing the sex ratio in the 0-6 age group, which declared that the child sex ratio in India has dropped to 914 females, the lowest since Independence. Population in the 0-6 year's group during

1. Morality In Law, 2012 Edition by Eastern Book Company, Lucknow.

2001-2011 registered minus 3.08 per cent growth with minus 2.42 for males and minus 3.80 for females. This was a clear reflection of the fact that the Indian society has continued the preference for boys. This figure stood at 927 in 2001. The comparative figure for Uttar Pradesh—the most populous State of our country stood at 916 as per the census figures of 2001 saw a sharp decline by dropping to 899 in 2011. This means while the national average dropped by 13 basis points, the same in the case of Uttar Pradesh was of 17 basis points.

It's all the more shocking, that hereto areas which were largely unaffected in Uttar Pradesh *i.e.,* Central & Eastern region, have seen the sharpest decline. For example, districts of Hardoi, Balia and Sidharthnagar have seen a decline of more than 42 basis points, with this being highest in case of Hardoi, where it was 51.

All this has happened despite their being a slew of laws, particularly the Pre-conception and Pre-Natal Diagnostic Techniques (Prohibition of Sex-Selection) Act, 1994 and even international conventions like the United Nations Conventions on the Right of the Child, 1989 (UNCRCT) to which India is a signatory; Article 6 of (UNCRCT) provides that, "Every child has the inherent right to life and the State has an obligation to ensure the child survival & development."

The anguish of the judiciary in the matter is best reflected in what was so succinctly stated by the Supreme Court of India in *Centre for Enquiring into Health & Allied Themes (CEHAT)* v. *Union of India,* (2003) 8 SCC 298. It is an admitted fact that in Indian Society, discrimination against girl child still prevails, may be because of prevailing uncontrolled dowry system despite the Dowry Prohibition Act, as there is no change in the mindset or also because of poor education and/or tradition of women being confined to household activities. Sex selection/sex determination further adds to this adversity... The misuse of modern science and technology by preventing the birth of girl child by sex determination before birth and thereafter abortion is evident from the (2001) census figures which reveal this decline in sex-ratio in the 0-6 age group... Despite this, it is unfortunate that law which aims at preventing such practice is not implemented and, therefore NGOs are required to approach... Court for implementation of PNDT Act, 1994".

One of our Health Minister has stated in Parliament that sex determination techniques to determine the sex of the foetus and subsequent abortions if the foetuses were females are used in India since 1975. Earlier, systematic elimination of girl child, through female infanticide in various parts of the country is a well-known fact. Dr. Amartya Sen long back estimated that, even in 1990, 100 million fewer women were alive than were projected in demographic studies. In the process, the Indian society and in particular the family have denied the girl child the most basic and fundamental of all human rights, the right to take birth and right to live.

In 1986, a forum against Sex Determination Sex Pre-Selection, a social action group based in Mumbai made a systematic attempt to initiate a campaign on this issue, pressuring the Maharashtra Government to enact the first ever law in India. The Maharashtra Pre-Natal Diagnostic Techniques Act was enacted in 1988. This formed the basis of the PC PNDT Act, 1994 which was brought into operation from the 1st January, 1996.

The Act prohibits sex selection before and after conception. Pre-natal diagnostic techniques are regulated to be used only to detect genetic and metabolic disorders, chromosomal abnormalities, congenital malformations, haemoglobin apathies and sex-linked disorders. The PC-PNDT Act states that sex selection, either before or after conception, is prohibited by anyone and by any means. However, while regulating the misuse of technology, the Act does not deny technology either. It allows for pre-natal sex diagnosis (not selection), for purposes of detecting chromosomal abnormalities, genetic disorders and congenital abnormalities. The Act requires the filling-up and regular submission of a Form, duly signed by the pregnant women.

However, under the law, ultrasound clinics, clinics for carrying out medical termination of pregnancy, and clinics for assisted reproductive technologies and facilities are allowed for the use of the technology provided they are licensed. The Preamble talks of prohibition and regulation of pre-natal techniques required for pregnant women. Definitions include the varieties of clinics, etc., which are eligible and the qualifications of doctors. Portable machines are also included. The Act has a Central and State level supervisory Board, an appropriate authority, and supporting advisory committee. The function of the Board is to monitor the Act, which included making amendments from time to time as may be required. The appropriate authority is required to oversee the registration of clinics, administrative details, inspections, investigations and imposing of penalties. The advisory committee provides technical support to the appropriate authority, which in turn is expected to advise the Central or State medical councils in the matter of taking action against culpable doctors. The Act prohibits sale of equipment to unregistered clinics. No parental tests may be done unless reason is recorded. The appropriate authorities have the following functions:

1. Granting/rejecting/suspending/cancelling registrations;
2. conducting inspections and investigations;
3. Initiating legal action;
4. Creating public awareness;
5. Recommending changes in the Act and the rules for better implementation;
6. Preparing quarterly reports on implementation of the Act.

The Act provided a well-knit legislative scheme for ensuring a strict and vigilant enforcement of the provisions of the Act directed against female foeticide and misuse of pre-natal diagnostic techniques. In fact, the use of those techniques are restricted to the purpose of detection of any of the abnormalities or diseases enumerated in sub-section (2) of section 4 of the Act. The provisions are stricter in case of conduct of pre-natal diagnostic techniques on a pregnant woman, requiring her written consent and determination of sex of a foetus is prohibited by the provisions contained in sections 5 and 6. Constitution of "appropriate authority" under section 17 is clearly meant to ensure proper and vigorous implementation of the Act; and it is expressly prescribed as one of its functions to take legal action against the use of any sex-selection technique. That authority, where appointed for the whole of a State or Union Territory, should consist of three members. But when it is appointed for the part of a State or Union Territory, it could consist of an officer of such rank as the Government concerned may deem fit.

The provisions of section 28 clearly provide for taking cognizance of an offence under the Act only upon a complaint being made by any of the four categories of complainants, *viz*:

1. The appropriate authority concerned;
2. Any officer authorized in that behalf by the Central Government or State Government;
3. Any officer authorized in that behalf by the appropriate authority; and
4. A person, which includes a social organization, who has given notice as prescribed in section 28(1)(b). According to a new Government Order (G.O.) dated 30th November, 2007, District Magistrates have been appointed as the appropriate authority in place of the Chief Medical Officer in Uttar Pradesh.

The Act does not provide any role to the police in its implementation. In order to conduct investigative procedures, appropriate authority have been vested with the investigative powers of a civil court. The Act clearly prohibits disclosure of the sex of the unborn child. The only way to catch the guilty is by checking the records, but a guilty doctor is unlikely to keep good records. However, abnormalities in the unborn child would come out in the genetic lab where one can easily find out if the MTP was essential. Gender-based violence is a public health issue as well as a rights issue. Ethical questions connected with the practice of female foeticide arise from the point of view of sociology and medicine, but the criminal nature of the practice is not highlighted. The punitive measures are ordinarily not enforced by the administrative machinery.

Amniocentesis and Ultra-Sonography are misused as sex determining techniques. This misuse of these technologies has increased particularly in private clinics, hospitals and diagnostic centres in the country. While, according to the Act only registered institutions can provide genetic counselling, genetic tests and clinical services, still the implementation of sex selection and sex determination lies squarely within the purview and discretion of the medical practitioner. To perform sex determination and abortions for the sole purpose of female feticide constitute the breach of medical ethics, in which both the doctors and their authority. *i.e.,* the Medical Council may be indicted.

Based on the amendments carried out under the Act in the year 2003, the Rules framed thereunder have also been amended. Under the amended Rules:

1. A provision for appeal has been made: Any person having against the sub-district level appropriate authority can make an appeal to the district level appropriate authority and similarly for grievance against the district level appropriate authority an appeal can be made to the State/UT level appropriate authority.
2. 23 indications, prescribed by ICMR, have been included in the PC-PNDT Rules for which ultrasound scanning can be conducted during pregnancy for the well being of the pregnant woman and foetus.
3. Forms have been simplified and Consent is required only in case of invasive techniques.

Under the Act specific role and responsibilities of different authorities are not specified. The difficult accessibility of most of the District Magistrates to maintain law and order being their busy schedule has led to certain laxity in its implementation. As a follow-up to this Government order and the State appropriate authority meeting, another order was passed whereby the CMO has been designated the role of the upkeep of the records and other formalities concerning the registration, renewal and cancellation of the ultrasound centers. This has streamlined the implementation process to some extent.

Unfortunately despite this landmark enactment of immense social significance having been in force ever since 1996, the female foeticide is increasing day by day, resulting in the female sex ratio coming down at an alarming scale.

Supreme Court of India recently in the case of Voluntary Health Association of Punjab[1] shown its deep concern to the female foeticide in the country. Supreme Court of India observed that *"female foeticide has its roots in the social thinking which is fundamentally based on certain erroneous notions, ego-centric traditions, pervert perception of societal norms, and obsession with ideas which are totally individualistic sans the collective good. All involved in female foeticide deliberately forget to realize that when the foetus of a girl child is destroyed, a woman of future is crucified. To put it differently, the present generation invites the sufferings on its own and also sows the seeds of suffering for the future generation, as in the ultimate eventuate, the sex ratio gets affected and leads to manifold social problems. I may hasten to add that no awareness campaign can ever be complete unless there is real focus on the prowess of women and the need for women empowerment."*

Supreme Court[1] further observed that *"it is not out of place to state here that the restricted and constricted thinking with regard to a girl child eventually leads to female foeticide. A foetus in the womb, because she is likely to be born as a girl child, is not allowed to see the mother earth. In* M.C. Mehta *v.* State of Tamil Nadu,

1. *Voluntary Health Association of Punjab* v. *Union of India,* (2013) 4 SCC 1.

[3], a three-Judge Bench, while dealing with the magnitude of the problem in engagement of the child labour in various hazardous factories or mines, etc., speaking through Hansaria, J., commenced the judgment thus: [(1996) 6 SCC 756 (759), para 1]—

> *"I am the child.*
>
> *All the world waits for my coming.*
>
> *All the earth watches with interest to see what I shall become.*
>
> *Civilization hangs in the balance.*
>
> *For what I am, the world of tomorrow will be.*
>
> *I am the child.*
>
> *You hold in your hand my destiny.*
>
> *You determine, largely, whether I shall succeed or fail,*
>
> *Give me, I pray you, these things that make for happiness.*
>
> *Train me, I beg you, that I may be a blessing to the world."*

The aforesaid lines from Mamie Gene Cole were treated as an appeal by this Court and the Bench reproduced the famous line from William Wordsworth "child is the father of the man". I have reproduced the same to highlight that this Court has laid special emphasis on the term "child" as a child feels that the entire world waits for his/her coming. A female child, as stated earlier, becomes a woman. Its life-spark cannot be extinguished in the womb, for such an act would certainly bring disaster to the society. On such an act the collective can neither laugh today nor tomorrow. There shall be tears and tears all the way because eventually the spirit of humanity is comatosed."

Supreme Court[1] further recapitulate the Indian thought where woman has been given very high status in the family life referring its earlier cases in the case of *Nikku Ram*[2] and

1. *Voluntary Health Association of Punjab* v. *Union of India,* (2013) 4 SCC 1.
2. *State of Himachal Pradesh* v. *Nikku Ram,* AIR 1996 SC 67: 1995 Cr LJ 4184: (1995) 6 SCC 219.

has reproduced the first line of ancient scripture *i.e.* the shloka and the second line of the same shloka is as under:—

Recapitulating from the past, I may refer to certain sayings in the Smritis which put women in an elevated position. This Court in Nikku Ram's *case (supra) had already reproduced the first line of the "Shloka". The second line of the same which is also significant is as follows:—*

"यत्र तास्तु न पूज्यन्ते सर्वास्तत्राफलाः क्रियाः"

[*Yatra tastu na pujyantc sarvastatraphalah kriyah]*

A free translation of the aforesaid is reproduced below:—

> "All the actions become unproductive in a place, where they are not treated with proper respect and dignity."

Another wise man of the past had his own way of putting it:

भर्तृभ्रात पित जाति श्रवश्रुश्वसुर देवरैः।

बन्धुभिश्च स्त्रियः पूज्यां भूषणाच्छादनाशनैः

[Bhartrbhratr pitrijnati swasruswasuradevaraih।
Bandhubhisca striyah pujyah bhusnachhadanasnaih]

A free translation of the aforesaid is as follows:—

> *"The women are to be respected equally on par with husbands, brothers, fathers, relatives, in-laws and other kith and kin and while respecting, the women gifts like ornaments, garments, etc. should be given as token of honour."*

20. Yet again, the sagacity got reflected in following lines:—

"अतुलं तत्र तत्तेजः सर्वदेवशरीरजम् ।

एकस्थं तदभून्नारी व्याप्तलोकत्रयंत्विषा ।।

[*Atulam yatra tattejah sarvadevasarirajam।*
Ekastham tadabhunnari vyaptalokatrayam tvisa]

A free translation of the aforesaid is reproduced below:—

> "The incomparable valour (effulgence) born from the physical frames of all the Gods, spreading the three worlds by its radiance and combining together took the form of a woman."

Supreme Court[1] further referred the ofquoted lines of Lord Denning, to quote:—

> *From the past, I travel to the present and respectfully notice what Lord Denning had to say about the equality of women and their role in the society:—*
>
> *"A woman feels as keenly, thinks as clearly, as a man. She in her sphere does work as useful as man does in his. She has as much right to her freedom – to develop her personality to the full as a man. When she marries, she does not become the husband's servant but his equal partner. If his work is more important in life of the community, her's is more important of the family. Neither can do without the other. Neither is above the other or under the other. They are equals."*

The Court[1] held that mere awareness will not serve the purpose. A cosmetic awareness campaign would never subserve the purpose. The authorities of the Government, the Non-Governmental Organisations and other volunteers are required to remember that there has to be awareness camps which are really effective. The people involved with the same must take it up as a service, a crusade. They must understand and accept that it is an art as well as a science and not simple arithmetic. It cannot take the colour of a routine speech. The awareness camps should not be founded on the theory of Euclidian geometry. It must engulf the concept of social vigilance with an analytical mind and radiate into the marrows of the society. If awareness campaigns are not appositely conducted, the needed guidance for the people would be without meaning

1. *Voluntary Health Association of Punjab* v. *Union of India,* (2013) 4 SCC 1.

and things shall fall apart and everyone would try to take shelter in cynical escapism.

Supreme Court[1] issued certain guidelines and called action taken report from different states of the country. Those guidelines are as under:—

In such circumstances, the following directions are given:

1. *The Central Supervisory Board and the State and Union Territories Supervisory Boards, constituted under sections 7 and 16A of PN&PNDT Act, would meet at least once in six months, so as to supervise and oversee how effective is the implementation of the PN&PNDT Act.*
2. *The State Advisory Committees and District Advisory Committees should gather information relating to the breach of the provisions of the PN&PNDT Act and the Rules and take steps to seize records, seal machines and institute legal proceedings, if they notice violation of the provisions of the PN&PNDT Act.*
3. *The Committees mentioned above should report the details of the charges framed and the conviction of the persons who have committed the offence, to the State Medical Councils for proper action, including suspension of the registration of the unit and cancellation of licence to practice.*
4. *The authorities should ensure also that all Genetic Counselling Centres, Genetic Laboratories and Genetic Clinics, Infertility Clinics, Scan Centres etc. using pre-conception and pre-natal diagnostic techniques and procedures should maintain all records and all forms, required to be maintained under the Act and the Rules and the duplicate copies of the same be sent to the concerned District Authorities, in accordance with Rule 9(8) of the Rules.*
5. *States and District Advisory Boards should ensure that all manufacturers and sellers of ultra-sonography machines do not sell any machine to any unregistered centre, as provided*

1. *Voluntary Health Association of Punjab* v. *Union of India*, (2013) 4 SCC 1.

under rule 3A and disclose, on a quarterly basis, to the concerned State/Union Territory and Central Government, a list of persons to whom the machines have been sold, in accordance with rule 3A(2) of the Act.

6. *There will be a direction to all Genetic Counselling Centres, Genetic Laboratories, Clinics etc. to maintain forms A, E, H and other Statutory forms provided under the Rules and if these forms are not properly maintained, appropriate action should be taken by the authorities concerned.*
7. *Steps should also be taken by the State Government and the authorities under the Act for mapping of all registered and unregistered ultra-sonography clinics, in three months' time.*
8. *Steps should be taken by the State Governments and the Union Territories to educate the people of the necessity of implementing the provisions of the Act by conducting workshops as well as awareness camps at the State and District levels.*
9. *Special Cell be constituted by the State Governments and the Union Territories to monitor the progress of various cases pending in the Courts under the Act and take steps for their early disposal.*
10. *The authorities concerned should take steps to seize the machines which have been used illegally and contrary to the provisions of the Act and the Rules thereunder and the seized machines can also be confiscated under the provisions of the Code of Criminal Procedure and be sold, in accordance with law.*

The various Courts in this country should take steps to dispose of all pending cases under the Act, within a period of six months. Communicate this order to the Registrars of various High Courts, who will take appropriate follow-up action with due intimation to the Courts concerned."

The social mindset of having fuelled by the globalization of modern technology, which as a matter of fact has taken place at a rapid pace, with around 4,000 ultrasound clinics in the State of Uttar Pradesh, systematic elimination of the female foetus has taken place throughout the State resulting in skewed sex ratio. Law enforcing agencies have to act very fact to arrest this phenomenon, which is already showing very adverse impact. The girls in the State are being bought from States like Orissa, West Bengal, Jharkhand etc. This may create distinct social and cultural mismatch. Evil practices like polyandry in that all the brothers in a family sharing a common wife/women is emerging. Crimes like rape, kidnapping, abducting, sexual assault against women is bound to increase in future. All the more this is certainly going to lead to further degradation of the status of women in the society.

The status report with regard to implementation of PC-PNDT Act in the State of Uttar Pradesh prepared by 'Vatsalya',[1] shows the action of the executive to check the foeticide and sex determination and sex selective abortion far from satisfaction. The number given is like drop of water in the ocean where the population of the State of Uttar Pradesh is almost 20 crores. Peoples obey the law ordinarily for three reasons:

1. Being a self-conscious citizen leading an honest life with impeccable character. Such peoples always abide by law.
2. Religious compulsion. The persons who are religious by core of heart (not hypocritic), shall never indulge into foeticide. The fear of God or Almighty in any form, keep them to lead life in a dignified manner with due respect to child in womb.
3. The fear of punishment. Citizen feel that they will be punished in case they indulge into foeticide immediately after commission of offence within short span of time, they shall ordinarily not indulge into female foeticide.

Sofaras the first and second reason is concerned, they require no elaboration. Survey shows that maximum female foeticide took place in States where the citizens are

1. A. NGO at Lucknow, U.P., India.

prosperous. The peoples are prosperous and may pay hefty amount to doctors. The doctors or persons involved in female foeticide from their clinic or nursing home ordinarily have their social set up. The majority of them may have in depth relationship with bureaucracy or police personnel. They influence the system and sometimes, share the income. While adjudicating such controversies, courts should not forget the ground realities of our country. The quick trial and punishment should be maximized and deterrent.

While expanding article 21, Supreme Court settled that children have fundamental right to full development.[1] Article 39(e) and 39(f) under the Directive Principles command for welfare of women and children. The journey of child starts from womb of the mother.

India is a country where institutional credibility is at lowest stage. Now, public interest depend upon individual credibility. I could not find any institution against whom the peoples are not raising finger. Every complaint may not be wrong or manipulated. There appears to be something wrong with our system of governance. The punishment depends how fair the investigating agency is. Why the female foeticide has not been treated as homicide calling for registration of case under section 302 or 304 IPC and prosecution therein.

Professional assisting in a planned manner by sex determination may also be prosecuted as co-accused or conspirator.

Once right to life has been extended to child in womb, there appears to be no reason to make the female foeticide outside the purview of criminal prosecution for homicide and consequential major penalty under Indian Penal Code or any other law for the time being in force. The child in womb whether male or female, is our future progeny and has right to take birth, live natural life and enjoy the natural

1. *Vide. Shantistar Builders* v. *Narayan Khimalal Totame,* (1990) 2 SCJ 10: AIR 1990 SC 630: JT 1990 (1) SC 106; *Lakshmi Kant Pandey* v. *Union of India,* AIR 1984 SC 469: 1984 Cri LR (SC) 127: (1984) 2 SCC 244; *Vishal Jeet* v. *Union of India,* AIR 1990 SC 1412: 1990 Cr LJ 1469.

resources of our country. The Government must think over it for appropriate change in the law with regard to foeticide. Power must be conferred on police to register first information report and charge for homicide in case doctor or any person whosoever may be, plans or acts deliberately for foeticide. The close proximity of the culprit must not come in the way to charge and decide a case with regard to female foeticide. Unless the mighty hands of law is applied equally with major penalty of life imprisonment or a like punishment, the message shall not go that "no one shall be spared".

I have been told, that presently there are only 33 cases, which have been registered in the courts which are under trial. This is very surprising, where facts without doubt reflect a large-scale illegal sex determination and sex selective abortions, where violation of the law in all certainty is going on with impunity. The only reason for this may be the state of prolonged hibernation of the concerned authorities who have to take action under the Act.

The law has to act very fast, we cannot wait for the mindset of the people to change. No doubt women empowerment, development of positive thinking amongst the people, more and ethical education etc., are important; But before all this happens, the implementation of the PC PNDT Act has to be done in letter and spirit with further amendment to check the menace of female foeticide.

I welcome the efforts of Vatsalya[1] and the UPSLSA. I believe that the CJMs participating in this workshop are going to become sensitized towards the importance of this law in arresting the phenomenon of systematic elimination of the girls. Only after doing this, we shall earn the right of calling ourselves to be a civilized society.

While parting with my exposition, I reiterate that law on the subject requires further change and foeticide whether female or male should not be permitted except on medical

1. *Ibid.*

ground and punishment should be more harsh at par with homicide. Vatsalya should take up the matter with the Government for appropriate change in PC-PNDT Act to make the punishment more harsh making the offence cognizable under the Indian Penal Code with right to police to register case and prosecute culprit.

In the end, I recite a hymn of Atharvaveda,[1] to quote:—

> *"The whole of this Universe*
> *Is stationed in the Omnipresent*
> *And Omnipresent God.*
> *We see Him in various forms.*
> *He brings to light*
> *All these worlds.*
> *Him they call the Kala Infinite.*
> *Pervading the vast sky."*

Whether in the child in womb, the Omnipresent is not present?

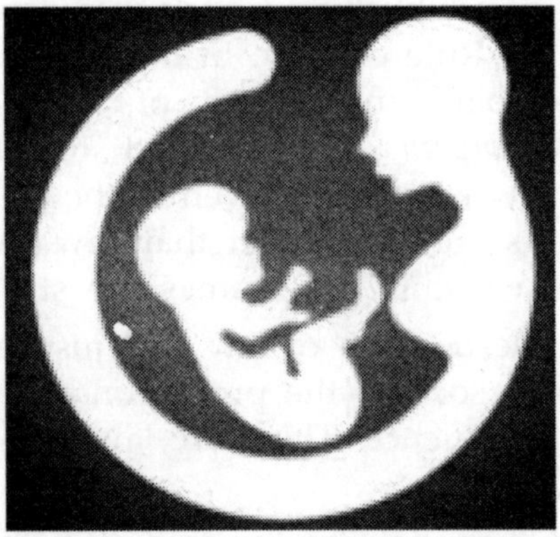

1. [Atharva. 19.53.3].

Legislative Overruling

"It is wrong to imply....that having identified the power of change—all manner of constitutional change is possible. Significant constitutional change may indeed possible where recognition (by the courts) can confidently be predicted, as with the devolution legislation and constitutional independence legislation, however on more controversial matters, the proposed constitutional change is only confirmed when the courts eventually shed light on the rule of recognitions previously penumbral area".[1]

The purpose of establishing Courts in a democratic set up is to maintain the Rule of Law. In Indian concept, law and justice are the part and parcel of a civilised society. According to *Shatpath Brahman* and the *Brihad-Aranyak Upnishad* " the law is the ruler even of the rulers and kings. Therefore there is nothing higher than law. With the aid of the law even a weakling overcomes the strong."

Manu says, "destruction of law and justice brings about the destruction of society; the protection of law and justice has a protective influence. Therefore law and justice should not be destroyed."

A western philosopher Bracton said, "The Kind ought not to be under a man, *non debet esse sub homine,* but under God and the law, *sed sub Deo et lege.* What the Upnishad said about 2500 years back, same was virtually repeated by

---

1. Oliver in Independence, page 304.

Bracton, relying upon which Charles I was executed in England in 1649.

According to Dicey the doctrine of the concept of the Rule of Law had three aspects. *First*, "it means the absolute supremacy or predominance of regular law as opposed to the influence of arbitrary power, and excludes the existence of arbitrariness, of prerogative, or even of wide discretionary authority on the part of the Government. According to Dicey, the Englishmen are ruled by the law, and by the law alone; a man may be punished for a breach of the law, but he can be punished for nothing else. Since we have inherited British parliamentary system, the essence of English law is, 'what is done officially must be done in accordance with law.'

By catena of judgments now it is settled proposition of law that right to life, right to live with dignity, right to quality of life, right to privacy, right to free and fresh air and water and so many other rights are the fundamental rights protected by article 21 of the Constitution of India. The apex court has extended the arena of article 21 of the Constitution to the extent which covers every sphere of human life correlating with the dignity of a person.[1] On account of expansion of the periphery of article 21 of the Constitution the higher judiciary while dealing with the matter involving public interest decide cases which may sometimes become unpleasant to a section of society. The public interest or social welfare is broad term and covers many facets of life not only human beings but also other creatures of God like animals, trees, plants and other living creatures including the environment. Thus, the public welfare or public interest means what is commonly spoken of a public policy, the good of collective body. In such cases the collective interest is to be protected, may be at the cost of individual interest. We may not find a single term to cover the public interest or social welfare. The public interest or social welfare does not mean that the interest is

1. *Kapila Hingorani* v. *State of Bihar*, (2003) 6 SCC 1: JT 2003 (5) SC 1.

based on unethical immoral sultry foundation. According to Dean Pound, "perhaps the most significant advance in the modern science of law is the change from the analytical to the functional attitude."

The emphasis has changed from the content of the precept and the existence of the remedy to the effect of the precept in action and the availability and efficiency of the remedy to attain the ends for which the precept was devised." The famous American Chief Justice Benjamin N. Cardozo had approved that judges should legislate law but ordinarily within the interpretative field. To quote:—

> I recognize without hesitation that judges must and do legislate, but they do so only interstitially; they are confined from molar to molecular motions. A common-law judge could not say, I think the doctrine of consideration a bit of historical nonsense and shall not enforce it in my court. This conception of the legislative power of a judge as operating between spaces is akin to the theory of "gaps in the law" familiar to foreign jurists. The general framework furnished by the statute is to be filled in for each case by means of interpretation, that is, by following out the principles of the statute. In every case, without exception, it is the business of the court to supply what the statute omits, but always by means of an interpretative function. If the statute is interpreted by the method of "free decision."

To quote again Benjamin N. Cardozo:—

> "Constitutions are more likely to enunciate general principles, which must be worked out and applied thereafter to particular conditions. What concerns us now, however, is not the size of the gaps. It is rather the principle that shall determine how they are to be filled, whether their size be great or small. The method of sociology in filling the gaps puts its emphasis on the social welfare."

The Parliament and Assembly of the State and their procedure to pass Bills are being regulated by various provisions of the Constitution. List I of the 7th Schedule deals with the Union List. However, under the entry 97 of the Union List residuary power has been given to Parliament to legislate law on any topic, which are not covered by lists II & III. List II relates to State items relating to which only State legislature has got power to legislate law. Lists III of Schedule 7 is the concurrent list in respect of which the State and Central Government may frame law. However, the law framed by Central legislature has got overriding effect to the extent of repugnancy. Those State and Central legislatures have got power to legislate law within their sphere. The validity of law in the form of Act, Statute, Rules or Regulations is ordinarily touched keeping in view the Constitutional mandate. Under article 226 of the Constitution of India the High Courts and under article 32 of the Constitution the apex court may declare any law of the State or Central Government as invalid and *ultra vires* in case it is violative of any constitutional provision. The provisions contained in Rules and Regulations may be declared invalid in case they are repugnant to a State legislature. Against the judgments of Court sometimes the States amend the law to invalidate the judicial decision, which is called doctrine of.

Thomas Jefferson and James Madison were the two prominent American judges behind old court of thought that Courts do not have right to legislate law. According to Jefferson, 'prudence of public functionaries and authority of public opinion should be trusted. In 1820 Jefferson attacked the notion that judges are the "ultimate arbiters of all constitutional questions" as a very dangerous doctrine indeed, and one which would place us under the despotism of an oligarchy. According to Jefferson only people could be trusted to exercise "the ultimate powers of the society." However, gradually all those countries where a written Constitution exists, keeping in view the abuse of power by majority the views of Jefferson was found to be not correct. Gradually it was visualized by the jurists that an abusive majority could not be checked once it had been formed, constitutional enforcement necessitated prevention of its formation in the first place.

It was thought that an abusive majority remained the greatest danger to constitutional maintenance in a republic. There was no solution to majority abuse of power except to protect the public interest by constitutional courts. That is why in the famous case of *Keshvananda Bharti,* Supreme Court held that basic structure of the constitution cannot be changed by constitutional amendment. In the famous case of *Eakin* v. *Raub,* Marshall, a great judge of his time, propounded the judicial invalidation of legislation being necessary to enforce the Constitution. After all, there is no effectual guard against legislative usurpation of power. Ordinarily it is public opinion, which force the government to move in a right direction but history shows that on account of division on the basis of caste, creed, religion and group or the corrupt State of mind or because of fear of persecution by government agencies sometime public in general do not raise voice against the unconstitutional 'State action' as we have noticed the State of affairs during emergency in 1975. In such situation the higher judiciary cannot shirk from its responsibility of judicial review of an Act, Statute, Rule, Regulation or order of the State or Central Government.

It is settled proposition of law that jurisdiction of High Courts is much wider than the power conferred by article 32 of the Constitution of India on the Supreme Court. Being the Court of record, the Supreme Court and High Courts have got power to punish for contempt of own court. Under article 141 of the Constitution of India the law declared by the Supreme Court is binding on all Courts of India and under article 144 of the Constitution all civil and judicial authorities have to act in aid of Supreme Court. The Constitution has given ample power to meet out the changes with the pace of time that is why the Chief Justice Kania had said that the Constitution is the living organism to meet out the challenges, which may arise in due course of time.

Keeping in view the aforementioned broader principle in two recent judgments,[1] the Supreme Court reaffirmed the power of judicial review by the higher judiciary as a part and parcel of basic feature of our Constitution. The former relates to Parliamentary privileges and later relates to power of judicial review relating to the matter falls within the domain of 9th Schedule of the Constitution.

The Courts and the Parliament, though, occupy different fields but the aim and object is to serve the people. *Prima facie,* the role of higher judiciary is to interpret law within the ambit of the Constitution. The role of the legislature is to legislate law for the welfare of the people of the country. Whenever the controversy relating to private dispute or public interest crops up in a proceeding before the higher judiciary or the people approach under the garb of public litigation, in the absence of effective legislated law or on account of apathy to deal with a matter of public importance by legislature or bureaucracy or sometimes in the absence of any remedial measure to sort out a problem the higher judiciary play its role to serve the public or private interest and meet out requirement. However, to that extent ordinarily objections are not raised, but when an issue is decided affecting a politico-social or personal right affecting identically situated large section of society, right of a section of the society or covering the manifesto of a political party to some extent the political scenario of the country boils up.

The Supreme Court of India came into existence on 26th January, 1950. The inaugural sitting of the Supreme Court of India on 28th January, 1950, was a truly memorable function. I would like to refer what the first Chief Justice of India (Justice Kania) had said regarding the role of Bench and Bar including higher judiciary in this country. To quote:—

---

1. *Rajaram Pal* v. *Hon'ble Speaker, Lok Sabha,* JT 2007 (2) SC 1; *I.R. Coelho* v. *State of Tamil Nadu,* (2007) 2 SCC 1: AIR 2007 SC 861: 2007 AIR SCW 611.

> "In a democratic country, the people make the law through their legislature. It is not the function of the Court to supervise or correct the laws passed by the legislature as an overriding authority. It is its function and duty to point out, when examining the acts of individuals or of the executive authority purporting to be done under some Act of the legislature, the lacunae or loopholes only with the object that, if so desired, the legislative authority may put matters right. As it is often stated, in cases of hardship, the Court tries its best to do justice between the parties; but if a clear provision of law exists, it has to administer the law, and not make one. The Court is thus working always in co-operation with the legislature and at no time its work can be considered obstructive or its attitude antagonistic."

Referring to the role of the Court in interpreting the Constitution, he said:

> "The duty of interpreting that Constitution with an enlightened liberality falls on the Supreme Court. The Supreme Court will declare and interpret the law of the land, and, with the high traditions behind the judiciary of this court, we are convinced that the work will be done in no spirit of formal or barren legalism. It will be our endeavour to interpret the Constitution, not as a rigid body, but, as a living organism, having within itself the force and power of self-government. We trust, that, in doing so, we shall allow the constitutional usages and conventions recognized in an civilized independent countries to be respected. The Supreme Court, however, under the colour of interpretation, cannot alter or amend the law. But, within the limits prescribed, we are quite sure that the Supreme Court will be able to make a substantial contribution towards the formation of India into a great unit retaining its own civilization, traditions and customs. With the establishment of the Supreme Court of India, we shall develop our own

jurisprudence based on our historical background and we trust that that will be an important and useful contribution to the creation of International Law. The Federal Court, as interpreting the constitution of the country, had earned the confidence of the country. In endowing the Supreme Court of India with very wide powers, the Constituent Assembly – the Assembly representing the voice of the people through its elected representatives – has shown complete confidence in the Court as the final body for dispensing justice between individuals and also between States and States, and the States and the Centre. We hope to deserve that confidence. We trust that the people of India will also maintain the independence, honour and dignity of the Supreme Court."

Inviting the co-operation of the Bar in the Court's lofty endeavour he said:

> "The Indian Bar has maintained the high tradition of the profession. Different conditions in different provinces have so far prevented the creation of one Bar with one good reliable standard of advocacy, knowledge and etiquette. With the inauguration of the independent Republic of India and the States Union Courts attaining the status of the States High Courts, one can look forward in time to the existence of one Bar for India, with a very high standard of efficiency to assist the Courts in the administration of justice."

He also emphasized the great duty which developed on the lawyers on the advent of Independence:

> "The lawyers equipped with knowledge of law are expected to fight for the freedom of the citizen and also the maintenance of law and order. While in the name of Independence confusion or disorder in society cannot be permitted, the lawyer's profession will naturally resist encroachments attempted in the

> name of law and order on the liberty of the subject and on fundamental human rights."

Finally he envisaged the Court playing an independent and impartial role in the life of the country:

> "The Supreme Court, an all-India Court will stand firm and aloof from party politics and political theories. It is unconcerned with the changes in the government. The Court stands to administer the law for the time being in force, has goodwill and sympathy for all, but is allied to none. Occupying that position, we hope and trust it will play a great part in the building-up of the nation, and in stabilizing the roots of civilization which have twice been threatened and shaken by two world wars, and maintain the fundamental principles of justice which are the emblem of God."

Subject to discussion made hereinabove, the doctrine of legislative overruling should be considered. In the case of *Shri Prithvi Cotton Mills Ltd.*[1] where legislature validated a Tax Law which was declared by the Court to be illegal with retrospective effect. Hon'ble Supreme Court upheld the power of legislature to validate statutes and to pass retrospective laws but such power cannot be used to carry out its avowed object. To quote;—

> "If this section is valid then the imposition cannot be questioned and the short question which arises in this case is as to the validity of this section. It is not denied that a legislature does not possess the power to validate statutes and to pass retrospective laws. It is, however, contended that the Validation Act is ineffective in carrying out its avowed object. This is the only point which falls for consideration in these appeals."

1. *Shri Prithvi Cotton Mills Ltd.* v. *Broach Borough Municipality*, AIR 1970 SC 192: 1970 (1) SCJ 288: (1970) 1 SCR 388.

The Constitution Bench of Hon'ble Supreme Court in a case *Ujager Prints (II)*,[1] held that legislatures can always validate a law which can be declared by the Court to be invalid. To quote:—

> "65. There is really no substance in the grievance that the retroactivity imparted to the amendments is violative of article 19(1)(g). A competent legislature can always validate a law which has been declared by courts to be invalid, provided the infirmities and vitiating infactors noticed in the declaratory judgment are removed or cured. Such a validating law can also be made retrospective. If in the light of such validating and curative exercise made by the legislature – granting legislative competence – the earlier judgment becomes irrelevant and unenforceable, that cannot be called an impermissible legislative overruling of the judicial decision. All that the legislature does is to usher in a valid law with retrospective effect in the light of which earlier judgment becomes irrelevant. (See *Sri Prithvi Cotton Mills Ltd.* v. *Broach Borough Municipality*).
>
> 66. Such legislative expedience of validation of laws is of particular significance and utility and is quite often applied, in taxing statutes. It is necessary that the legislature should be able to cure defects in statutes. No individual can acquire a vested right from a defect in a statute and seek a windfall from the legislature's mistakes. Validity of legislations retroactively curing defects in taxing statutes is well recognized and courts, except under extraordinary circumstances, would be reluctant to override the legislative judgment as to the need for and wisdom of the retrospective legislation. In *Empire Industries Limited* v. *Union of India*[2] this Court observed:
>
> ....not only because of the paramount governmental interest in obtaining adequate

1. *Ujagar Prints (II)* v. *Union of India*, AIR 1989 SC 516: JT 1988 (4) SC 330: (1989) 3 SCC 488.
2. 1985 Supp (1) SCR 292

> revenues, but also because taxes are not in the nature of a penalty or a contractual obligation but rather a means of apportioning the costs of government amongst those who benefit from it."

In other cases[1] the Supreme Court had reiterated the aforementioned proposition of law to upheld the power of legislature to validate an Act with the rider that the validation should be done either retrospectively or prospectively. Unless the amendment provide retrospectively the validation shall always be prospective in nature.

Similar proposition of law emerges from the case of *Bhubaneshwar Singh.*[2] In the case of *Bhubaneshwar· Singh* (supra) again the Supreme Court held that the power of legislatures to validate an Act cannot be questioned in case the intention of legislature is clearly expressed with it purports to introduce the legislation or to amend the existing legislation retrospectively. However, it has been further held that validating legislation must remove the cause of invalidity. To quote:—

> "From time to time controversy has arisen as to whether the effect of judicial pronouncements of the High Court or the Supreme Court can be wiped out by amending the legislation with retrospective effect. Many such amendment Acts are called Validating Acts, validating the action taken under the particular enactments by removing the defect in the statute retrospectively because of which the statute or the part of it had been declared *ultra vires*. Such exercise has been held by this Court as not to amount to encroachment on the judicial power of the courts. The exercise of rendering ineffective the judgments or orders of competent courts by changing the very basis by legislation is a well-known device of validating legislation. This Court has repeatedly

1. *K.S. Pariapoornan* v. *State of Kerala,* (1992) 1 SCC 684: 1992 AIR SCW 1580: AIR 1992 SC 1488; *Delhi Cloth & General Mills Co. Ltd.* v. *State of Rajasthan,* AIR 1996 SC 2930: 1996 AIR SCW 855: (1996) 2 SCC 449.
2. *Bhubaneshwar Singh* v. *Union of India,* (1994) 6 SCC 77.

pointed out that such validating legislation which removes the cause of the invalidity cannot be considered to be an encroachment on judicial power. At the same time, any action in exercise of the power under any enactment which has been declared to be invalid by a court cannot be made valid by a Validating Act by merely saying so unless the defect which has been pointed out by the court is removed with retrospective effect. The validating legislation must remove the cause of invalidity. Till such defect or the lack of authority pointed out by the court under a statute is removed by the subsequent enactment with retrospective effect, the binding nature of the judgment of the court cannot be ignored."

However, there seems to be exception to some extent to the principle, discussed hereinabove. In the case of *S.R. Bhagwat*[1] where the dispute arisen during the creation of State of Mysore the statutory provision was declared *ultra vires*. The power of the State legislature and the rights of the employees were settled in pursuance to judgment of the Court. Another validating legislation of the State Government was not found to be *intra vires* on the ground that binding judicial pronouncement between the parties cannot be made ineffective with the aid of legislative power, where the rights of the parties and employees have been settled and seniority has been finalized in their respective States in pursuance to judgment of High Court. Such rights cannot be undone by the State Government through invalidating Act. To quote:—

"11. Having given out anxious consideration to rival contentions we have reached the conclusion that the impugned provision of the Act, namely, section 11 sub-section (2) is clearly *ultra vires* the powers of the State Legislature as it encroaches upon the judicial field and tries to overrule the judicial decision

1. *S.R. Bhagwat* v. *State of Mysore,* (1995) 6 SCC 16: AIR 1996 SC 188: 1995 AIR SCW 3918.

binding between the parties and consequently the relevant sub-sections of section 4 which are also in challenge will have to be read down as indicated hereinafter in this judgment. Before we advert to the relevant provisions of the impugned Karnataka Act it will be appropriate to keep in view the settled legal position governing the present controversy.

12. It is now well-settled by a catena of decisions of this Court that a binding judicial pronouncement between the parties cannot be made ineffective with the aid of any legislative power by enacting a provision which in substance overrules such judgment and is not in the realm of a legislative enactment which displaces the basis or foundation of the judgment and uniformly applies to a class of persons concerned with the entire subject sought to be covered by such an enactment having retrospective effect. We may only refer to two of these judgments."

In a case where Trade union and Life Insurance Corporation of India entered into settlement with an agreement for payment of bonus and the same was discontinued for year 1975-76 in pursuance to circular a writ petition was filed by the workmen in the Calcutta High Court. Calcutta High Court had allowed the writ petition holding that it recognise the right of petitioners for payment of bonus for the year 1975-76 with the finding that it shall become payable alongwith salary of April 1976. Bonus was treated as the part of right of petitioner workmen to be property protected by article 19(1)(F) and article 31(1) of the Constitution. On 29th May, 1976 Parliament had amended the law by an Act namely Life Insurance Corporation Modification and Settlement Act 1976 denying the right of workmen which was recognised by settlement followed by the verdict of Calcutta High Court. Controversy gone to Supreme Court. The Constitution Bench[1] of Supreme Court held that the benefit

1. *Madan Mohan Pathak* v. *Union of India,* AIR 1978 SC 803: (1978) 2 SCC 50: (1978) 3 SCR 334.

of rights recognised by the judgment of Calcutta High Court could not be indirectly taken away by section 3 of the amending Act, selectively being directed against the specified settlement only. While concurring with the leading judgment pronounced by Hon'ble Mr. Justice Bhagwati, the then Chief Justice of India Hon'ble Mr. Justice M.H. Beg while rendering the last judgment of his judgeship proceeded to be observed as under:—

> "I find myself in complete agreement with my learned brother Bhagwati that to give effect to the judgment of the Calcutta High Court is not the same thing as enforcing a right under article 19 of the Constitution. It may be that a right under article 19 of the Constitution becomes linked-up with the enforceability of the judgment. Nevertheless, the two could be viewed as separable sets of rights. If the right conferred by the judgment independently is sought to be set aside, section 3 of the Act, would, in my opinion, be invalid for trenching upon the judicial power.
>
> 9. I may, however, observe that even though the real object of the Act may be to set aside the result of the *mandamus* issued by the Calcutta High Court, yet, the section does not mention this object at all. Probably this was so because the jurisdiction of a High Court and the effectiveness of its order derived their force from article 226 of the Constitution itself. These could not be touched by an ordinary act of Parliament. Even if section 3 of the Act seeks to take away the basis of the judgment of the Calcutta High Court, without mentioning it, by enacting what may appear to be a law, yet, I think that, where the rights of the citizen against the state are concerned, we should adopt an interpretation which upholds those rights which had passed into those embodied in a judgment and became the basis of a *mandamus* from the High Court could not be taken away in this indirect fashion.

> 13. I have, however, no doubt, that the conclusion reached by my learned brother Bhagwati is quite correct inasmuch as the benefits of the rights recognised by the judgment of the Calcutta High Court could not be indirectly taken away by section 3 of the Act selectively directed against specified settlements only."

Mr. Justice Bhagwati while delivering the judgment on behalf of Hon'ble Mr. Justice V.R. Krishna Iyer and Hon'ble Mr. Justice D.A. Desai observed as under:—

> "It does not say that whenever any factual or legal situation is altered by retrospective legislation, a judicial decision rendered by a court on the basis of such factual or legal situation prior to the alteration, would straightway, without more, cease to be effective and binding on the parties. It is true that there are certain observations in this decision which seem to suggest that a court decision may cease to be binding when the conditions on which it is based are so fundamentally altered that the decision could not have been given in the altered circumstances. But these observations have to be read in the light of the question which arose for consideration in that case. There, the validity of the Gujarat Imposition of Taxes by Municipalities (Validation) Act, 1963 was assailed on behalf of the petitioners. The Validation Act had to be enacted because it was held by this court in *Patel Gordhandas Hargovindas* v. *Municipal Commissioner, Ahmedabad*, (1964) 2 SCR 608: AIR 1963 SC 1742: 1965 (1) SCJ 15), that since section 73 of the Bombay Municipal Boroughs Act, 1925 allowed the Municipality to levy a 'rate' was confined to an imposition on the basis of annual letting value, tax levied by the Municipality on lands and buildings on the basis of capital value was invalid. Section 3 of the Validation Act provided that notwithstanding anything contained in any judgment, decree or order of a court or tribunal or any other authority, no tax

assessed or purported to have been assessed by a municipality on the basis of capital value of a building or land and imposed, collected or recovered by the municipality at any time before the commencement of the Validation Act shall be deemed to have invalidly assessed imposed, collected or recovered and the imposition, collection or recovery of the tax so assessed shall be valid and shall be deemed to have always been valid and shall not be called in question merely on the ground that the assessment of the tax on the basis of capital value of the building or land was not authorised by law and accordingly any tax so assessed before the commencement of the Validation Act and leviable for a period prior to such commencement may be collected or recovered in accordance with the relevant municipal law. It will be seen that by section 3 of the impugned Act the Legislature retrospectively imposed tax on building or land on the basis of capital value and if the tax was already imposed, levied and collected on that basis, made the imposition, levy, collection and recovery of the tax valid, notwithstanding the declaration by the Court that as 'rate' the levy was incompetent. This was clearly permissible to the Legislature because in doing so, the legislature did not seeks to reverse the decision of this court on the interpretation of the word 'rate' but retrospectively amended the law by providing for imposition of tax on land or building on the basis of capital value and validated the imposition, levy, collection and recovery of tax on that basis. The decision of this court holding the levy of tax to be incompetent on the basis of the unamended law, therefore, became irrelevant and could not stand in the way of the tax being assessed, collected and recovered on the basis of capital value under the law as retrospectively amended. That is why this court held that the Validation Act was effective to validate imposition, levy, collection and recovery of tax on land or building on the basis of capital value. It is difficult to see how this decision given in the context of a validating statute can be of any held to the Life Insurance Corporation..........

.............It is by reason of retrospective alteration of the factual or legal situation, the judgment is rendered erroneous, the remedy may be by way of appeal or review, but so long as the judgment stands, it cannot be disregarded or ignored and it must be obeyed by the Life Insurance Corporation. We are, therefore, of the view that, in any event, therefore, of the view that, in any event, irrespective of whether the impugned Act is constitutionally valid or not, the Life Insurance Corporation is bound to obey the writ of *mandamus* issued by the Calcutta High Court and to pay annual cash bonus of the year 1st April, 1975 to 31st March, 1976 to Class III and Class IV employees."

In view of *Madan Mohan Pathak's* case (supra), it is clear that under the particular facts and circumstances, a legislation which override the judgment of court may be nullified in case its constitutional validly is impugned on the ground that the legislation was aimed only to nullify the judgment without application of mind but it shall depend upon the facts and circumstances of each case.

The sum and substance of the law settled by Supreme Court does not question the competence of legislature to invalidate the judicial decisions but it should be subject to rider that while invalidating the judicial decision the defect noticed by the Court must be removed by amending Act. The amendment must be specific relating to it prospectively or retrospectively. Simple invalidation of a judicial decision by legislature is not permissible under law.

Though the State has got right to invalidate a judicial decision but still the High Courts as well as Supreme Court has got power of judicial review to scrutinise the action of legislatures. As I have said, Constitution is an organic instrument reflecting quality of impartiality, safeguarding the interest of the people. The House of Parliament or State legislature function in a derivative capacity as delegated authorities. They are only creators of the Constituents. Whether it is State legislature or Central legislature the amending Act passed by them overriding the judicial decision may always be subjected to test provided under Part III of the Constitution of India. In case an invalidating Act has been passed with colourable exercise of power violating fundamental rights guaranteed under Part III of the Constitution of India or rights of the parties have been settled in such a manner which cannot be undone then such invalidating Act may be held as *ultra vires* to the Constitution. The imperative command contained in article 13(2) of Part III of the Constitution is wide enough to out law any unjust invalidating Act, which may fall outside the purview of power of Parliament, or State legislature. Though morally and ethically once a law has been invalidated by a Court being unconstitutional ordinarily it should not be validated by amending Act but it is said that morality does not decide the legislative intent. It is the legislatures own dent of mind, political compulsions, administrative demands and so many other requirements prompt to invalidate a judicial decision.

Quest for Good Governance

"The city in which those who are to rule are least eager to hold office must needs be the best governed and freest from strife."[1]

The principles of justice, liberty, equality, human rights, due process of law or equal protection of law enshrined in the constitution are based on experience of human race of ages. While framing the Indian constitution, the members of constituent assembly had taken note of more than 60 constitutions governing the set-up of various countries of the world. One of the biggest constitution possessing 395 articles has almost successfully completed more than 56 years. Though the economic, agricultural and scientific developments achieved by the country are remarkable but when we compare our development with some other developing or developed countries our proud for the achievements diminishes. The achievements of some of the countries who attained freedom from colonial rule later than India are much better than ours.

Amartya Sen a Lamont University Professor at Harvard who was awarded Nobel Prize in Economics in the year 1998 has shown his deep concern towards the India's development being not up to the mark. Amartya Sen in his book[2] had observed as under:—

> "The weakness of Indian social policies on education, health care, land reform and gender equity is as much a failure of the opposition parties as of the

1. Plato in Republic page 520.
2. *THE ARGUMENTATIVE INDIAN,* by Amartya Sen; page 199.

governments in office. In comparative terms, the political commitment of leaders of some of the less democratic countries has often led to more achievement in these fields than has been produced by the working of democracy in India."

Even if, we accept that country's achievement is commendable then whether in view of present achievements the citizens of the country are enjoying fruits of independence without fear and favour. Right to live, right to live with dignity, right of fresh air and unpolluted water, right to live a fearless dignified life, right to quality of life and several other rights have been preserved and protected by the apex court from time to time by expanding the horizon of article 21 of the Constitution of India. Let us visualize the plights of common people. Whether those who have earned a lot of wealth and prosperity are leading fearless dignified life? Whether bread and butter is available to common citizens? Whether people of the country are enjoying a peaceful life from their own source of livelihood? Whether the poverty has been eradicated? Whether Nehru's "Tryst with Destiny" has been achieved? Whether the member of judicial fraternity (Bar and Bench both) have successfully discharged their duties to provide good to the people? In case we deeply study and feel the societies' plight we may take note that casteism, corruption, communalism and criminalism and intrusion of criminals in our democratic institutions is moving with upward trend. When the constitution was framed, it was expected that the constitutional functionaries shall discharge their duties with utmost honesty, integrity and commitment to nation within the boundaries of law. The supervision of the judiciary, on two wings should be effective to compel the government to discharge duties within the four corners of the constitutional provisions. It was also expected that since the elected representatives who form the government changes from time to time, the bureaucracy shall tender correct and firm advise to the government for the maintenance and enforcement of due process of law. Elected representatives being directly associated with the people of the country have got much experience with the plight of people. Accordingly it is their rights to legislate law keeping in view the ground realities of the society. But during the course of framing of law, duty cast upon the bureaucracy and Law department to tender correct and firm advise (without yielding to political pressure) so that the legislation which is being passed by the assembly or Parliament may not be abused or used for extraneous purposes and must be within the ambit of constitutional provisions. But recent experience shows that the bureaucracy is yielding to the pressures of elected bodies. Consequently, while exercising power under article 162 of the Constitution of India or legislating certain laws sometime things are done in such a manner which affects the country and society adversely. Rapid amendments done in the State and Central Acts for one or other reason is the indicative of fact that everything is not going on well within our system. Sometimes laws are made or amendments in statute done to meet out immediate requirement adversely affect the country's long-term interest and public good.

I invite attention to an alarming situation creeping to our electoral system. According to Newspaper report[1] a Dalit lady Balamani Veeman elected president of the Village Panchayat Kodikulam District Madurai of the State of Tamilnadu was auctioned for Rs. 2.16 lakh, inspite of assurance given by her that she will handover all her "earnings" to the Village Committee. In case news item is correct then it is not only deplorable but also horrible. About 3,500 years back Manu said; to quote:—

> "destruction of law and justice brings about the destruction of society; the protection of law and justice has a protective influence. Therefore law and justice should not be destroyed".

It is the solemn duty of State to implement the judgments of court in letter and spirit. But for the enforcement of

1. Indian Express dated 19-11-2006 published from Lucknow, U.P.

substantial number of orders of court, provisions under Contempt Law is invoked frequently under compulsion. No one is higher than law. Law is supreme. In Brihad-Aranyak Upnishad, it has been said that nothing is higher than law; to quote:—

> "The law is the ruler even of the rulers and kings. Therefore there is nothing higher than law. With the aid of the law even a weakling overcomes the strong."[1]

Sometime it comes to our mind as to whether our system has been partially failed to protect the citizens or has been failed to provide a fearless dignified life. We belong to a great country and has got several thousand years of civilization. But it is unfortunate that the old ancient law has not been explored to solve the problems. Rise in flesh trade coupled with forbidden relationship, rise of criminalisation, casteism as well as corruption in our system of governance requires a second look. Recent report of Transparency International is an eye-opener. It will be too late in case some effective step is not taken to eradicate the corruption, casteism and criminalisation from our system. It is unfortunate that even after lapse of 59 years of independence in various parts of the country people dies because of starvation. In an article "India and the Constitution" delivered by Hon'ble Mr. Justice M. Katju, Judge of Hon'ble Supreme Court of India printed in the September part of AIR, has shown his deep concern to the present state of affairs of the country, to quote:

> "At present there appears to be total confusion of what is happening in the country, in which way the nation is heading etc. Some say that India is shining, but others point out to the poverty, and unemployment among the masses, the large number of farmers who committed suicide in various parts of the country, the price rise, acute shortage of water and electricity and infrastructure in the cities, etc. All

1. *Shatpath Brahman* (XIV. 4.2.26).

> this requires the patriotic intellectuals of the country to get together and think seriously about the welfare of our country and to suggest ideas for progress"

I have also occasion to know the plight of peoples and influence of mafias and criminals in our system while deciding a case of *Chandrika Prasad Nishad*.[1] The ground realities which emerges from the report of one-man committee chaired by the then Principal Secretary of the Government of Uttar Pradesh, Shri G.B. Patnaik which has been considered and relied upon in the case of *Chandrika Prasad Nishad* (supra) gives alarming signal. While considering the plight of country Hon'ble Justice Katju has opined to develop a nationalist feeling in the country. How the patriotism can be developed in the intellectuals or people of the country, when state has not taken any step to that direction even after lapse of 59 years of independence. Please read the judgments of House of Lord, Privy Council and books written by Lord Denning and other European scholars or jurists. Everywhere we find that the intellectuals and jurist of the United Kingdom and other European countries have given much stress to preserve, protect and propagate their culture, literatures and related works. Though we have adopted British system but we have failed to adopt those goods which have kept united, the United Kingdom since several hundred years with the feeling of proud.

Secularism does not mean that every good thing, knowledge and literature of ancient India should be made untouchable. Those materials which create hatred, discrimination or feeling of inequality may be made redundant and ignored. But the old ancient treatise containing the collection of thousands years of experience of human race are still relevant and may be still good for the country and should be studied and must be utilised for public good. They should be part of our research work,

---

1. *Chandrika Prasad Nishad* v. *State of Uttar Pradesh*, 2006 (24) LCD 1243.

study and use. I would like to discuss in brief some of our old ancient scriptures relating to law and justice.

The scriptural writings of our ancient India have been divided mainly in the two classes namely; Sruti or what is heard and Smriti or what is remembered. Veda belongs to the former. In it the words of revelation are preserved in their original form. All laws, civil and religious, which regulate the life and conduct of ancient Indians contains in sacred appellation of Sruti. According to old Indian belief Smriti possess divine origin.

Manu has been held to be one of the first Indian jurist who codified in his Samhita *i.e.* Manusmriti the essence of Vedas. Though some of the verse creates hatred and untouchability in society but substantial portion of Manusmriti are still seems to have got practical utility to run a Government or Society. Some author says 20 and some says 36 or more Samhitas were written at various times in pre - Christian era. Some of the great authors and their works are, Atri composed and remarkable law treatise, Vishnu the author of excellent law treatise, Yajnawalkya had delivered his precept in the audience of ancient philosophers in Mithila. The statutes of Yajnawalkya is second in importance to Manusmirit and have been arrayed in three books. Ushana, Manu, Angira Yama and Jama, Apastamva, Katyayana, Parasara Vyasa, Sankha, Likhita, Daksha, Goutama, Satatapa and Vasishtha, Narad and Kautilya are some of the great Indian jurists who had written various Samhitas. Majority of them can provide material or guidelines to solve our problems. I would like to refer some of the verse or axioms from few Samhitas, which still hold the field.

For appointment in the government service Yajnawalkya says; *"he (king) should appoint devoted, clever and honest men in posts suited to them and energetic men in the works of collection and disbursement"*[1].

1. Verse 322.

For corrupted employees Yajnawalkya says; *"having deprived the bribe-takers of their possession, he should banish them, and should, always, settle the Srotriyas with honour, gifts and good treatment.*[1]*"*.

While commanding the king not to spare anyone for his or her misdeed even if such persons belong to his own family Yajnawalkya says, to quote; *"whether a brother, a son, a preceptor, a father-in-law or a maternal uncle, none can escape from the punishment of king, if he deviates from the performance of his own duties (verse 358). The king, who punishes those who deserve punishment and kills those who deserve death, reaps the fruits of sacrifices well-performed with a thousand sacrificial presents.*[2]*"*

Narad in his Samhita while laying down the condition for a good judgeship of judicial officer said to quote; *"as an experienced surgeon extracts a dart by means of surgical instruments, even so the chief judge must extract the dart (of iniquity) from the lawsuit. That is not a judicial assembly where there are no elders. They are not elders who do not pass a just sentence. That is not a just sentence in which there is no truth which is vitiated by error"*.

While deprecating the unfairness on the part of judges Narad says; to quote, *"he who, having entered the court, delivers a strange opinion, ignoring the true state of the case, resembles a blind man who regardless swallows fish together with the bones"*.

The Maxwell's "Principle of Interpretation" is a recognised book used by court in U.K. and our country. He had laid down certain principles for interpretation of statute. In ancient India Mimansa Rules of Interpretation was applied. Mimansa Rules of Interpretation was for the first time published in the year 1909 containing lectures of Professor K.L. Sarkar. Few years back *i.e.* in the year 2003 second edition was published with utmost efforts of Justice M. Katju, former Judge of Allahabad High Court and presently Judge of Hon'ble Supreme Court. On the basis of

1. Verse 339.
2. Verse 359.

lectures of Professor K.L. Sarkar six axioms of interpretation have been given; to reproduce:—

"(1) the Sarthakyata axiom, which means that every word and sentence must have some meaning.

(2) the Laghava axiom (Gauravah doshah), which states that the construction which makes the meaning simpler and shorter is to be preferred.

(3) the Arthaikatva axiom, which states that a double meaning should not be attached to a word or sentence occurring at one and the same place. Such a double meaning is known as a Vakyabheda, and is a fault (dosh).

(4) The Gunapradhan axiom, which states that if a word or sentence purporting to express a subordinate idea clashes with the principal idea the former must be adjusted to the latter, or must be disregarded altogether.

(5) the Samanjasya axiom, which states that all attempts should be made at reconciliation of apparently conflicting texts. Jimutvahana has utilized this principle for reconciling conflicting texts of Manu and Yajnavalkya on the right of succession (*see* K.L. Sarkar's Mimansa Principles.' Second Lecture).

(6) The Vikalpa axiom, which states that if there is a real and irreconcilable contradiction between two legal rules having equal force, the rule more in accordance with equity and usage can be adopted at one's option (it must be clarified here that where one of the rules is a higher legal norm as compared to the other, *e.g.* a Shruti is a higher norm than a Smriti, then by the Badha principle the former will prevail)."

Western jurist had propounded the Rules of Interpretation in last 200 or 300 years back whereas Indian jurist applied Mimansa Rule of Interpretation much before the advent of Christian era. Recently Hon'ble Supreme Court in a case of Ispat Industry Limited,[1] had applied the

1. *Ispat Industry Limited* v. *Commissioner of Custom,* JT 2006 (12) SC 379.

Mimansa Rules of Interpretation. We may find good collection of Indian ancient juristic science in a book Legal and Constitutional History of India by Justice M. Rama Jois.

From the discoveries made by Archeological Department of the country at Mohenjodaro and Harappa, Indus Valley and later on at Lothal and Rangpur in southern Narmada Valley the antiquity of Rigveda has been established beyond doubt. Research work shows that the age of Vedic Samhitas and other works is approximately 4000-1000 BC. Some of the Vedic hymns are older then 4000 BC. The intrinsic evidence in Shruti reveals that the peoples of Vedic age had robust concept of lawful duties of men and women. The practice of dharma signify the privileges, duties and obligations of a man, his standard of conduct as the community member or as the member of respective castes or as a person belonging to particular community. On account of fact that western scholars had held Indian scriptures being made up of sages and saints, they have being imparted with step-motherly treatment. Virtually in present context all the Ancient Indian scholars like Yajnawalkya, Manu, Katyayan, Angira, Yama, Atri, Goutama, Narad, Kautilya and others should be treated as jurist or law-makers while considering their treatise in the present context or within the parameter of Indian Constitution. Some of the provisions contained in Kautilya's Arthsashtra are still relevant for good governance. Certain measures taken by Indian rulers like Chandragupta Maurya, emperor Ashoka and Akbar for smooth and secular administration also requires consideration. We should utilise our ancient knowledge on the basis of writings of great scholars of various castes and creed and religion. In case, we will search out apart from Sanskrit we may find very useful and remarkable materials in writings of various languages of the country like Tamil, Kannad, Oriya, Bengali, Maharashtrian, Gujarati, Urdu, Hindi and so on, which can be very useful to solve our problems. However, it requires research work with utmost commitment and dedication.

The Indian Scholars and Jurists have not been given proper place in our literature, science, administrative and judicial field inspite of fact that we have attained independence in the year 1947. That is why for one or the other reason we have been failed to develop patriotism or nationalism. King Charles 1 of the England was tried and executed relying upon what Bracton had said almost 400 years back; to quote Bracton: *"The King is under no man save under God and the law."* On the other hand, about 2,500 years back Upanishad said *"The law is the ruler even of the rulers and kings and nothing is higher then law."*

When we go through various books written by Lord Denning like Leaves from my library, Landmarks in the law, The closing chapter, The due process of law and the discipline of law we will find reference of works done by various English scholars in the field of Art, Science, literature and polity. In the "Leaves from my library" Lord Denning had referred with proud and appreciation, Winston Churchill, Lord Nelson, John Buchan, Lord Macaulay, Thomas Hardy, Charles Dickens, Shakespeare and others. But in case, we introspect our conduct we will be disappointed. No effort has been made to consider, interpret, the ancient law within the ambit of Indian constitution inspite of lapse of almost 56 years of its enforcement.

I have occasion to go through certain books available in the library of our High Court at Lucknow. F. Maxmuller in 1880's had edited series of books under the title of *The Sacred Books of the East* published by Oxford at the Clarendon Press. John D. Mayne had written a commentary on Hindu Law in 1878. We will find a large number of work done by the Britishers in 18th and 19th century exploring the old Indian literature, science and art but it is unfortunate that after independence our country had failed to take note of works done by Ancient Indian scholars. Rich history of 5000 years of our civilization has been dumped because of two evils *i.e.* casteism and untouchability. The outcome of excavation which has come out from Indus Valley

Mohenjodaro and Harappa shows how civilized our country was. The civilization was maintained and perpetuated because of great laureates whose writings were followed in letter and spirit and some of them are still available, requires research and exploration. We will find one thing common in old ancient scriptures that our jurist have given much emphasis for adherence by king to a honest simple life with good character. They were well aware that peoples of a country suffers because of misdeed of rulers. I am not using word "sages" or "saints" for the ancient Indian Scholars or jurists to confine their knowledge only to Hindus. In case we will go through the Kautilya Arthshastra written during in Maurya Dynasty (about 300 B.C.) we will find sufficient material for good governance.

Dr. Bheem Rao Ambedkar as well as Dr. Rajendra Prasad both were of the view that a constitution is never good or bad. In case a person who manned the country is good the constitution shall be good but in case the person occupying high offices is not of good character, knowledge and integrity then the constitutional provision shall not deliver goods and shall be bad. There shall always be good and bad people in a country.

Krishna in Gita says there are only two types of human being namely; Dev (divine) of whom the heart is dominated by noble traits and other Asur (devil) whose evil traits dominate the hearts. In this entire creation there is no other type of human beings. It is the combined duty of State consisting legislature bureaucracy and judiciary to protect the people from Asur and punish them.

Our justice delivery system contains almost 7,00,000 of lawyers, 12,205 members of subordinate judiciary, 647 Judges of High Courts and 31 Judges of Hon'ble Supreme Court.

10.5 Judges have been provided to every 10 lakhs people of India. Between 1999-2001 on an average about 50,00,000 criminal cases were registered in each year in the State and Union Territory. Almost one-third are under Indian Penal

Code and rest under other special and local laws. The strength of police force is between 12 lakhs and 13 lakhs. The pendency of criminal cases in the subordinate court is about 1,32,00,000 are pending for disposal at the shoulder of 12,205 members of subordinate judiciary. Throughout the country about 2,00,000 under-trials are in prisons. About 65 lakhs peoples are arrested every year for one crime or other and 13,000 persons are victim of custodial violence including death and torture in police custody. The budget for legal services is about 300,000,000 (three hundred crore) in a year for all the States and Union Territories. The pendency of civil cases are also in several lakhs throughout the country. No attention has been given by the various governments since independence to provide sufficient infrastructure manned by able persons to strengthen our judicial system. Any development done by the government in the absence of quick, fair and independent judicial system shall not be able to give the citizens a happy, dignified and peaceful life.

In May 2005, a five-judge Bench of the Supreme Court referred to a seven-judge Constitution Bench the question relating to the interpretation of the word 'industry' in the Industrial Disputes Act, 1947. Almost eight years later, the matter is still pending in the apex court.

Similarly, on March 30, 2011, a three-judge Bench headed by then Chief Justice of India Justice S.H. Kapadia referred the *Mineral Area Development Authority* v. *Steel Authority of India Ltd.* case, which dealt with the important issue of royalty on minerals, to a nine-judge Bench. This case has also not been heard till date.

Another important matter that is awaiting the constitution of a larger Bench is the Presidential reference in the *Sutlej Yamuna Link (SYL) canal* case, pending since 2004.

The data compiled by the Supreme Court itself states that there are over 66,800 cases pending in the apex court, 66,809 as on March 1, 2013, there seems to be paucity of time to decide 750 constitution Bench matters which have to be heard by a Bench of five or more judges, which now is 754 as in November 2010, according to figures collected by academic Nick Robinson of the Centre for Policy Research.[1]

This, however, includes cases that may not involve an important law point, but have been referred to larger Benches because judges on smaller Benches were unable to reconcile their contrasting judgments.

Pendency of 754 Constitution Bench matters in Supreme Court of India is itself indicative of some flaw in the system. Sometimes even pendency of one *Constitution Bench* case has wide repercussion or of wide ramification, but here 754 Constitution Bench cases are pending, which is alarming .

Plato while considering the just and unjust judgment and decision-making process in the administration of justice observed, to quote:—

> *"They say, then, that to be unjust is good, and to suffer injustice is bad, and the excess of evil in suffering injustice is greater than the excess of good in being unjust; so that when people do and suffer injustice in dealing with one another, and taste both, those who cannot both escape the one and take the other think it profitable to make an agreement neither to do nor to suffer injustice; from this they begin to make laws and compacts among themselves, and they name the inaction of the law lawful and just. This, they say, is the origin and nature of justice, which is something between the best, namely to do wrong and not to be able to get vengeance. Justice, they say, is between these two, and they are content with it not as a good, but as honoured in the weakness of injustice; since one who was able to do injustice, if he were truly a man, would never make an agreement with anyone neither to wrong nor to be wronged – He would be mad to do so. Then this and such is the nature of justice, Socrates, and such is its origin as they say."*
>
> *"But we would perceive most clearly that those who practise justice do so unwillingly and because they cannot*

1. The Indian Express, April 22, 2013.

> *do injustice, if we should put a case in imagination; let us grant licence to each, both just and unjust, to do whatever he wishes, and let us follow this up by seeing where his desire will lead each. Then we should catch the just man in the act; he would go the same way as the unjust through self-seeking, the way which every creature naturally follows as a good, only the law leads him forcibly astray to honour fair dealing."*[1]

Plato's opinion requires consideration in the matter of selection and appointment in the administration of justice.

We are facing complex problem but one thing is certain that apart from insufficient infrastructure one of the root cause of backlog of cases is the lack of effective 'work culture' in our system. Whether it is Bar or Bench substantial number of persons on both sides are not discharging their duties with up to mark achievements. While searching the solutions to these problems we should give second look to our system and should get some inspiration from old Indian scriptures. We can consider the treatise of great jurist of Ancient India in present context. Constitution of India was amended for more than hundred times in last 56 years. We are ready to amend the constitution from time to time though its origin is 60 years back.

Why not the old ancient law propounded by great scholars, academicians and jurists of our country may be considered within the parameter of our constitution with the appropriate amendment to solve our problem. In case Law Institutes, Universities and Institutions related with Bar and Bench and persons related to our system of governance, do some research work from the available material in the country or abroad and manuscript is prepared keeping in view the ancient law on various subjects within the parameter of our constitution, it shall be a great service to the nation. Propagation of literature, art, science, culture and works done by great Indian scholars

---

1. Great Dialogues of Plato by W.H.D. Rouse.

shall enhance patriotism or nationalism to meet out the challenges. Let us separate the grain from chaff.

It was in around 1925, while delivering series of lectures in Yale University, a great American Judge, Benjamin N. Cardozo noticed that Bar has been commercialised. American Supreme Court took step to develop research oriented law institutes like Howard, Yale and other universities. The Howard Law Review reveals how extensive research is done by these American universities in the field of law to meet the challenges keeping in view the American ground realities. Research work done by them may not suit to India and they require modification keeping in view our social structure. The question cropped up why India has been failed to establish an university at par with Howard, Yale etc? Why still 'work culture' has not been developed in our law institutes, thereby creating an assisting body enlighting the Judges on different issues. Every judgment of higher judiciary including the Supreme Court must be scanned by the law institutes of the country. They (judgments) should be carefully looked into, constructively discussed, criticized or appreciated with due publication in journals and newspapers. But our law institutes are mute spectator to the folly which we (Judges) may commit under the overburdened court management.

Cardozo says, to quote:

> "History, in illuminating the past, illuminates the present, and in illuminating the present, illuminates the future."[1]

The comment of Cardozo has universal application. The Indian courts and law students, the teachers, Professors and research scholars must look into past literatures, historical fact, rise and fall of kingdoms and the literatures available, written centuries ago to meet the challenges in administration of justice.

---

1. The Nature of the Judicial Process by Benjamin N. Cardozo, page 53.

Whether because of failure of our system, there is rise in crime and corruption? The teachers of Law Universities and students should also go back to the historical events right from Chandragupta and Kautilya (321 B.C.) or earlier, followed by Great Ashoka, Akbar and Jahangir. What we can borrow from Kautilya's 'Economics' and success of emperor Akbar in the matter of governance may be looked into while developing the law of the country. It is unwise to solve our problems merely on western jurisprudence.

Cardozo was critical of the system and the manner in which students are taught in the classroom keeping in view the current and future problems only without looking to the past experience.

Development of law is not only legislative act but also judicial act. Judicial pronouncements are also law on the subject involved therein. "Constitutions are more likely to enunciate general principles, which must be worked out and applied thereafter to particular conditions. What concerns us now, however, is not the size of the gaps. It is rather the principle that shall determine how they are to be filled, whether their size be great or small. The method of sociology in filling the gaps puts its emphasis on the social welfare.[1]"

The governing principle for the judicial legislation or even legislative enactment should be backed by scripts written by experts based on research work. Every legislative enactment or the judicial legislation should be well considered and thoughtful pronouncements which may in terms of western philosophers, guide and carry on the country for at least 50 years or centuries. Our Constitution, even statutes are amended like changing of cloths. The amendments are done to solve immediate problem without taking into account its effect on generations to come.

Though the constitution as well as statutory provisions are organic body and they may be amended to suit a

1. Extract taken from the Nature of the Judicial Process by Benjamin N. Cardozo, page 71.

situation but it should be done rarely and the people may be permitted to become accustomed to the constitutional and statutory provisions even if some hardship causes. Frequent amendments in the Constitution or statutory provisions or changes made by judicial legislation to the principle of law creates uncertainty and destabilize a country.

While deciding the case of *Chandrika Prasad Nishad* (supra) I have occasion to consider certain available literatures and material in text books and Internet. It requires further studies and research work on the basis of up-to-date law relating to crime in the country. Even if appropriate training is given to judicial officers or Judges of the higher judiciary and they delivers judgments for public good it shall remain on paper for the lack of implementation by executive. In spite of good talent and training we cannot deliver good to people unless member of judicial fraternity discharges duties with honesty, fairness and commitment to nation without being influenced by element of corruption which includes caste, creed and political corruption. In the same way judicial verdict should be honoured by bureaucracy and legislature in its letter and spirit. Recently, a Division Bench of High Court at Allahabad during the course of hearing of a writ petition came to know that thousands of criminal cases of serious crime pending in the subordinate courts of the Uttar Pradesh and have been held up since more than decades in which political persons and bureaucrats are named as accused. Even records of some of the criminal cases pending in the subordinate courts have been misplaced obviously for extraneous reasons and considerations to prolong the litigation. It is necessary to work out the modalities to eliminate or reduce the effect of corruption, casteism and influence of criminals in our system *i.e.* all the three wings of the Government in appropriate manner.

Fali S. Nariman, a Senior Counsel of apex court had rightly said in a recent book "India's Legal System: Can it be Saved?" that the government has not done right thing by not accepting the report of Justice Malimath Committee for appropriate amendment in article 21 of the Constitution of India to curtail the "right of silence of the accused" during the trial of a criminal case.

In pursuance to report of All India Bar Committee (1951) headed by Justice S.R. Das as its chairman followed by 14th report of Law Commission headed by Shri M.C. Setalvat (1958) and after long battle autonomy was given to Bar in the year 1961 by promulgating Advocates Act. Thus, unified Bar was created by the Act of Parliament. It is said that Bar is the judge of judges. Rather it is the watchdog of our system. It is the Bar alone which can take revolutionary steps to streamline our system and eradicate the evils, which I have referred earlier, but there is word of caution. My experience as a member of Bar Council of Uttar Pradesh and as its Chairman, for about a decade shows that everything is not good with the Bar. Elections are contested on the basis of caste, creed and religion. Sometime functioning of courts are stopped because of lawyers' strike. Cases are adjourned for no reasonable cause. Cooperation of lawyers to expedite the cases is not up to mark. A section of Bar indulge into the malpractices. Bar Council has been failed to punish the guilty which is expected being the statutory body. Without effective assistance of Bar nothing can be done solely by judiciary. Accordingly, it is also necessary to sort out some means and measures so that courts may get effective assistance from the members of Bar.

One of the reason of failure of governance is the loss of moral values and sticking to post in spite of inability to discharge duty or facing charges of corruption. One of the most instructive episode of Mahabharat comes out when Yudhishthir meets Bhishma Pitamah to learn lessons of good governance. At the time when he was on deathbed, questioned by Yudhishthir, Bhishma Pitamah tells him "O King, just as the foot of an elephant covers every other foot, so does 'raj dharma' (duty assigned to constitutional functionaries) cover every aspect of dharma (law). In all conditions among all dharmas, Raj dharma is supreme, as it provides welfare and security to entire society".

Dharma does not mean religion as is commonly misunderstood, but it means righteous performance of duty in accordance to constitution and law. Thus, if king performs his dharma, it helps and prompts all others in society to perform their own respective duties righteously. Similarly, if the king resorts to adharma, it encourages others to do the same even more brazenly.

Bhishma Pitamah further tells Yudhishthir which sounds even more contemporaneous: "For kings nothing except adherence to truth becomes the cause for the trust placed in them."

In case king cannot discharge his duties righteously or fairly then what is to be done? The advice of Bhishma Pitamah to Yudhishthir is "sacrifice your office, but don't subject it to sacrilege."

Means the constitutional functionaries should abdicate the office in case they are charged for indulgence in corruption on the basis of *prima facie* material on record or they have been failed to discharge their duty fairly and honestly.

Time has come when it is necessary for the Bar and Bench both to introspect and search out the remedial measures to restore and strengthen the people's confidence. Otherwise time is not far away when our system relating to administration of justice shall be at par with other two wings of the Government in the people's eyes.

Instead of discussing the problems only academically or in speeches or in lectures, it is high time when we have to convert and enforce our knowledge into effective practice for public good. I wish to conclude in the words of great saint of the country Kabir Sahab; to quote:—

कथनी काची होय गयी, करनी करी न सार ।
स्त्रोता बक्ता मरि गया, मूरख अनंत अपार ।।

"If an advantage of putting the knowledge to practice is not gained, the mere saying then remains unripe (incomplete). Without practice (conduct), numerous highly foolish speakers and listeners were lost in the current of illusory mundane affairs."

"Apparently many companies experience problems including: a lack of direction, poor accountability, lack of respect among members, pushing personal agendas, poor communication..."

Right to Information Act

"The most basic principle is that democracy should treat people as political equals. That does not just means that there should all have a vote and that their vote should count the same, but they should have the same access to information on which to make their decision.[1]"

Right to Information Act enforced from 12-11-2005, is revolutionary, empowering the common man of the country to pierce the iron curtains encircling the government offices. Citizens have been blessed with a tool with the help of which, mighty government is now, liable to discharge its obligations with openness. The secrecy in the administration promotes and encourages corruption, oppression, the abuse and misuse of power and in due course of time, results with the serious consequences. The action shroud in the veil of secrecy without any public accountability, makes the system corrupt and deprives the peoples of their rightful claim. The more openness in the administration, the lesser would be abuse of power.

The majority of people lives in misery, hunger, and ignorance and still owe the major problems. The pervasive corruption aggravated by the use of money and muscle powers by some persons either to win the election or to make individual member more rich, is worsening the situation. The growing divide between the super rich and the down-trodden has given impetus to unemployed youth to adopt unethical unlawful ways and means to serve themselves. Sometimes, it is said that only 19% of the fund

1. Martin Linton in Public Law 760-63 referred by Ian Ward in The English Constitution Myth and Realities at page 172.

of public exchequer reaches to people and sometimes it is reduced to 15%. No one bothers about the remaining 85% as to where it goes. No effective and corrective step has been taken to ensure that each and every penny of the government, reaches to its destination. This is alarming state of affair.

The father of Nation Mahatma Gandhi said that civilisation has got direct link with the code of conduct. Citizens should not be deprived of the information as to how the government fund is invested and how their representatives and public servants are discharging their obligations. The Right to Information Act as a source of power, in case used effectively, it can make sea change in the system and check the misappropriation of the fund of public exchequer as well as abuse of power.

In the oft-quoted judgment of *Raj Narain,*[1] Supreme Court, has observed, to quote:—

> "In a government of responsibility like ours, where all agents of the public must be responsible for their conduct, there can be but few secrets. The people of this country have a right to know every public act, everything that is done in a public way, by their public functionaries... to cover with veil of secrecy the common routine business, is not in the interest of public"
>
> ...Mathew J. on behalf of the Bench.

In the case of *S.P. Gupta,*[2] Supreme Court of India ruled, to quote:—

> "The concept of an open Government is the direct emanation from the right to know which seems to be implicit in the right of free speech and expression guaranteed under article 19(1)(a). Therefore, disclosure of information in regard to the functioning

---

1. *State of Uttar Pradesh* v. *Raj Narain,* (1975) 4 SCC 428: AIR 1975 SC 865: (1975) 3 SCR 333.
2. *S.P. Gupta* v. *President of India,* AIR 1982 SC 149: 1982 Rajdhani LR 389: 1981 Supp SCC 87, etc. [Para 66].

> of Government must be the rule and secrecy an exception justified only where the strictest requirement of public interest so demands. The approach of the Court must be to attenuate the area of secrecy as much as possible consistently with the requirement of public interest, bearing in mind all the time that disclosure also serves an important aspect of public interest"

It is the right of citizen to have a watch over the conduct of their representatives or public servant, and to ensure and preserve the public cause and keep their representatives and public servants within the four corners of law and discharge their obligation in a just and fair manner. The Right to Information Act is a boon. In a democratic polity, no one is inconsequential and, self-proclaimed monarch on account of public money or office and may be compelled to shred their flesh by wide application of Right to Information Act. The more it is invoked, the more public fund will be saved with the lesser abuse of power.

According to report, Roman Catholic Church has been delinquent in handling widespread sexual abuse of members of its flock by some or several of its priests and faces a wave of paedophiliac scandals and faces prospect of eroding credibility and moral authority leaving Catholics demoralised throughout Europe and U.S.A. Almost 11,750 allegations of child abuse featured in actions settled by individual archdioceses in United States.

Judge Murphy's Commission in Ireland found sexual abuse in boys institutions not only endemic but the church hierarchy protected the perpetrators. Pope Benedict XVI apologised for the heinous crime and met victims in U.S., and Australia. Now a decision has been taken for a departure from decade old practice to make rules more transparent.[1]

Virtually, every person possesses animal instinct and in case he or she is permitted to discharge his or her worldly

---

1. Hindu newspaper, dated 6-4-2010.

or statutory obligations in secrecy, beyond reasonable limit, it results into disastrous consequences in due course of time. Man becomes beast under the veil of secrecy of more than a reasonable limit. It is said that in the darkness of night, evils come out with full of their strength. Unless there is openness in system, we cannot combat the monster of corruption, casteism or abuse of power.

There is one alarming situation. Now, there is backlog of applications before the Information Commissioners. It is happening either because of appointment of incompetent person as Information Commissioners or because of lack of infrastructure in the hands of Information Commissioners or non-cooperation from the Government. With due respect, a system works on the capability of person holding the post. A bad system may work good in case a person is committed to his job and a good system shall become bad in case the person managing the affair is not competent and committed to his duty. The increasing backlog in the offices of Information Commissioners at the moment as revealed from newspapers, is alarming.

According to recent news item, containing the statement of the Information Commissioner Sri Shailesh Gandhi, the national average of disposal of cases under Right to Information Act is, 600 while in the State of Uttar Pradesh, Tamil Nadu and Karnataka, there is backlog of six months. The Information Commissioner has rightly shown his anguish stating that because of growing number of pending cases, under the Right to Information Act, the country poses threat of killing the very spirit of law. In case, cases take years for disposal, it will mar and collapse the system. He rightly stated that there is no excuse on the part of the Commissioners in disposal of cases.

In case backlog is taken into account, then it appears that the office of Chief Information Commissioner or State Information Commissioners, are not discharging their obligations fairly with devotion to duty.

Let us consider the mode of appointment and the process of removal in brief. Under section 15 of Right to

Information Act, a committee consisting of Chief Minister of the State as Chairperson, the leader of opposition in the Legislative Assembly and a Cabinet Minister to be nominated by the Chief Minister, appoints the State Chief Information Commissioner and the State Information Commissioner. Ordinarily, the Information Commissioner is to obtain and re-direct the information as required by the citizen. The Government is the main body around which the Office of State Chief Information Commissioner moves to collect the information. There appears to be no doubt that a Cabinet Minister being nominated by Chief Minister, shall always share the Chief Minister's views. In such situation, virtually, it is the Government which takes a decision under section 15 of the Act to appoint the State Chief Information Commissioner or State Information Commissioners affecting its own rights and privileges. Decision of the committee should not only be just and fair, based on merit but also it should seem to be fair to avail and inspire peoples confidence.

It is settled law that no one should be judge for his own cause. Hence provisions contained under section 15 of the Act, requires second look to give autonomy to selection committee provided under sub-section (3) of section 15 of the Act so that the State Chief Information Commissioner and the State Information Commissioners may be selected and appointed by an autonomous body, choosing independent, learned and upright persons to discharge their statutory obligations.

Under section 17 of the Act, power of removal has been conferred to the Governor of the State. In case a person is adjudged as insolvent or convicted of an offence, engaged in paid employment outside the duties of his Office or in the opinion of Governor, is unfit to continue in office by reason of infirmity of mind or body, or has acquired financial or other interest likely to affect his functioning as State Chief Information Commissioner and State Information Commissioners, may be removed.

Sub-section (1) of section 17 of the Act provides that removal by the Governor, may be on the ground of proved misbehaviour or incapacity to hold Office after approval from the Supreme Court. The incapacity to hold the Office includes, dereliction in discharge of duty, not discharging duty whole of the time during working hours or not discharging statutory obligations being influenced by the Government or political parties or for any other extraneous reasons whatsoever.

It may be noted that Office of State Chief Information Commissioner and State Information Commissioners, is statutory in nature. They are not constitutional functionaries. Under section 15 of the Act, only those persons may be appointed to hold the Office who are the persons of eminence in public life with wide knowledge and experience in law, science and technology, social service, management, journalism, mass media or administration and governance. The qualification prescribed for the purpose is so wide that anyone can be appointed on the post of State Chief Information Commissioner or State Information Commissioners showing certain experience in his or her field. The qualifications provided under sub-section (5) of section 15 of the Act, are vague and give an option to fill-up the vacancies choosing a person to carry out the Government's views. It also requires appropriate amendment so that persons appointed to hold Office, should be upright, non-political person having zeal to serve the society. The Office of State Chief Information Commissioner as well as the State Information Commissioners being statutory in nature, the appointment shall be subject to judicial review under writ jurisdiction though, on very limited ground. The higher judiciary has got power to interfere against the appointments made by the Government in case it is demonstrated that it has been done by colourable exercise of power or person appointed for political or extraneous reason or the person appointed, lacks basic merit necessary for the post.

In case persons appointed for the posts are not discharging their statutory duty, working for extraneous reasons, then also higher judiciary may issue appropriate order for misdemeanour of office or misconduct or request the Governor to look into allegations.

It shall be appropriate for the Union of India, to consider for appropriate amendment in sections 15 and 17 of the Act to streamline and make effective the process of appointment and removal to inspire people's confidence in the system.

In a Writ Petition,[1] Supreme Court of India being conscious with the present scenario and with intention to access more information with the aid of skilled persons from judiciary had issued following directions:—

"1. The writ petition is partly allowed.

2. The provisions of sections 12(5) and 15(5) of the Act of 2005 are held to be constitutionally valid, but with the rider that, to give it a meaningful and purposive interpretation, it is necessary for the Court to 'read into' these provisions some aspects without which these provisions are bound to offend the doctrine of equality. Thus, we hold and declare that the expression 'knowledge and experience' appearing in these provisions would mean and include a basic degree in the respective field and the experience gained thereafter. Further, without any peradventure and veritably, we state that appointments of legally qualified, judicially trained and experienced persons would certainly manifest in more effective serving of the ends of justice as well as ensuring better administration of justice by the Commission. It would render the adjudicatory process which involves critical legal questions and nuances of law, more adherent to justice and shall enhance the public confidence in the working of the Commission. This is the obvious interpretation of the language of these provisions and, in fact, is the essence thereof.

3. As opposed to declaring the provisions of sections 12(6) and 15(6) unconstitutional, we would prefer to

---

1. *Namit Sharma* v. *Union of India,* 2012 AIR SCW 5523, Writ Petition (Civil) No. 210 of 2012, decided on 13-9-2012.

read these provisions as having effect 'post appointment'. In other words, cessation/termination of holding of office of profit, pursuing any profession or carrying any business is a condition precedent to the appointment of a person as Chief Information Commissioner or Information Commissioner at the Centre or State levels.

4. There is an absolute necessity for the legislature to reward or amend the provisions of sections 12(5), 12(6) and 15(5), 15(6) of the Act. We observe and hope that these provisions would be amended at the earliest by the legislature to avoid any ambiguity or impracticability and to make it in consonance with the constitutional mandates.
5. We also direct that the Central Government and/or the competent authority shall frame all practice and procedure related rules to make working of the Information Commissions effective and in consonance with the basic rule of law. Such rules should be framed with particular reference to sections 27 and 28 of the Act within a period of six months from today.
6. We are of the considered view that it is an unquestionable proposition of law that the Commission is a 'judicial tribunal' performing functions of 'judicial' as well as 'quasi-judicial' nature and having the trappings of a Court. It is an important cog and is part of the court-attached system of administration of justice, unlike a ministerial tribunal which is more influenced and controlled and performs functions akin to the machinery of administration.
7. It will be just, fair and proper that the first appellate authority (*i.e.* the senior officers to be nominated in terms of section 5 of the Act of 2005) preferably should be the persons possessing a degree in law or having adequate knowledge and experience in the field of law.

8. The Information Commissions at the respective levels shall henceforth work in Benches of two members each. One of them being a 'judicial member', while the other an 'expert member'. The judicial member should be a person possessing a degree in law, having a judicially trained mind and experience in performing judicial functions. A law officer or a lawyer may also be eligible provided he is a person who has practiced law at least for a period of twenty years as on the date of the advertisement. Such lawyer should also have experience in social work. We are of the considered view that the competent authority should prefer a person who is or has been a Judge of the High Court for appointment as Information Commissioner. Chief Information Commissioner at the Centre or State-level shall only be a person who is or has been a Chief Justice of the High Court or a Judge of the Supreme Court of India.
9. The appointment of the judicial members to any of these posts shall be made 'in consultation' with the Chief Justice of India and Chief Justices of the High Courts of the respective States, as the case may be.
10. The appointment of the Information Commissioners at both levels should be made from amongst the persons empanelled by the DoPT in the case of Centre and the concerned Ministry in the case of a State. The panel has to be prepared upon due advertisement and on a rational basis as afore-recorded.
11. The panel so prepared by the DoPT or the concerned Ministry ought to be placed before the High-powered Committee in terms of section 12(3), for final recommendation to the President of India. Needless to repeat that the High-Powered Committee at the Centre and the State levels is expected to adopt a fair and transparent method of recommending the names for appointment to the competent authority.
12. The selection process should be commenced at least three months prior to the occurrence of vacancy.

13. This judgment shall have effect only prospectively.
14. Under the scheme of the Act of 2005, it is clear that the orders of the Commissions are subject to judicial review before the High Court and then before the Supreme Court of India. In terms of article 141 of the Constitution, the judgments of the Supreme Court are law of the land and are binding on all courts and tribunals. Thus, it is abundantly clear that the Information Commission is bound by the law of precedence, *i.e.*, judgments of the High Court and the Supreme Court of India. In order to maintain judicial discipline and consistency in the functioning of the Commission, we direct that the Commission shall give appropriate attention to the doctrine of precedence and shall not overlook the judgments of the courts dealing with the subject and principles applicable, in a given case.

    It is not only the higher court's judgments that are binding precedents for the Information Commission, but even those of the larger Benches of the Commission should be given due acceptance and enforcement by the smaller Benches of the Commission. The rule of precedence is equally applicable to intra appeals or references in the hierarchy of the Commission."

The aforesaid judgment has been reiterated by Supreme Court of India in *Manohar's*[1] case. Now it is expected that the members of judicial fraternity while discharging duties as Information Commissioner will deliver better and matured output to secure public interest.

It is true that in case, the Information Commissioners do not discharge their obligation effectively within reasonable time, it shall make the Right to Information Act, redundant and in due course of time, people will face same problem as in the courts with regard to backlogs. Problem should be

1. *Manohar* v. *State of Maharashtra,* AIR 2013 SC 681, decided on 13-12-2012 in Civil Appeal No. 9095 of 2012.

nipped in bud. It is a matter of deep concern that the applications moved by the citizens before the Information Commissioners are not decided within reasonable period.

I wish to quote a passage from Bible:—

> "To every thing there is a season, and a time to every purpose under the heaven:
>
> A time to be born, and a time to die...
>
> A time to weep and a time to laugh; a time to mourn, and a time to dance.[1]"

Accordingly, in case information is not provided immediately or within the reasonable period, it may loose its sanctity. Time is the essence of an information. Persons who are working as Information Commissioners, in case, they are not discharging their statutory duties effectively, then it shall be appropriate that some code of conduct may be framed to regulate their working and conduct. Those, who are inefficient in discharge of their obligations, should be removed.

Mere receipt of information, is not sufficient. The citizens who are active in this field, must form a body to protest within the ambit of law in case the information received by them, reveals misappropriation of fund or vice of arbitrariness, inaction of the authorities or abuse of power or the persecution of a citizen by the persons holding public office.

Provisions contained in Official Secrets Act, 1923, legislated during British Rule, was meant to preserve and protect their rights siphoning public fund in their pockets and continue with colonial rule. It should be appropriately amended to make it convenient for the peoples to exercise powers conferred by Right to Information Act effectively on various issues.

Information which are detrimental to national interest or integration or security of states or its commercial or economic and strategic interest may not be made public but

1. Bible: Ecclesiastics.

nothing should be held back just to sub serve the interest of bureaucrats, politicians or any other person holding public Office.

The openness in the Government functioning, as far as possible, is necessary to maintain people's confidence. It has been widely accepted that democracy is not only to exercise franchise at the interval of 5 years to choose representatives to run the State or the country and after casting votes, retire in passivity without taking any interest as a washed off in the functioning of the Government but democracy possesses more positive content and its orchestration has to be continuous and pervasive. It means that people should not only cast intelligent and rational votes but should also exercise sound judgment on the conduct of the government and the merits of public policies, so that democracy does not remain merely a sporadic exercise in voting but becomes a continuous process of government— a attitude and habit of mind. For this, full access to information with regard to the functioning of the government is necessary.

In every democratic country to some extent, there exists certain amount of public suspicion and distrust in the governmental bodies depending upon its performance and it prompts people to insist upon maximum exposure of its functioning. It is axiomatic that every action of the government must be actuated by public interest but even then there are number of examples where governmental action is not taken for public good but for personal gain or other extraneous considerations. Sometimes, governmental action is influenced by political and other motivations and pressures and at times, there are also instances of misuse or abuse of authority on the part of the executive. In such a situation, secrecy in the governmental functioning shall result into oppression.

In *S.P. Gupta* (supra), Supreme Court of India after considering the abuse of power by governmental bodies, observed as under, to quote:—

> "Now, if secrecy were to be observed in the functioning of government and the processes of

> government were to be kept hidden from public scrutiny, it would tend to promote and encourage oppression, corruption and misuse or abuse of authority, for it would all be shrouded in the veil of secrecy without any public accountability. But if there is an open government with means of information available to the public, there would be greater exposure of the functioning of government and it would help to assure the people a better and more efficient administration. There can be little doubt that exposure to public gaze and scrutiny is one of the surest means of achieving a clean and healthy administration. It has been truly said that an open government is clean government and a powerful safeguard against political and administrative aberration and inefficiency."

In England, with regard to openness of government, the Franks Committee was constituted which observed that only a totalitarian government finds it easy to maintain secrecy.

The only exception to retain information is public or national interest.

Where the interest clashes, Court has to decide which predominates. The exception with regard to disclosure of document, has been noted in a judgment of *Burma Oil Co. Ltd.,*[1] where, the House of Lords observed, to quote:—

> "But, is the secretary of the inner workings of the government machine so vital a public interest that it must prevail over even the most imperative demands of justice? If the contents of a document concern the national safety, affect diplomatic relations or relate to some sate secret of high importance, I can understand an affirmative answer. But if they do not (and it is not claimed in this case that they do), what is so important about secret government that it must be protected even at the price of injustice in our courts?"

1. *Burma Oil Co. Ltd.* v. *Bank of England,* (1979) 3 All ER 700: 1980 AC 1090: (1979) 3 WLR 722.

Virtually, this broader principle has been accepted by the Indian Courts and Supreme Court from time to time, while interpreting article 74 of Constitution and sections 123 and 124 of the Evidence Act and ruled that it is not possible to lay down any general rule but while considering the immunity, it should seem clear that in the weighing process the Court has to decide which of the two aspects of public interest should be given predominance, keeping in view the ends of justice *vis-a-vis* national interest.

The report of transparency international, placed India at No. 84. Undoubtedly, the Right to Information Act must be used to full of its capacity but information availed so, should be made a point by the public or citizen to fight with the menace of corruption and casteism within the constitutional ambit and four corners of law, Merely securing the information, shall not fulfil the aims and object of the Act.

However, corruption is now international phenomenon. Simon Jekins in his article[1] writes:—

> "Democracy in both America and Britain is coming under scrutiny these days. Quite apart from the antics of MPs and Congressmen, it is said to be sliding toward oligarchy, with increasing overtone of autocracy. Money and its power over technology are making the elections unfair. The military-industrial-complex is as powerful as ever, having adopted "the menace of global terrorism" as its *casus belli*. Lobbying and corruption are polluting the government process. In a nutshell democracy is not in a good shape."

I wish to refer an incident of Mahabharata. Right to gather information was used by Pandavas. It is of common knowledge that the great warrior Bhishma was blessed with power to die as per his own wish. It was a challenge before the Pandavas to defeat Bhishma. They went to Bhishma Pitamaha and prayed to inform them the mode and manner which may make him die. In those days, ordinarily, people particularly, the great men, were not

1. Published in newspaper Hindu, dated 10-4-2010.

liars. Uprightness and truthfulness was in their blood. Bhishma told Pandavas the manner by adopting which, he will meet to death. It is known fact, that Bhishma died because of Shikhandi.

Let it not be repeated in present context. The Right to Information should be used in national interest and should be protected to be abused by miscreants with appropriate safeguards.

It is universally recognised that society owes to all its future members and nearly, whole of the civilised world is trying to meet its obligation in one way or the other. Apart from imparting good education to children to make them good future citizen, it is also necessary that our coming generation breathes in a corruptless atmosphere where they avail their due rights, in accordance with their capability or merit. It cannot be just one upsurge but a continuous search into cause and effect of unending effort to match the situation. Our planning and decision should be research based for long-term gain. Every system has scope of abuse including RTI Act. But it does not make out a case to curtail people's right under the Act. It is for Information Commissioner to check the abuse.

The Constitution is an organic body, so the law is, to meet out the requirement, by changes. We must concern ourselves not only with the kind of the world we want, but also with the kind of men, who inhabited it. We should have, thinking people, capable of spontaneous, self-directed activity, people who are entrusted and entrusting, and who are imbued with compassion for others with open heart and mind.

RIGHT TO INFORMATION

Terrorism – Key Challenges

"From all that terror teaches, From lies of
tongue and pen,
From all the easy speeches
That comfort cruel men,
From sale and profanation,
Of honour and the sword,
From sleep and from damnation,
Deliver us, good Lord![1]

Terrorism is not new phenomena. In the Indian mythology, there has been continuous fighting between the four-fold orders of the civilization with the fifth class termed as 'Rakshas'. There is no exact translation of the word "Rakshas" in English. By nature, they were possessing the evil design, crudeness, deceptive nature, saddish approach. Leaders of the clan of Rakshas were also having back-up of religious fervor. Rakshas were expansionist by nature and whenever civilized society weakened, they always try to expand their horizon by annexation. 'Devasur Sangram' in Indian mythology speaks the fight of civilized world with the fifth, the outlawed class of world population. The civilized world was always conscious, acquired knowledge and power to fight with these people who were in habit to persecute the civilised population by successive attacks, interfering with their rituals, worship, meditation etc. However, the collective effort and regular preparedness kept the fifth outlawed class cornered and in segregated situation.

1. 'A Hymn' (1915) by G.K. Chesterton, 1874-1936.

In modern concept, deliberate, planned and systemic use of terror either against a Nation or Society to fulfil certain aims and object drew the international attention only after 11th September, 2001 when the twin tower of World Trade Centre suffered the wrath of terrorists. Earlier, the terrorism was the concern of underdeveloped and developing country but after September, 2001, it has become the concern of international community. Terrorism, a politically and emotionally charged word was alien to Indian civilization seems to born outside India and later on smuggled with the aid of "sleeping partner". In Ancient India, criminals were moderately of personalised nature. Majority of rulers were honest and used to impose punishment proportionate to crime (Raghwansam by Kalidas). After passage of time in Third Century B.C., Fa-Hien visited India in the regime of Vikramaditya (Chandragupta II). He noted the charity works and free medical aids in Pataliputra. He noted that the peoples were in general rich in particular benevolent. Fa-Hien spent about six years in pursuit of authentic Buddha texts and observed that the country was peaceful, serious crime was rare and administration was mild in its treatment of the common people. The people in general were contented having peaceful life.

Historian A.L. Basham also observed that during Gupta Empire, India was perhaps the happiest and most civilized region of the world, for the effete Roman Empire was nearing its destruction, and China was passing through a time of troubles between the two great periods of the Hans and the T'angs.

Today's world is the creation of migrated peoples from one part to other. No country may claim its occupation exclusively by local inhabitants or native peoples. There is migration and mixture of civilization and because of propagation and assertion of individual rights and liberty, peoples become more conscious to their rights on the ground of ethnic, lingual, regional or religious sacraments etc. The old Ancient Indian Philosophy of the life of mutual co-existence and sharing of pleasure and sorrow is at back foot. Ego, envy and personal rights overriding the compassion, tolerance and common rights to share natural resources. Accumulation of property and natural resources in few hands gives mileage to misguided peoples to indulge into terrorism to fight for their cause.

Terror or terrorism were alien to Indian society. The word 'terror' comes from a Latin word which means "to frighten". The terror cimbricus was a panic and state of emergency in Rome in response to the approach of warriors of the Cimbri tribe in 105 BC. The word 'terrorism' was also originally used to describe the action of Jacobins Club during the reign of terror in the French revolution. In 1795 Edmund Burke denounced the Jacobins for letting "thousands of those hell hounds called terrorists" loose upon the people of France. In 1858, Italian patriot Felice Orsini threw three bombs in an attempt to assassinate French Emperor Napoleon III. Russian Sergey Nechayev describes himself as a terrorist. George. C. Marshall Center for European Security Studies by Carsten Bockstette defined terrorism, to quote:—

> "terrorism is defined as political violence in a asymmetrical conflict that is designed to induce terror and psychic fear (sometimes indiscriminate) through the violent victimization and destruction of noncombatant targets (sometimes iconic symbols). Such acts are meant to send a message from an illicit clandestine organization. The purpose of terrorism is to exploit the media in order to achieve maximum attainable publicity as an amplifying force multiplier in order to influence the targeted audience(s) in order to reach short and mid-term political goals and/or desired long-term end states".

Bruce Hoffman in his famous treatise "Inside Terrorism" defined the terrorism to quote:—

> "On one point, at least, everyone agrees: terrorism is a pejorative term. It is a word with intrinsically negative connotations that is generally applied to

one's enemies and opponents, or to those with whom one disagrees and would otherwise prefer to ignore. 'What is called terrorism,' Brian Jenkins has written, "thus seems to depend on one's point of view. Use of the term implies a moral judgment; and if one party can successfully attach the label terrorist to its opponent, then it has indirectly persuaded others to adopt its moral viewpoint.' Hence the decision to call someone or label some organization 'terrorist' becomes almost unavoidably subjective, depending largely on whether one sympathizes with or opposes the person/group/ cause concerned. If one identifies with the victim of the violence, for example, then the act is terrorism. If, however, one identifies with the perpetrator, the violent act is regarded in a more sympathetic, if not positive (or, at the worst, an ambivalent) light; and it is not terrorism."

The National Advisory Committee on Criminal Justice Standards and Goals (a task force) formed by Law Enforcement Assistant Administration United States had classified terrorism into six categories *viz.*

1. **Civil Disorders** – A form of collective violence interfering with the peace, security, and normal functioning of the community.
2. **Political Terrorism** – Violent criminal behaviour designed primarily to generate fear in the community, or substantial segment of it, for political purposes.
3. **Non-Political Terrorism** – Exhibits "conscious design to create and maintain high degree of fear for coercive purposes, but the end is individual or collective gain rather than the achievement of a political objective."
4. ***Quasi*-Terrorism** – The activities incidental to the commission of crimes of violence that are similar in form and method to genuine terrorism but which nevertheless lack its essential ingredient.

5. **Limited Political Terrorism** – Genuine political terrorism is characterized by a revolutionary approach whereas limited political terrorism refers to "acts of terrorism which are committed for ideological or political motives but which are not part of a concerted campaign to capture control of the State".
6. **Official or State Terrorism** –"Referring to nations whose rule is based upon fear and oppression that reach similar to terrorism or such proportions." It may also be referred to as **Structural Terrorism** defined broadly as terrorist acts carried out by governments in pursuit of political objectives, often as part of their foreign policy.

According to report of United State Intelligence the terrorist may be of several varieties like Nationalist-Separatist, Religious Fundamentalist, New Religious, Social Revolutionary. Apart from these, the terrorist activity may also be managed by Mafia involved in organized crime under the cover of some separatist demand or for their own vested interest.

The *perpetrators* of acts of terrorism may be individuals, groups, or states. The clandestine and semi-clandestine state actors may also carry out terrorist acts outside the framework of a state of war. However, the common image of terrorism is that it is carried out by small group or secretive *cells,* highly motivated to serve a particular cause.

The cause of terrorism may include *Secession* of a territory to form a new sovereign state, Dominance of territory or resources by various *ethnic groups* Imposition of a particular form of government, Economic deprivation of a population, Opposition to a domestic government or occupying army.

Apart from these factors the inequalities in distribution of scarce resources, hunger, starvation, poor financial condition, lack of basic amenities, mal-functioning of government, corruption and poverty may create grounds for establishment of terrorist organization.

According to newspaper report, Azmal Kasab joined the terrorist organization merely for Rs. 50,000. However, appropriate research is required as to under what circumstances a person joins the terrorist organizations. But I feel that in majority of the cases the persons holding gun in their hand as the members of terrorist organization belongs to poor family who does not possess the basic amenities for survival. Poverty and unemployment compel a weak statured person to move in wrong direction.

Samuel P. Huntington in his celebrated treatise *"The Clash of Civilizations and The Remaking of World Order"* had expressed that the western universalism could lead to a major inter-civilizational war. Learned author observed to quote:—

> "Much evidence exists in the 1990s for the relevance of the "sheer chaos" *paradigm* of world affairs; a global breakdown of law and order, failed states and increasing anarchy in many parts of the world, a global crime wave, transnational mafias and drug cartels, increasing drug addiction in many societies, a general weakening of the family, a decline in trust and social solidarity in many countries, ethnic, religious, and civilizational violence and rule by the gun prevalent in much of the world. In city after city – Moscow, Rio De Janeiro, Bangkok, Shanghai, London, Rome, Warsaw, Tokyo, Johannesburg, Delhi, Karachi, Cairo, Bogota, Washington – Crime seems to be soaring and basic elements of Civilization fading away. People speak of a global crisis in governance."

The grim situation of the world is because of materialistic approach in general and high level of corruption, casteism, nepotism and communalism in politically and financially influenced group, all over the world. Burden to maintain the respective civilizational qualities, broadly has been shifted to judiciary within the Constitutional ambit, so far as democratic countries are concerned.

Keeping in view this scenario and brief sketch depicting the varieties of terrorism and their cause the effectiveness of statutory provisions of India should be judged.

In India, there has been continuous debate over safeguarding liberty of citizen juxtaposed to the security of people and the integrity of India. Number of statutes framed in post-independent India deals with not only terrorism but also habitual offenders involved in organised crime like Preventive Detention Act, 1950, Reinvented as Maintenance of Security Act, 1971 (MISA) and thereafter National Security Act, 1980 (NSA), TADA, 1987 and POTA in 2002. UAPA Act, 1967 amended in 2004 to combat the terror keeping in view 26/11 terror strike. The Government of India was blamed as soft State on terrorism and called for stringent law and to create necessary instrumentality to abet terrorism. The Government shared the public opinion and responded with two enactments, namely Unlawful Activities (Prevention) Amendment Act, 2008 amending Unlawful Activities (Prevention) Act, 1967 (UAPA) and National Investigation Agency Act, 2008. These two legislations are complementary to combat terrorism and an effort has been made to address both *terror and terrorists activities*.

Section 15 of the Unlawful Activities (Prevention Act, 1967) (in short referred as to Act) defines the terrorist act. The Maintenance of Security Act, 1980 in India definition is wide enough to cover so many terrorist activities but it shall not be able to meet out the requirement to check every form of terrorism classified by the committee of United States (supra). Legislatures should reconsider the definition of terrorism keeping in view the pace with time. However, ordinarily the effective enforcement of the Act and quick disposal of cases registered under the Act may to some extent check the menace of terrorism. The appointment of Tribunal should be expeditious and must be presided by Judge having impeccable character. The decision should be quick and burden to proof of the 'prosecution case', on the shoulder of prosecution, under common law should be relaxed. In case, *prima facie,* case is made out involving a person in terrorist act then burden should be shifted on the accused to establish that he is not a terrorist.

The most important thing in the criminal justice system is the *"investigation"* and *"quick trial"*. The National Investigation Agency Act, 2008 (in short referred as to 2008 Act) promulgated by Parliament to establish a National Investigation Agency (in short referred as to NIA) is the latest in line to check terrorism. Though the spirit behind the Act is to ensure quick investigation and disposal of cases related to terrorist activities, but a close scrutiny of the 2008 Act shows it to be "half-hearted Act". Though the Central Government had tried to set-up an investigation agency at the pattern of FBI (Federal Bureau of Investigation) of the United States of America and some other western countries but it seems to be far away to achieve its object.

Section 6 of the 2008 Act empowers the Officer In-charge of a Police Station to register a FIR of the scheduled offence. Though section 15 of the Act gives wider meaning to some extent to the Terrorist Act but section 6 of the 2008 Act confines the power to register a FIR only to scheduled offences, empowering the State Government to forward a report to the Central Government and in lieu thereof it is for the Central Government to consider as to whether it is a fit case to be investigated by the agency (NIA). Section 10 of the NIA empowers the State Government also to investigate and prosecute any Scheduled Offence. NIA has been also given power under section 7 either to make a request to State Government to associate itself with the investigation or transfer the case to the State Government for investigation and trial. The provision contained in NIA Act are neither seems to clear nor effective to cope up with the situation which may arises because of terrorists activities in due course of time.

While deciding a case with regard to organized crime (Mafia) I have occasion to consider the machinery to deal with organized crime in a case of *Chandrika Prasad Nisad*[1]. While deciding the said case, I have observed that appropriate legislation should be promulgated at the pattern of RICO Act operating in the United States of America. I have also observed that the investigation agency should be established at par with FBI of America. For FBI it is not necessary to seek permission for investigation of a case involved in inter-state crime or terrorist activities. The National Investigation Agency should be conferred with power to take up *suo motu* a crime under the Act or a case involving inter-state or international criminal links which includes terrorist activities also. At least keeping in view the ground realities of our country it shall not be possible to have a quick decision keeping in view the letter and spirit of provision contained in Chapter 3 of the NIA Act. Because of the red tapism, political anomalies and interest, Government shall not be able to take a quick decision to refer a matter to NIA .

The offence falling under the 1967 Act are also punishable under the Indian Penal Code. Once a FIR is lodged for crime under the Penal Code, the investigating officer need not require to seek permission or green signal from any superior authority under the Code of Criminal Procedure, then why so much hurdle has been created under the NIA Act. NIA should be empowered to take up *'suo motu'* every terrorist incident or the organised crime for investigation and prosecution.

In due course of time NIA Act shall show its ineffectiveness in case appropriately not amended. Ultimately law is not what is written in the textbook but the law is, how it is implemented effectively to redress the public grievance.

It is often said that the Parliament lacks jurisdiction to legislate law with regard to criminal investigation affecting States' right to deal with criminal cases. *Prima facie*, it seems to be unfounded. The organized crime as well as terrorist

---

1. *Chandrika Prasad Nisad* v. *State of Uttar Pradesh*, 2006 LCD 1243.

activities ordinarily possessed the sphere of working in more than one State. Their members have got active as well as sleeping partners not only in one State but more than one State. Sometimes it may be noticed that they originate in one foreign country, trained in other country hit the target in other country and similarly prepare their base in one state of our country and indulge into terrorist act in other State. They have got sleeping partners in more than one States. Accordingly though public order and police falls in the State list *i.e.* list 2 of the 7th Schedule but it does not mean that Parliament does not have got power to legislate law with regard to an offence relating to organized crime or Terrorist Act committed by a person or antisocial body having members in more than one state or outside the country.

A close and collective reading of entries 1, 2, 5, 8, 9, 21, 94, 95 of the List I of the 7th Schedule of the Constitution read with entries 1, 2 and 4 of the List II shows that Parliament may legislate law with regard to investigation and trial of a crime like organized crime and terrorist activities where the roots of body involved in such activity have got interstate or international links. *Prima facie* it shall not amount to the interference with the states subject.

There is one other aspect of the matter as to why Parliament may legislate law on the subject. In view of article 5 of the Constitution of India, there is single common citizenship in India unlike other federal Constitutions like USA which provides dual citizenship. There is nothing like domicile of the State. After *Pradeep Jain*[1] there is only one domicile *viz.* the domicile of the territory of India and there is no separate domicile for a State. Every citizen has right to move freely throughout the territory of India, to reside and settle in any part of the country, to own property and to carry on any trade or business or occupation (article 19).

The Government of India is signatory to universal declaration of human rights and other UN Charters. It is

1. *Pradeep Jain* v. *Union of India,* (1984) 3 SCC 654: AIR 1984 SC 1420: 1984 Ed Cas 237.

prime duty of Government to ensure fraternity, sovereignty and integrity of India.

Otherwise also, under article 355 of the Constitution of India, it is the duty of the Union Government to protect every State not only against external aggression but also against internal disturbance and to ensure that the Government of every State is carried on in accordance with the constitutional scheme.

Needless to say that deliberate, planned and repeated terrorist incidents creates fear psychosis in public and causes internal disturbance. In such a situation, it is the solemn duty of the legislature to legislate law, to meet out the challenges. Almost every terrorist group has got inter-State links, sleeping partners and some of them have got foreign associations. In such a situation, more teeth should be given to NIA and UAPA at par with FBI to deal with terrorist *suo motu* without the consent of the State Government.

As observed, the quick investigation and speedy trial is necessary to check terrorism. The overloaded judiciary by backlog of cases has shaken the people's faith to some extent in the administration of justice. The per capita civil case filing in India is much less than the developed country. According to Robert Moog, litigation rate in Uttar Pradesh from 1951 to 1976 is falling dramatically from early days of independence, when there were 1.63 per 1000 persons in 1951 to 1976, now it is only 0.88 per thousand. The available data contravene the perception that India is an increasingly litigious country but neither investigation nor disposal of cases by the Courts has touched the satisfactory bench mark. There appears to be some fault at entry point in Bar and Bench and maintenance of work culture in the system. Supreme Court of India in the case of *P.N. Eswara Iyer*,[1] observed, to quote:

1. *P.N. Eswara Iyer* v. *Registrar of the Supreme Court of India*, (1980) 4 SCC 680: 1980 (2) SCJ 119: AIR 1980 SC 808.

"It is fair to confess that the scientific method of undertaking research and study into public problems as prelude to legislation is lamentably lacking; and court......management is currently beyond the ken of scientific research. Where awareness is absent, ad-hocism is inevitable......Here experiential evidence makes do for empirical research."

In a judgment of Ram Jethmalani,[1] Supreme Court of India while deciding the writ petition with regard to large amount of unaccounted money stashed in oversea countries has shown deep concern with regard to feeble governance in country. Supreme Court noted how India is treated as "soft State". It shall be appropriate to reproduce the observation made by Supreme Court from the case of *Ram Jethmalani* (supra); to quote:

"7. Security of the nation, infrastructure of governance, including those that relate to law-making and law keeping functions, crime prevention, detection and punishment, coordination of the economy, and ensuring minimal levels of material, and cultural goods for those who may not be in a position to fend for themselves or who have been left by the wayside by the operation of the economy and society, may all be cited as some examples of the kinds of public goods that the State is expected to provide for, or enable the provision of. Inasmuch as the market is primarily expected to cater to purely self-centered activities of individuals and groups, markets and the domain of purely private social action significantly fail to provide such goods. Consequently, the State, and government, emerges to rectify the coordination problem, and provide the public goods.

9. Consequently, the issue of unaccounted monies held by nationals, and other legal entities, in foreign banks, is of primordial importance to the welfare of

---

1. *Ram Jethmalani* v. *Union of India*, reported in JT 2011 (7) SC 104.

the citizens. The quantum of such monies may be rough indicators of the weakness of the State, in terms of both crime prevention, and also of tax collection. Depending on the volume of such monies, and the number of incidents through which such monies are generated and secreted away, it may very well reveal the degree of 'softness of the State.'

10. The concept of a 'soft state' was famously articulated by the Nobel Laureate, Gunnar Myrdal. It is a broad based assessment of the degree to which the State, and its machinery, is equipped to deal with its responsibilities of governance. The more soft the State is, greater the likelihood that there is an unholy nexus between the law-maker, the law-keeper, and the law-breaker."

Needless to say that in case India wants to combat terrorism, then the image with regard to 'soft State' should be reasonably toned-up to *"Firm and Decisive State"*.

There has been successive terrorist attack and bomb blast in India and recent one was on 13.7.2011 again in Bombay. Why India has been failed to check terrorism though the United States of America after 9/11 attack on World Trade Centre in 2001 has successfully secured its terror by adopting certain stringent regulatory method manned by its upright bureaucracy imbibed by 'work culture' without any political interference to protect its Nation.

After 9/11 incident in United States of America, a Committee was constituted headed by Thomas H. Kean and the committee after thorough investigation has submitted its report which has been published by W.W. Norton & Company Limited. According to the report, the committee has recommended that the terrorism should be dealt with treating the incident as more than war with successive measuring success efforts made for the purpose. The committee recommended to attack terrorists and their organisation and make preparation and be ready to face terrorist attack. The committee opined for setting-up of priorities for national preparedness with a definite command, control and communication system.

In nutshell, the Committee recommended as under:

1. Though expert agencies cannot always prevent determined, suicidal attackers from reaching a target but the American peoples are entitled to expect their government to do its very best. They should expect that officials will have realistic objectives, clear guidance, and effective organisation. They are entitled to see some standards for performance so they can judge, with the help of their elected representatives, whether the objectives are being met;
2. The United States Government, joined by other governments around the world, is working through intelligence, law enforcement, military, financial, and diplomatic channels to identify, disrupt, capture, or kill individual terrorists;
3. United States must build the capacities to prevent a 9/11 scale plot from succeeding, and those capabilities will help greatly to cope with lesser but still devastating attacks;
4. Time, space, and ability to perform competent planning and staff work;
5. A command structure able to make necessary decisions and possessing the authority and contacts to assemble needed people, money, and materials;
6. Opportunity and space to recruit, train, and select operatives with the needed skills and dedication, providing the time and structure required to socialize them into the terrorist cause, judge their trustworthiness, and hone their skills;
7. A logistics network able to securely manage the travel of operatives, move money, and transport resources (like explosives) where they need to go;
8. Access, in the case of certain weapons, to the special materials needed for a nuclear, chemical, radiological, or biological attack;

9. Reliable communications between coordinators and operatives; and opportunity to test the workability of the plan.

America being a super power and having capacity to strike anywhere in the world, the Committee has opined to strike the terrorist bases wherever are they situated. The Committee observed that America should specifically ask as if you were a terrorist leader today where would you locate your base. Some of the places cope up again and again in their lists are, western Pakistan and the Pakistan-Afghanistan border region, southern and western Afghanistan, the Arabian Peninsula especially Saudi Arabia and Yemen, and the nearby Horn of Africa, including Somalia and extending southwest into Kenya, Southeast Asia, from Thailand to the southern Philippines to Indonesia, West Africa, including Nigeria and Mali and some of European cities. The Committee further opined that United States Government must identify and prioritize actual or potential terrorist sanctuaries. For each, it should have a realistic strategy to keep possible terrorists insecure and on the run, using all elements of national power. America should reach out, listen to, and work with other countries which may be helpful.

The United States Government must define *what the message is and what it stands for*. It should offer an example of moral leadership in the world community to treat people humanely abide by rule of law and be generous. The Committee further opined that America's Borders and immigration system including law enforcement ought to send a message of welcome, tolerance and justice to members of immigrant communities in the United States and in their countries of origin. *It is elemental to border security to know who is coming into the country.* The secure identification should begin in the United States. The Federal Government should set standard for issuance of *'birth certificates'* and source of identification, such as driver's licenses. The government should identify and evaluate transportation assets that need to be protected.

The plan must take into consideration the full array of possible enemy tactics, such as use of insiders, suicide terrorism or standoff attack. Each layer must be effective in its own right.

There are several other recommendations to check terrorism effectively has been made by the committee which may be looked into by the Indian Government in Indian context keeping in view the ground realities.

Overall assessment made by the Committee after 9/11 incident of 2001 in U.S.A. speaks for "zero tolerance" on the part of the government. In India, recommendation may be taken into account while combating with the terrorists. Some of the other features which requires are:

1. A back-up of research team consisting scientifically trained persons to suggest preventive measures and assist in investigation with regard to terrorist activities and time bound investigation by country's 'prime agency' within statutory specified period.
2. Zero tolerance to check, prevent and punish the incident of terrorism with intelligence back-up.
3. Mercy petitions or application for the grant of sanction must be decided within specified period without hesitation, discrimination or appeasement to secure National Interest.
4. Quick and speedy trial in notified court on day to day basis, within specified period.

Keeping in view the overburdened High Court and subordinate judiciary and moral dilution in the society, statutory "multiple member tribunal" may be constituted for trial of the accused, charged of terrorism within a specified period on day to day basis by amending statutory provisions, relaxing the burden of proof under the Evidence Act. Tribunals may be permitted to regulate its own procedure subject to strict compliance of the principle of natural justice.

5. Creation of autonomous independent investigation agency having jurisdiction throughout the country and power to take up any heinous crime, with terror link – *suo motu*.

Terrorism is not uncombative. It may be checked and prevented but for that requires 'will power' and 'rigorous enforcement of law' with a commitment to national security.

Mediation in Commercial and Matrimonial Dispute

"Every one has the duty to run to the help of a neighbour in distress............
Every one shall contribute his share to the building of common facilities.............
People of a village shall obey the orders of any one who propose any activity beneficial to all.[1]"

Former US Supreme Court Chief Justice Warren Burger in his keynote address in the "National Conference on the Causes of Popular Dissatisfaction with Administration of Justice", conducted way back in the year 1976, remarked:

"The notion that ordinary people want black-robed judges, well dressed lawyers and fine courtrooms as settings to resolve their disputes is incorrect. People with problems, like people with pain, want relief, and they want it as quickly and inexpensively as possible".

ADR or "Alternative Dispute Resolution" often described by many international authors as "Appropriate Dispute Resolution" and involving mediation as one of its tool, has taken deep roots in the legal system around the world, be it the United States, United Kingdom, Australia and even in small countries like Sri Lanka and Hong Kong.

Thus the need, efficacy and importance of mediation in modern dispute resolution system has risen above scholarly debates and dialectic discussions. Therefore, in line with the

1. 'Kautilya in Economics'.

topic of this session, that is, "Mediation in commercial and matrimonial disputes", I would attempt to analyse the feasibility of mediation in the domains of commercial and matrimonial disputes. It is my preliminary submission that the fields of commercial and matrimonial disputes by their nature rest on two different poles. A commercial dispute is evidently a winner takes all battle, whereas a matrimonial dispute merely involves couple in confrontation over social and emotional issues. Therefore, I deem it proper to discuss the topic of mediation in these two differing areas one by one.

I would prefer to begin with matrimonial dispute since development in this area in our country has been really encouraging.

Woodrow Wilson, 28th President of United States of America, once remarked, "A dispute is a problem to be solved, together, rather than a combat to be won."

His words perfectly describe the irony attached to matrimonial cases.

It is clear that more often than not, matrimonial litigants who "go all the way" really do end up being losers.

What are the real problems that confront a divorcing couple? Let me begin with the definition of divorce. Black's Law Dictionary defines divorce as "the legal separation of man and wife." Interestingly, however, marriage has a much broader definition. Britannica—Webster defines marriage as "the institution whereby a man and a woman are joined in a special social and legal relationship for the purpose of making a home and raising a family."

Thus, it is interesting to see that marriage is viewed as a legal and social union of two people; however, divorce is merely viewed as the legal termination of said marriage. These definitions in and of themselves highlight one of the basic problems that occur when a couple chooses to divorce. Namely, although the legal system is equipped to deal with the legal problems that the couple embroiled in matrimonial dispute faces, it does not address nor is it equipped to deal with the social and emotional issues that confront the couple.

Once the emotional or social issues are dealt with, it makes the resolution of the legal issues that much easier. Further it is also clear that matrimonial litigation is unduly burdensome to our courts. Perhaps mediation is a means to solve the problem.

The sanctity of mediation to remedy such issues is best described by D.K. Sampath, Faculty National Law School, Bangalore who observes, "Mediation restores the shattered faith and human relations, upholds harmony as a social value and removes impediments to access to justice."

Taking it a step further, what most people really are arguing about, in a matrimonial dispute, is not legal or financial issues, but rather arguments fuelled by their desire to get some form of revenge for a perceived wrong by his/ her spouse. This feeling can alone be dealt through mediation. To quote Sampath again in this context, "Mediation never allows an individual to build-up his success by humbling his adversary...When each individual's thinking is anchored in cooperation, psychological orientation towards harmony is ensured."

Thus in my humble submission there is no other legal mechanism as noble and befitting as mediation to remedy matrimonial disputes.

The need to foster mediation in matrimonial dispute has been recognised at all level. While the legislature on its part has enacted section 89 in the CPC, the courts have supported it through positive interpretation for example in *Salem Advocates Bar Association's* case.[1] Further, various reports, including Law Commission of India 129th Report titled "Urban Litigation: Mediation as Alternative to Adjudication", have mooted the proposition of using mediation techniques.

1. *Salem Advocate Bar Association* v. *Union of India,* (2005) 6 SCC 344: AIR 2005 SC 3353: 2005 AIR SCW 3827.

However, we still need to amplify the efforts in this field. I humbly suggest that the couple involved in the matrimonial dispute, particularly divorce mediation, may need more than one mediator to help them arrive at a mutually acceptable agreement. Different people have different needs. One's emotional or social issues are best handled by mental health mediators such as psychiatrists, psychologists or social workers. Financial issues are best dealt with by specially trained mediators such as accountants, financial planners and lawyers. Legal issues are best dealt with by attorney-mediators. Thus I put my proposal to adopt a "mediation team approach" which may effectively enable a couple to have what might be called 'a successful or positive solution'.

Coming to Commercial matters, mediation in recent past has emerged as a highly effective means to settle commercial disputes, often more quickly and more cheaply than by normal litigation, arbitration and negotiation.

The later half of 20th century witnessed many national legal systems making sweeping commitments to three areas of substantive political and economic reform. *First,* traditionally authoritarian political systems have sought to achieve greater democracy through popular elections, more accountable and transparent public service. *Second,* governments have loosened their grips on economic systems and embraced a free marketplace. *Third,* the international community has embarked on a nearly uncontrollable and irreversible process of globalization. Unprecedented daily flows of capital, goods, services, information, as well as technology, and people currently permeate national borders. In pursuit of these commitments countries have generated an enormous amount of new substantive law, including civil rights, criminal justice reform, commercial legislation, constitutional law, and free trade agreements and regional economic unions. But with that has come true warning of Roscoe Pound about the limits to ability of law to remedy every social evil. In Pound's words, " When men demand much of law, when they seek to devolve upon it the whole burden of social control,...enforcement of law comes to involve many difficulties".

The institution to enforce law

The right asserting society backed by commercial laws of the globalized world has also imposed new burdens on courts.

New rights create new forms of legally cognizable claims and disputes. In most market-oriented or democratic countries, case filings are on the rise; yet, most countries are not close to keeping pace. India is far from alone on this single index: in many countries from Latin America to Eastern Europe case filings (roughly) doubled over a single decade. Notwithstanding the common need for institutional reform, these backlogs occur not only because the courts do not have the institutional resources to shoulder these new burdens, but also because the society has heightened expectations of getting justice from the courts.

Further the attitude of parties in commercial dispute is very peculiar which makes a simple dispute a hard and long fought battle.

Commenting on the fighting parties in a commercial dispute William Sheffield[1] in his article "Dispute among the business partners should be mediated or arbitrated, not litigated" has very aptly remarked:

> "Hire 'big guns, seek out the friendliest courtroom available and begin hammering the other side in a winner-take all, give no quarter, war. This is litigation. This is 'the adversarial system.' Litigation, if it ever was useful, has outlived its usefulness as a way to resolving most disputes."

Such tendency of parties drains both money and time in reaching a resolution.

Thus in such a scenario when the court are at the verge of what is being termed as 'Docket Explosion', finding quick

1. Judge, Superior Court of California (Retd.)

and amicable settlement of commercial disputes is not only necessary for administration of justice but also *sine qua non* to maintain efficiency of industries.

Prof. Amartya Sen has emphasized in a broader context, "our opportunities and prospects depend crucially on what institutions exist and how they function."[1] And there appears need to maintain efficiency of dispute resolution. The need to find alternative to adversarial litigation, the need to find alternative dispute resolution.

The experience of other countries.

Probably this is the reason that need for commercial mediation was felt first in industrialized west. The recent developments in several countries and institutions are both noteworthy and encouraging.

The United Nations General Assembly while adopting UNCITRAL Conciliation Rules, 1980, recorded that 'the establishment of conciliation[2] rules that are acceptable in countries with different legal, social, and economic systems would significantly contribute to the development of harmonious international relations.' Further the United Nations Commission on International Trade Law (UNCITRAL) drafted Model law, which was adopted by General Assembly in 2002, to bring procedural uniformity in commercial mediation.

The European Union on its part approved in 2008, Directive on Mediation primarily on five key areas, namely,

1. to provide for training of mediators and devise code to regulate functioning of the process;
2. to encourage courts to refer parties to mediation;

---

1. Amartya Sen, Freedom As Development 142 (1999).
2. Read also as mediation, article 1(3) of Model Law, "For the purposes of this Law, 'conciliation' means a process, whether referred to by the expression conciliation, mediation or an expression of similar import, whereby parties request a third person or persons ('the conciliator') to assist them in their attempt to reach an amicable settlement of their dispute arriving out of or relating to a contractual or other legal relationship...".

3. to put enforcements machinery in place, for example by providing settlement agreement status of court decree;
4. to ensure confidentiality and promote faith of parties in mediation;

provisions to suspend the period of statutory limitation when parties are at mediation.

The United States of America with a view to encourage faster, less costly ways to resolve disputes in cases where federal Government was a party, passed The Administrative Dispute Resolution, Act in 1996. Now United States federal agencies extensively use ADR, mainly mediation to settle dispute.

In USA probably, 80 to 90% civil and commercial matters are resolved by mediation, sometimes during the pendency of the litigation, and sometimes even before going to a Court of Law. The Office of Dispute Resolution (ODA), Department of Justice, United States in its annual report 2010 mentions that 80% of the cases in voluntary mediation proceedings were resolved whereas ratio in court ordered proceedings stood at 46%. The ODA estimates that it saved $11,662,500 (approx 11 million) worth of Litigation or Discovery expenses and 930 months of litigation time.

The traditional United Kingdom also woke-up to the changes and introduced its Civil Procedure Reforms in 1999 to enable courts to deal with cases "justly" through active case management, partly defined as encouraging the use of Alternative Dispute Resolution procedures.

The enormous potential of mediation has been recognised at the very highest level in the English judiciary for some time. In May 2008 Lord Clarke (Sir Anthony Clarke, as he then was) was equally unequivocal:

> ....ADR in general and mediation in particular, where it is the appropriate ADR mechanism, must become an integral part of our litigation culture. It must become such a well established part of it that when considering the proper management of

litigation it forms as intrinsic and as instinctive a part of our lexicon...[1]

Indian Scenario

The concept of mediation, in which a neutral third party, the mediator helps disputing parties to reach an agreement, has been in vogue in our villages from time immemorial. We had the system of "Madhyamasi", the reference of which is found in Rig Veda. Kautilya in his famous treatise, Arthashastra, dated as back as 321 B.C. has emphasised the graceful solution of dispute between parties by literate persons having impeccable character. Later in the "Dispute Resolution Panchayats" wisdom of the village wise men acting as Panchayatdar, enabled villagers to find mutually acceptable solutions to their dispute. Also, in pre-British India, ADR was popular among businessmen. For example, in Ahmedabad, leading cloth merchants banded together to form a business association "Maskati Mahajan", as it was called, to resolve disputes between members by respected businessmen.

Supreme Court of India in the case of *K. Srinivas Rao*[2] had directed for implementation of its order with regard to matrimonial matters by the courts and mediation centers. The order of the Supreme Court is as follows:—

36. We, therefore, issue directions, which the courts dealing with the matrimonial matters shall follow:

(a) In terms of section 9 of the Family Courts Act, the Family Courts shall make all efforts to settle the matrimonial disputes through mediation. Even if the Counsellors submit a failure report, the Family Courts shall, with the consent of the parties, refer the matter to the mediation centre. In such a case, however, the Family Courts shall set a reasonable time limit for

---

1. Sir Anthony Clarke, Master of the Rolls, the Second Civil Mediation Council National Conference 'The Future of Civil Mediation', Birmingham 8 May, 2008.
2. *K. Srinivas Rao* v. *D.A. Deepa,* in Civil Appeal No. 1794 of 2013, decided on 22-2-2013.

mediation centres to complete the process of mediation because otherwise the resolution of the disputes by the Family Court may get delayed. In a given case, if there is good chance of settlement, the Family Court in its discretion, can always extend the time limit.

(b) The criminal courts dealing with the complaint under section 498A of the IPC should, at any stage and particularly, before they take up the complaint for hearing, refer the parties to mediation centre if they feel that there exist elements of settlement and both the parties are willing. However, they should take care to see that in this exercise, rigour, purport and efficacy of section 498A of the IPC is not diluted. Needless to say that the discretion to grant or not to grant bail is not in any way curtailed by this direction. It will be for the concerned court to work out the modalities taking into consideration the facts of each case.

(c) All mediation centres shall set-up pre-litigation desks/clinics; give them wide publicity and make efforts to settle matrimonial disputes at pre-litigation stage.

Thus reformers have grown increasingly interested in reviving or extending traditional forms of dispute resolution and integrating them into the formal litigation system which to make mention of is the distinctive form of evaluative Chinese mediation known as *tiaojie.*

Legislative recognition

Efforts have been made by the legislature in India to include mediation in our legal framework. The concept of mediation got legislative recognition for the first time in the Industrial Disputes Act, 1947. The conciliators appointed under section 4 of the Act are "charged with the duty of mediating in and promoting the settlement of industrial disputes". A complete machinery for conciliation proceedings is provided under the Act.

The Arbitration and Conciliation Act, 1996 has made elaborate provisions for conciliation of disputes arising out of legal relationship, whether contractual or not, and to all proceedings relating thereto.

Finally the introduction of ADR mechanisms in the Code of Civil Procedure, 1908 is one more radical step taken in recent times by Indian legislature. Section 89 and Order X rules 1A, 1B and 1C provide for ADR machinery even in cases pending before the civil courts and further authorize the High Courts to frame rules for the purpose. Thus, now the Indian legislature has made sufficient provisions in law to facilitate introduction of court annexed mediation.

Conclusion

However, we cannot deny the fact, standing tall before us, that even after the enactment of the Arbitration & Conciliation Act, 1996, mediation has not gained required momentum in our country. Even though some mediation training and familiarization programs were conducted it did not create the real effect. Although some success has been achieved at the level of High Courts it is almost nil in subordinate courts, the courts of first instance.

In our country with huge population, a large part of which is poor and illiterate, it is imperative that mediation both in concept and institution is taken to grass-root level. It is necessary to create awareness among the litigants and particularly in class litigants like businessmen.

This can be effectuated by organizing seminars and conferences at district and taluka level because such activities have till now largely remained confined to major cities basically at the seats of High Court.

At such conferences direct participation of citizens should be ensured through proper advertisement in newspapers and electronic media.

It is my humble submission that in increasing awareness of the process amongst legal circles, law schools should be an important target. For law students who are trained and lectured only about the workings and merits about the adversarial system of justice, such an exposure will be an absolute necessity to carry forth mediation in the future.

Further there has been wide scepticism both in lawyers and litigants about the results of mediation to their benefit, even without making resort to such noble technique.

Even in court ordered mediation, the lack of confidence in the process has led parties to failure and withdrawal from the proceedings. To make mention of data from Mediation and Conciliation Centre at Lucknow Bench, Allahabad High Court, starting from 2007 out of total 1165 cases referred for mediation, excluding the pending 115, a startling 748 cases (approx. 64%) ended either in failure of mediation or parties withdrawing from proceeding.

A further split of this data shows that in matrimonial disputes failure rate is high (almost 64%). Though in property disputes between private parties success was reached in 75% matters, yet these cases were limited to 20 in numbers. At the same time in Company matters out of 69 cases mediated, the data tells that 67, that is almost 97%, failed due to non-appearance or cooperation from the parties.

I most humbly urge that this mentality has to be overdone. I remind, that in March 2008 Lord Phillips, now President of the Supreme Court of England and Wales, very aptly expressed that:

> ...It is madness to incur the considerable expense of litigation [...] without making a determined attempt to reach an amicable settlement. The idea that there is only one just result of every dispute, which only the Court can deliver is, I believe, illusory....

Friends, our society has transformed more in the past fifty years than it has over the past few centuries. Efficiency in terms of quality, time and money in dispute resolution has become one of the most fundamental goals that modern society is working towards.

Now, Supreme Court has re-affirmed the common belief that there is trust deficit between the people governing and the people to be governed. Therefore, in days to come, the judiciary is likely to be over-burdened by plenty of cases involving disputes between the Government and the governed. We have to find out the ways and means to cope up with the situation apart from clearing the backlog of pending cases.[1]

Roscoe Pound pointed out, forms of dispute redressal have to change along with the society it serves.

However, our legal system has failed to respond effectively enough to these demands of modern society. When we compare the United States and Indian system, over the last twenty (20) years, American lawyers and judges have warmly embraced mediation as a primary tool for resolving conflicts in court and out of court, while Indian lawyers and judges are still warily examining mediation, discussing whether and in which types of cases mediation should be used – similar to what was happening in the United States in the 1980's.

To conclude, I find no better words than to quote Justice V.R. Krishna Iyer,

> "...Law and Justice can no longer remain distant neighbours, if the increasing deficiencies and distortions of the legal system and the challenge to the credibility of the judicature are to be adequately met. The lawlessness of the old original law, judged by the new dharma, can be corrected either by radical reform or by surrender to the direct action. The choice is obvious and the hour is late. Let us begin."

---

1. Judgment of Supreme Court dated 23-2-2012 in the case of *Ramlila Maidan Incident* v. *Home Secretary, Union of India (UOI).*

State's Focus on Water Conservation, Safe Drinking Water and Sanitation Programme

The devine waters, the purifiers of hundreds,
Rejoicing in their innate nature;
Pursue the paths of Nature's forces; They never violate
The sacred laws of the Resplendent Lord:
May you offer to rivers Your tribute
Rich in affection and love![1]

Since ages, this Country (India) had attracted the inhabitants of other parts of the world because of its green lustre, forest, fertile land and rivers well suited to mankind to live a happy life. Ancient Indians knew their sub-continent as Jambudvipa or Bharatavarsa and also called Aryavarta. More than two thousand years before the Christ the fertile plain of the Punjab watered by five great tributaries of the Indus the Jhelam, Chenab, Ravi, Beas and Sutlej had a high culture, which spread as far as the sea along the western seaboard at least as far as Gujarat. The basin of Indus is occupied by Ganga and since ages right from Haridwar to Culcutta, densely-populated cities were grown up at its bank. In far east Brahamputra in South Kaveri and other rivers have attracted the peoples of the world to migrate and settle in this sub-continent. Western

1. The Holy Vedas, Rig. 7.47.3.

Historians used to say that India was blessed by bounteous nature, who demanded little of man in return for sustenance because of rich natural resources, and that is why the Indian character has tended to fatalism and quietism, accepting fortune and misfortune without any complaint. However, it appears to be not correct in its totality. The great genius of the Indian traditions lies in the concept of the divine power that pervades every atom of the universe, visible and invisible, manifest and unmanifest. According to ancient Indian scholars, the divinity is, in the ultimate analysis, seated within each individual. Indian civilization has unlike Egypt, Mesopotamia and Greece, preserved its tradition and culture without a break down to present day. It happened because of emotional attachment with the nature and worship of, ponds, lakes, hills and trees and nature-related objects. In one or other form, Indian enjoyed the nature's blessing, since ages because of preventive and preservative steps taken by our forefathers.

The earliest evidence of urban sanitation was seen in Harappa, Mohenjodaro and the recently discovered Rakhigarhi of Indus Valley Civilisation. This urban plan included the world's first urban sanitation system. Within the city, individual homes or groups of homes obtained water from wells. From a room or from a place earmarked for bathing, wastewater was directed to cover drains, which lined the major streets. Homes opened only to inner courtyards and smaller lanes. Romans had some elements of sanitation systems, especially related to waste water collection and transport away from populated areas. According to historians, the unsanitary conditions were widespread throughout the Europe and Asia in the Middle Ages. Very high infant and child mortality prevailed in Europe throughout medieval times. In India, river Ganga since ages, has been personified as Goddess whereas, river Saraswati has been referred to as the Goddess in Vedas. Also water is one of the "panch-tatvas" (basic 5 elements, others including fire, earth, space, air). Alternatively, Gods can be patrons of particular springs, rivers, or lakes: for example in Greek and Roman mythology, Peneus was a river God, one of the three thousand Oceanids. In Islam, not only does water give life, but every life is itself made of water. "We made from water every living thing."

The excavations shows that the Indus Civilization (2500-3000 B.C.) covering most part of the Punjab and Baluchistan to Gujarat were possessing well-planned cities. According to historian, Mr. Irfan Habib (The Indus Civilization, page 24), Indus Civilization is the first culture, known where access to underground water was secured by wells. On rivers, lakes and bunded reservoirs, the lever-lift based on stone counterweights were used to provide drinking water as well as to irrigate the field. Mohenjodaro was built as a planned city on a large platform above the flood level. Spaces for roads were marked well before houses were built. Mohenjodaro had long broad roads running parallel with other roads, with lanes meeting them at right angles. No encroachments or construction on roadside was allowed showing detailed lay out of a planned city with sumptuous drinking water facility and sanitation (supra). The excavation of the Lothal (Gujarat) also shows that there was water reservoir to provide drinking water as well as irrigation facility.

Water is considered a purifier in most religions. Major faiths that incorporate ritual washing (ablution) include Hinduism, Christianity, Islam, Judaism, and Shinto. Water baptism is a central sacrament of Christianity. It is also a part of the practice of other religions, including Judaism (mikvah) and Sikhism (Amrit Sanskar). In Islam the five daily prayers can be done in most cases after completing washing certain parts of the body using clean water (wudu). In Shinto water is used in almost all rituals to cleanse a person or an area (*e.g.,* in the ritual of misogi). Water is mentioned in Bible 442 times in the New International Version and 363 times in the King James Version: 2 Peter 3:5 (b) states, "The earth was formed out of water and by water". Many religions also consider particular sources or bodies of water to be sacred or at least auspicious. Water is often believed to have spiritual powers. A Greek philosopher Empedocles held that water is one of the four classical elements along with fire, earth and air, and was regarded as the ylem or the basic substance of the universe. Historically, civilization has flourished around rivers and major waterways.

A.L. Basham, Professor of Asian Civilization in the Australian National University, Canberra in his book *"The Wonder That Was India"* said, to quote:—

> In 3000 B.C. the climate was very different. The whole Indus region was well forested, providing fuel to burn bricks and food for wild elephant and rhinoceros, and Baluchistan, now almost a waterless desert, was rich in rivers. This region supported many villagers of agriculturists, who had settled in the upland valleys of Baluchistan and in the then fertile plain of the Makran and the lower Indus.

According to A.L. Basham, when, in 326 B.C. Alexander of Macedon crossed the Indus, the climate of North West India was much as it is today, though perhaps a little moister. The river valleys were fertile and well wooded, though the coastal strip to the west of the Indus, now called the Makran and much of Baluchistan, were already dry and desolate. Indian used to live vigorous corporate life which continued into the Middle Ages. Tamil and Sanskrit inscriptions show that the village councils took an active interest in the communal welfare, dug and renewed reservoirs, made canals, improved the roads, and cared for the village shrines. This strong sense of the community was one of the chief factors in the survival of Indian culture (supra).

There is no dispute that in vedic period, the great Indian scholars had made great inventions and co-related the pleasure of human life with nature. The knowledge acquired in the vedic period has been codified in four veds.

Western historian believes that vedic period runs around 1500 B.C. and some of the Indian historian says that it is between 5000 B.C. and 6000 B.C. However, without entering into this controversy the hymns of Rigveda and Atharvaveda indicates the keen interest of our forefather in nature and its conservation.

Rigveda is the oldest manuscript in the world. Its secular credentials has been recognised all over world.

I wish to quote three hymns of Rigveda:—

"(I) Water contain
All disease-dispelling medicaments,
Useful for the upkeep of our body,
So that we may live long
To enjoy the bright sun.
(Ref: 1.23.2)

(II) That there is ambrosia in waters,
There is healing balm in them,
And there are medicinal herbs,
Know this all,
And by their proper use become wiser."
(Ref: 1.23.19)

(III) Some waters collect together,
Others join them.
As rivers they flow together
To a common reservoir (ocean).
The pure waters have gathered
Round the hydrodynamic power.
(Ref: 2.35.3)

In Atharvaveda also the importance of water, its purity and medicinal value have been noted, to quote from Atharvaveda:—

(1) "May the divine Waters be weal for us, for our aid and bliss. May they stream unto us health and strength. Within Waters lie all healing balms. Soma has told me, and Agni, good for all.

(2) O Waters, teeming with medicine, keep my body safe from harm that long I may see the Sun. O Waters of the plains, those of the marshes, and those got by digging, bestow weal on us and also that brought in a vessel and those of the rain be propitious to us all."

In Yajurveda the importance of water has been noticed in hymn, to quote:—

> "All-pervading and quick-reaching Wind is the Gandharva. The Waters and Saps which sustain life, are his Apsaras. May they guard us. All hail to them!

A great Indian King Bhartrhari who ruled in 7th century AD, in later period of life became saint and poet, in his splendid poem, addresses the five elements *i.e.,* Panchtatva of the Indian physics, to quote:—

> "Oh Earth, my mother, Air, my father, Oh Fire, my friend,
>
> Water, my kinsman, Space, my brother,
>
> here do I bow before you with folded hands!
>
> With your aid I have done good deeds and found clear knowledge,
> and, glorious, with all delusion past, I merge in highest Godhead."

The period of Chandragupta Maurya in Indian History is one of the golden period regulated by orderly life and strict discipline in administration. Chandragupta Maurya when ascended to throne around 321 B.C. had managed the affairs of the country with the help of Kautilya, who is also called Chankaya. The Arthshastra of Kautilya is valuable piece of, treatise dealing with political and administrative law to run the country. Its secular credentials are recognised in every walk of life. According to the Kautilya's Arthshastra (compiled by L.N. Rangarajan) it was mandatory for the villagers to subscribe from their own fund for construction of ponds or lakes within their area for water conservation.

The rules relating to sanitation were strict and mandatory for compliance by inhabitants of a city, to quote from Kautilya's Arthshastra:—

> "The rules on precautions against fire show that fire was a major hazard in a densely packed city (2.36.15-25). Craftsmen, like smiths, who worked with fire were concentrated in a separate quarter of the city (2.36.20). Maintenance of cleanliness, sanitation and hygiene was a part of house building regulations (2.36.26-33); so was privacy (3.8.17). The people were expected to contribute to building common facilities, not obstruct their use nor destroy them (3.8.26.27). Causing harm to an entire neighbourhood attracted a fine of 48 panas (3.20.15) (Kautilya, The Arthashastra, *L.N. Rangarajan* page 57).

However, rules relating to sanitation was relaxed in certain circumstances which includes illness or other infirmity of a person, to quote:—

> "The punishment prescribed for passing urine or faeces in public places is mitigated if the person did so due to illness, medication or fear {2.36.29}. The rules about sanitation in private dwellings in the city were relaxed during child birth {3.8.6}. Reduced punishments could be awarded for some offences if there were mitigating circumstances such as mistake, intoxication or temporary insanity (3.18.5; 3.19.4) (Kautilya, The Arthashastra, *L.N. Rangarajan* page 37)

The three characters of the Seminar namely conservation of water, safe drinking water and sanitation are interlinked. Without proper conservation of water citizens will not able to get safe drinking water and without proper sanitation management, the life of the citizens shall become unhygienic and prone to disease. Part IV of the Constitution of India under the head Directive Principle of State Policy contains mandate for the State while dealing with the welfare activities. Article 38 commands the State to secure social order for promotion of welfare of people. Article 39(B) relates to ownership and control of material resources and article 48 A of the Constitution of India compels the State to protect the environment and safeguard forest and wild life. Water harvesting is part and parcel of the environmental protection. article 51A(g) of the Constitution of India which relates to citizen's fundamental duties, provides that "it shall be the duty of every citizen to protect the natural environment including forest, lakes, rivers and wild life and to have a passion for living creatures". While expanding the horizon of article 21 of the Constitution of India by catena of judgment Supreme Court had settled the law that not only right to life but right to live with dignity and quality of life are fundamental rights guaranteed under Constitution of India.[1]

It has further been settled by apex court that right to life enshrined in article 21 means right to have something more than survival and not mere existence or animal existence. It includes all those aspects of life which go to make a man's life meaningful complete and worth living. Right to life also includes protection from all things, which causes health hazards due to pollution or use of harmful drugs. The right conferred under Part III of the Constitution of India *i.e.* Fundamental Rights and Directive Principle of State policy under Part IV are complementary to each other. It is the duty of State to ensure that citizens get unpolluted clean drinking water and lay out plan of the cities should be chalked out in such a manner which may provide hygienic condition in the cities and town areas of the State. In the case of *Kesavananda Bharati* v. *State of Kerala*,[2] and *Minerva*

1. *Kapila Hingorani* v. *State of Bihar,* (2003) 6 SCC 1: JT 2003 (5) SC 1.
2. Reported in *Keshvananda Bharati* v. *State of Kerala,* (1973) 4 SCC 225: AIR 1973 SC 1461.

Mills Ltd. v. *Union of India,*[1] Supreme Court held that Part III (Fundamental Rights) and Part IV (Directive Principle of the State Policy) of the Constitution of India together constitute the core of commitment of social revolution and combine to form its conscience of the Constitution. It is to be traced for deep understanding of the scheme of Indian Constitution. This principle has been reiterated by Supreme Court in a recent judgment of *I.R. Coelho* v. *State of Tamil Nadu,*[2] Meaning thereby it is the liability of State not only to take necessary steps to ensure the protection of natural resources including lakes, ponds, hill tops but also it is State's liability to see that citizens gets safe and clean drinking water and cities must be provided with an effective sanitation system to provide hygienic condition and to ensure the quality and dignity of life protected by article 21 of the Constitution of India. By catena of judgment the apex court[3] ruled that even under garb of planned and sustainable development of cities, the fundamental rights guaranteed by Part III of the Constitution of India particularly article 21 of the Constitution of India cannot be diluted or abrogated. I.R. Coelho (supra) says that the Constitution cannot be amended which may abrogate the fundamental rights of the citizens.

Various acts namely Uttar Pradesh Urban Planning and Development Act, 1973 and Uttar Pradesh Nagar Mahapalika Adhiniyam, 1959, Uttar Pradesh Municipalities Act and other statutes cast duty upon the State and local bodies to ensure that the citizens get safe drinking water and the Urban Development must consist the proper

1. (1980) 3 SCC 625: AIR 1980 SC 1789: 1980 Ker LT 573.
2. (2007) 2 SCC 1: AIR 2007 SC 861: 2007 AIR SCW 611.
3. *Vide; M.C. Mehta* v. *Union of India,* (2004) 12 SCC 118: AIR 2004 SC 4016: 2004 AIR SCW 4033; *Subhash Kumar* v. *State of Bihar,* (1991) 1 SCC 598: AIR 1991 SC 420: 1991 AIR SCW 121; *T.N. Godavarman Thirumulpad* v. *Union of India,* (2006) 1 SCC 1: AIR 2006 SC 4256: 2005 AIR SCW 5110; *Hinch Lal Tiwari* v. *Kamala Devi,* (2001) 6 SCC 496: AIR 2001 SC 3216: 2001 AIR SCW 2865; *Intellectuals Forum, Tirupathi* v. *State of Andhra Pradesh,* (2006) 3 SCC 549: AIR 2006 SC 1350: 2006 AIR SCW 1309.

sanitation system to provide hygienic condition. Every State of the country possess identical statutes to regulate urban planning. However, once we take notice of the ground realities we will find that in most part of the country during rainy season citizens suffer with serious consequences because of water logging in view of bad sanitation. Whether it is Bombay, Delhi, Lucknow, Hyderabad, Kolkata or other cities of the country the executive has been failed to take care with preventive steps and maintain the sanitation system by enforcing the law with firm hand in its letter and spirit. Newspaper reports reveal the death of citizen in various parts of the country because of epidemic or bad sanitary system with water-born disease including in Lucknow is not uncommon.

According to report of WHO, almost more than 1000 children die every day due to diarrhoea. Infant mortality disease because of bad sanitation rates highest and in Uttar Pradesh, it is 72 out of 1000 because of bad sanitation. The worst effected segment of our society are women and children especially poor and down-trodden segments of society. Though, hand pumps have been installed in urban and rural areas but because of lack of maintenance the majority of them are non-functional. However, time is not far when majority of hand pumps and tubewells and wells shall become non-functional because of receding of underground water level. It is unfortunate that inspite of lapse of 60 years, the post-independent India has been failed to provide safe and pure drinking water and good hygienic condition. According to report, 55,000 children upto the age of one year, die every year in the State of Uttar Pradesh Needless to say that water-born disease is not uncommon, not only in the State of Uttar Pradesh but other parts of the country also.

Waterbodies which are natural resources, are being encroached not only by the land mafia, individual persons but also by the State instrumentalities. The *modus operendi* for destroying the lake or pond is simple and systematic.

The municipality starts with dumping garbage into the lake. Domestic and industrial effluents are let into the lakes. Grass, weeds and water hyacinth are never removed. The lake gradually dies and slums, colonies or other 'development projects' spring up near it. The nexus between persons affiliated with political parties, government agencies, land grabbers and criminals is strong and powerful, with adequate muscle and money power.

So far as the State of Uttar Pradesh is concerned, while deciding a case of *Rajendra* v. *Additional Commissioner, Devi Patan Mandal, Gonda,*[1] I have taken note of situations relating to encroachments over waterbodies. It is astonishing to note that waterbodies, ponds, lakes in the State of Uttar Pradesh have been encroached not only by common citizen or persons or land grabbers or mafia or villagers to construct houses but it has been also encroached by local bodies like Nagar Palika, Nagar Nigam and Development Authorities in systematic way. In a planned manner development authorities had sold the part of water bodies for construction of houses, buildings and commercial complexes. In pursuance to apex court judgment *Hinch Lal Tiwari* v. *Kamala Devi,*[2] State Government had issued an order dated 8-10-2001 for the restoration and protection of waterbodies but even then the developmental authorities like Lucknow Development Authority, Ghaziabad Development Authority, Gorakhpur Development Authority and others, continue to allot waterbodies to builders and other influential persons. The result is, almost in entire State of Uttar Pradesh the underground water level, is receding at the rate of 20 to 125 centimetre every year. In a judgment delivered by Hon'ble Mr. Justice S.N. Srivastava, at Allahabad, the State was directed to restore waterbodies of rural area. The State and its instrumentality or local bodies who are responsible to maintain the water reservoir, have become the wrongdoers and are the main

1. 2007 (25) LCD 565.
2. (2001) 6 SCC 496: AIR 2001 SC 3216: 2001 AIR SCW 2865.

violators of apex court judgment. It has been noticed that in pursuance of the judgment of apex court or orders of High Court, State after issuance of an order or circular forget its responsibility to enforce it. Law is not the black letter existing in statute books but it is the action taken by the authorities concerned to implement the law in real sense is the rule of law. More than three decades of experience at Bar and Bench, I have noticed that a trend has been developed ordinarily to implement only those judgments which are monitored by courts whether it is High Court or Supreme Court. The case of *Hinch Lal Tiwari (supra)* is an example where apex court judgment has been blatantly not complied with by the State authorities.

Bundelkhand and Agra regions of the State of Uttar Pradesh, are water scared regions where water-related crimes are much higher than the other parts of the State. In case, newspaper reports are believed, people use to guard their waterbodies in the night in groups and because of water shortage. Not only irrigation is seriously affected, the people are suffering from various water born diseases as well as scuffle took place to meet out the water requirements.

I have seen a special report of electronic media telecast by 17-8-2007 at 10:30 p.m. [by NDTV] covering the water crisis of Bundelkhand area having 7 districts of State of Uttar Pradesh namely, Jhansi, Mahoba, Lalitpur, Banda, Chitrakut, Hamirpur and Jalaun and 6 districts of State of Madhya Pradesh namely, Chhatarpur, Damoh, Datia, Panna, Sagar and Tikamgarh. According to live telecast of the electronic media [NDTV], the lower class of the society is using the same water which is extracted from pits for drinking as well as to fulfill other needs. It is not uncommon because of water-related disputes, murders took place between the parties and peoples fight with each other to get hold of wells, hand pumps and other water reservoirs in Bundelkhand area of Uttar Pradesh According to report, the reduction of underground water level in Bundelkhand area is more than 1.5 metre per year.

According to one other report published in 'Indian Express' newspaper (Lucknow Edn.) on 18-8-2007, due to frequent draughts excessive exploitation of land minor cracks have been noticed in the agricultural fields in a village Jigni of Rath Tahsil of district Hamirpur in Bundelkhand. Tensional cracks have been noticed in earth having depth of 4 ft. to 50 ft. and some of the villagers have deserted from their native place. Statement of Lavkush Tripathi, Tahsildar of Tahsil concerned as appeared in the newspaper reveals that out of 200 houses in the village, 50% villagers have deserted. However, some of them are gradually returning to their homes. It may be noted that Bundelkhand area was mostly forested until the late of 18th century when intensive logging of the forests accelerated. Deforestation accelerated after the consolidation of British control in the 19th century. The consequence of deforestation is one of the reason because of which the people of Bundelkhand are suffering today. The State has started to pay price of its animosity with the nature and because of ecological imbalance.

Dr. Rajendra Prasad as well as Dr. B.R. Ambedkar while making their concluding speeches in the constitution assembly were of the view that it is not the constitution which may be termed as good or bad but it is the person who manned it makes the Constitution good or bad. In case persons having foresight, sincerity, honesty and competence are at the helm of affair in a country, then even the bad constitution or law, may give good result. Because of corruption and casteism in our system, least interests are taken to chalk out developmental plan with foresightedness relying upon expert opinions. In case some positive steps are taken at particular point of time at later stage, such actions are made redundant.

We may take note of the fact that even the "master plan' prepared for cities are changed from time to time for extraneous reasons. For good sanitation instead of creating scientific drainage system, with sufficient infrastructure, old one-constructed decades before, have been encroached upon without any authority in violation of constitutional mandate, and their use is changed. The widths of drains and canals constructed before decades rather, a century back, are reduced for extraneous reasons and constructions are done on its banks by change of use of land. The residential areas are converted into commercial and commercial to residential for extraneous reasons and such actions on the part of authorities, badly affect the sanitation system which were originally planned, and such actions are contrary to spirit of planned development of a city.

Elected representatives have got their own problems. That is why, the scheme of permanent bureaucracy was adopted by constitutional framers for the planned development of the country, which may not be adversely affected by the change of Governments. It is always expected that bureaucracy shall not yield to the political pressure and shall stick to law and constitutional mandate. But things seem to be otherwise. That is why, India is likely to become water starved country in few decades.

Once Mahatma Gandhi said, civilisation is, the mode of conduct which points out to man the path of duty. Performance of duty and observance of morality are convertible terms. In constitutional purview it is the duty of every person to follow the pursuit of article 51A of the Constitution (Fundamental Duties).

The standard sanitation technology in urban areas is the collection of waste water in sewers, and treatment in "wastewater treatment plants" for reuse or disposal in rivers, lakes or the sea. Sewers are either combined with storm drains or separated from them as sanitary sewers. Combined sewers are usually found in the central, older parts or urban areas. Heavy rainfall, and inadequate maintenance can lead to combined sewer overflows or sanitary sewer overflows, *i.e.,* more or less diluted raw sewage being discharged into the environment. Industries often discharge wastewater into municipal sewers, which can complicate wastewater treatment unless industries pre-treat their discharges. Discharge of industrial wastewater into river is causing serious threat to various rivers of the country. We may take notice of the fact that millions of rupees have been invested in Ganga action plan and even for the river Gomti without any outcome. Reasons need not to be discussed being well-known. Disposal of solid waste in rivers and absence of recycling plans are causing hazards to public health.

UNESCO's World Water Development Report (WWDR, 2003) from its World Water Assessment Programme indicates that, in the next 20 years, the quantity of water available to everyone is predicted to decrease by 30%. 40% of the world's inhabitants currently have insufficient fresh water for minimal hygiene. More than 2.2 million people died in 2000 from diseases related to the consumption of contaminated water or drought. In 2004, the UK Charity Water Aid reported that a child dies every 15 seconds from easily preventable water-related diseases; often this means lack of sewage disposal and bad sanitation system. United Nations Development Programme sums up world water distribution in the 2006 development report, to quote:

> "While one part of the world sustains a designer bottledwater market that generates no tangible health benefits, another part suffers acute public health risks because people have to drink water from drains or from lakes and rivers".

Drinking water as well as fresh water for its extensive use in agriculture, now become more precious than ever in our history. Availability of water and to provide safe and pure drinking water coupled with efficient sanitary system, are two fields of the basic need of a civilised society.

Polluting water may be the biggest single misuse of water; to the extent that a pollutant limits other uses of the water, it becomes a waste of the recourse, regardless of benefits to public health. People pay price of water pollution, while the private firms' profits are not redistributed to the local population victim of this pollution. Pharmaceuticals consumed by humans often end up in the waterways and can have detrimental effects on aquatic life if they bio-accumulate and if they are not biodegradable.

It is high time when the Government should gear up and take remedial measures to provide safe drinking water and should make water harvesting compulsory and create artificial waterbodies, reservoirs and restoring the old one coupled with efficient sanitation system to maintain the underground water level. Old drainage system should be restored and renovated by removing encroachments. Efforts made by some of the countries for water harvesting and to regulate water supply have been discussed by me in the case of *Rajendra* (supra). Hence need not be repeated again.

There is one more reason why old waterbodies should be restored and new one should also be created. From research, it has been borne out that atmospheric temperature over the seas is less than the temperature of the area covered by land. Accordingly, restoration of waterbodies is also necessary to minimise the global warming as noticed by scientists by various research projects.

No doubt because of population growth, to some extent city planners compromise for one or the other reason by encroaching the waterbodies but we must keep in mind that we can live without multi-storied buildings by taking shelter in huts or in rural areas, but it is impossible to live without safe drinking water and good sanitation system and hygienic condition.

Francesco Sindico, a University research fellow had presented a lecture at the International Conference on Human Security and Climate Change. It was published in *New Zealand Journal of Environmental Law* Vol. 9 pp. 209-238 in the year 2005 and has also been published in *'The Icfai Journal of Environmental Law'*, January, 2007 Vol. VI No. 1 wherein he has observed that world is gradually moving towards a situation where the countries shall fight each other to get hold of waterbodies, rivers and reservoirs to meet out their requirements.

It is irony that we speak much, legislate too much, decisions are enormous but enforcement of law in their letter and spirit, is minimum.

Lord Denning in his famous treatise, *"The Discipline of Law'* (page 61) had rightly said, to quote:

> "Our procedure for securing personal freedom is efficient, but our procedure for preventing the abuse of power is not."

The observation of Lord Denning is more correct for India than England.

It is unfortunate that nothing has been done to provide efficient machinery to preserve and protect waterbodies and create new one and make water harvesting compulsory. Orders passed by Supreme Court or High Courts are not being implemented in their letters and spirit. Society at large is likely to face acute water crisis and may be, after 100 years or 200 years, State may be compelled to sell water through fair price shops as "essential commodity". It is possible that some of the cities of the country shall convert into desert in the manner the policy-makers and bureaucrats are functioning in our country. After 300 years substantial portion of our country including some part of the State of Uttar Pradesh, may become desert in case no remedial steps are taken. It is not the question of only present and coming generation but it is also the question of our survival after rebirth. It is not necessary that we shall achieve salvation or Moksh. Because of good deeds, some of us again may reborn as human being or some may reborn in the form of other creature of world at any place on this earth. Our soul in "new body" shall suffer because of our own faults or inactions in the form of coming generation. That is why in Rigveda, the author prays to Almighty in repentance to forgive for things done resulting in destruction of waterbodies to quote:—

O powerful waters
I might have violated
The laws of Nature
Knowingly or unknowingly,
Foolishly or impudently.
Take away whatever is wrong
Or deficient in me.

I wish to conclude with couplet of *Geetanjali,* written by Noble Laureate, nationalist and poet of this country Sri Ravindra Nath Tagore:

> "Where the mind is without fear and the
> head is held high............
> Into that Heaven of freedom my Father,
> let my country awake."

Swami Vivekanand—The Soul of India

"...................Him worship, and break all other idols!
Ye fools! who neglect the living God,
And His infinite reflections with which the world is full.

While ye run after imaginary shadows,
That lead alone to fights and quarrels,
Him worship, the only visible!
Break all other idols![1]

Vivekanand, the propagator of 'world religion', born on 12-1-1863. Mother Bhubaneswari Devi fervently visited Vishwanath temple of Varanasi with the prayer resulting incarnation of Vivekanand. Bhubneshwari Devi decided with the agreement of husband Bisvanath Datta, a successful lawyer of Calcutta High Court, that their son would be called Vireshwara, one of the many names of Lord Shiva, by whose blessings they owed their second son. Later, he became Narendranath, 'Narendra' or 'Naren' to his friends.

Vivekanand's grandfather Durgaprasad renounced the world when he was only 25 years old took to the ochre robe leaving behind wife and a son. Since, Vivekanand was born in the family of three generations of highly successful and rich lawyer, the professionalism alongwith spiritualism ran in his blood.

---

1. From 'The Living God' (Written to an American friend from Almora on 9-7-1987 by Swami Vivekanand).

The life of Swami Vivekanand is inseparable from his changing response to social condition of the Indian sub-continent as well as west. He was committed disciple of his Guru Ram Krishna Paramhans and vedanti in thought and action. He has given new meaning to Vedanta and repudiated in his teaching and also by his conduct the notion of sanyas based on renunciation of world. Even after sanyas he remain attached to his mother Bhubneshwari Devi till last breath of life. He was critical of collection of wealth by the temples without utilizing the fund to serve the downtrodden. He was greatest reverence of Lord Buddha in spite being disciple of Swami Ram Krishna Paramhans and Sharda Devi.[1]

Vivekanand lived and worked for less than forty years but his life may be judged from the intensity and expansiveness in the mode of his working. He spent life mostly in hardship and self-denial, often oblivious of basic need, dedicated to a cause which ultimately consumed it prematurely in early age. He was not a 'sadhak' for 'moksh' but given his life to philosophical disputation and to eradicate conservative way of life.

Swami Vivekanand was proud to say that his religion taught him the word 'tolerance' and 'universal acceptance'. He further proud to say that India have sheltered the persecuted and the refugees of all religions and all the nations of the earth. His reverberating calls to 'Arise', 'Awake' and 'Stop Not till the Goal is Reached' ignited the mind of young men.

While considering the cause of downfall of India, Swami Vivekanand opined that it is because of neglect of the masses. The uncared-for lower classes, the peasants and weavers, downtrodden, untouchability has resulted into defeat by foreigners.

Swami Vivekanand was of the view that the country carries on its legacy because of the masses who from time

1. Swami Vivekanand the living vedanta by Chaturvedi Badrinath.

immemorial have been working silently without even getting the remuneration of their labours.[1]

Swami Vivekanand observed, to quote:—

> "The poor, the low, the sinner in India have no friends, no help-they cannot rise, try however they may. They sink lower and lower every day, they feel the blows showered upon them by a cruel society and they do not know whence the blow comes."[2]

Swami Vivekanand further opined, to quote:—

> "The one thing that is at the root of all evils in India is the condition of the poor.....Priest-power and foreign conquest have trodden them down for centuries, and at last the poor of India have forgotten that they are human beings.[3]

Swami Vivekanand opined that in ancient India in one hand the priesthood stood between the lawless social tyranny of the princes over the masses, whom the Kshatriyas declared to be their legal food, on the other hand, the Kshatriya power was the one potent force which struggled with any success against the spiritual tyranny of the priesthood and the ever-increasing chain of ceremonials which they were forging to blind down the people with.[4]

While appreciating the Buddhistic movement and death of Buddhism in his own country with the advent of Sankara in quick succession by Ramanuja and Madhava and revival of vedanta, Swami Vivekanand observed, to quote:—

> "In the Buddhistic movement, the Kshatriyas were the real leaders, and whole masses of them became Buddhists. In the zeal of reform and conversion, the popular dialects had been almost exclusively cultivated, to the neglect of Sanskrit, and the larger portion of Kshatriyas had become disjointed from the

1. The complete works of Swami Vivekanand-Volume VII page 538.
2. Letters of Swami Vivekanand, page 40.
3. Letters of Swami Vivekanand, pages 117-118.
4. My India: The India Eternal, Swami Vivekanand, page 21.

Vedic literature and Sanskrit learning. Thus this wave of reform, which came from the South, benefited to a certain extent the priesthood, and the priests only. For the rest of India's millions, it forged more chains than they had ever known before.

The Kshatriyas have always been the backbone of India, so also they had been the supporters of science and liberty, and their voices had rung out again and again to clear the land from superstitions; and throughout the history of India they ever formed the invulnerable barrier to aggressive priestly tyranny.

When the greater part of their number sank into ignorance, and another portion mixed their blood with savages from Central Asia and lent their swords to establish the rules of priests in India, her cup became full to the brim, and down sank the land of Bharata, not to rise again, until the Kshatriya rouses himself, and making himself free, strikes the chains from the feet of the rest.[1]"

Vivekanand was of the view that no religion on earth preaches the dignity of humanity in such a lofty strain as Hinduism, and no religion on earth treads upon the necks of the poor and the low in such a fashion as Hinduism.[2]

Vivekanand was very critical to charitable associations in not discharging their obligation for the well being of the poor. He questioned, how many people really weep for the sorrows and sufferings of the millions of poor in India? The untouchability had ruined the entire system. He reminded the bane of India with "the greatest of all truths", discovered by ancestors, is that the universe is one. Can one injure anyone without injuring himself?

The chief cause of India's ruin has been the monopolizing of the whole education and intelligence of the land, by dint of pride and royal authority, among a handful of men.[3]

1. My India: The India Eternal, Swami Vivekanand, page 23.
2. The complete works of Swami Vivekanand-Volume V page 15.
3. Letters of Swami Vivekanand, page 328.

Swami Vivekanand was of opinion, for centuries Indian were taught theory of degradation. They have been so frightened for centuries, till they have nearly become animals. Never were they allowed to hear of the *atman*.[1]

Swami Vivekanand was of the view that all must get equal opportunity and leave the habit of not doing anything on own, to quote:—

> "We would do nothing ourselves and would scoff at others who try to do something-this is the bane that has brought about our downfall as a nation. Want of sympathy and lack of energy are at the root of all misery, and you must therefor give these two up. Who but the Lord knows what potentialities there are in particular individuals—let all have opportunities, and leave the rest to the Lord. It is indeed very difficult to have an equal love for all, but without it there is no mukti.[2]"

One other cause realized by Swami Vivekanand was narrow thought living in shell as the oyster and refusal to give the life-giving truths with thirsting nations outside the Aryan fold.

While speaking to eradicate untouchability and uplift the pride of Scheduled Caste, Swami Vivekanand said, to quote:—

> "No man, no nation, my son, can hate others and live; India's doom was sealed the very day they invented the word mleccha and stopped from communion with others."[3]

Vivekanand further questioned the hate perceived during centuries against large section of society, to quote:—

> "Whatever cloak ancient or modern sophistry may try to throw over it, the inevitable result—the vindication of the moral law, that none can hate

1. The complete works of Swami Vivekanand-Volume III, page 224.
2. The complete works of Swami Vivekanand-Volume VI, page 357.
3. The complete works of Swami Vivekanand-Volume V, page 52.

> others without degenerating himself-is that the race that was foremost amongst the ancient races is now a byword, and a scorn among nations.[1]

Vivekanand was critical of Indian masses lacking the faculty of organization. On account of lack of organization quality Indian suffered since centuries and the flaw still exists. He was upset from the fact that the country possessing greatness of Upanishad and Vedic text missing ancestral of sages in comparison to other ratio, it suffering from evils.

The laziness crept in India since centuries resulted into selfishness and downfall of civilization. The speaking and not doing has become a habit with Indians. He opined that Indians have two great evils *i.e.* trampling on the women and grinding the poor through caste restriction. The worshiper of Sakti does not know that God is the omnipresent force in the universe and in women the manifestation of those source exists.

Vivekanand predicted that India shall attain freedom in fifty years. He further predicted that proletariat revolution should take place either in Russia or in China. The third prediction was that India would carry prosperity and power far more than she had done in the past. However, present picture of India gives no hint of such a possibility. Far from such an augury, the India is beleaguered by problems which some think may very well spell her doom. The problems include poverty, illiteracy and casteism, corruption and criminalization of politics.

Vivekanand came to light and world accepted his ability, knowledge and spiritual power from the speech given on 2nd November, 1893 at Chicago (U.S.A) when he addressed the American as "brother and sister" there was clapping for more than two minutes. He placed the American giving due importance to women while reiterating with proud that he belong to religion which has sheltered and still fostering the remnant of grand Zoroastrian nation. He quoted in

1. Letters of Swami Vivekanand, page 172.

conference a hymn from Veda which according to him he repeatedly singing since childhood, to quote:—

> "As the different streams having their
> sources in different places all mingle their
> water in the sea, so, O Lord, the different
> paths which men take through different
> tendencies, various though they appear,
> crooked or straight, all lead to Thee...."
> I fervently hope that the bell that
> tolled this morning in honour of this
> convention may be the death-knell of all
> fanaticism, of all persecutions with the
> sword or with the pen, and of all
> uncharitable feelings between persons
> wending their way to the same goal.[1]"

Once he said that he would come again in about two hundred years when a Master comes along his own people. Swami Vivekanand has taken his last breath at Belur Math (Calcutta). During last days in Belur Math on 26-12-1900 he wrote, to quote:—

> "I look behind and after
> And find that all is right,
> In my deepest sorrows
> There is a soul of light.[2]"

Romain Rolland, French Nobel Laureate, written the Biography of Vivekanand and said, to quote:—

> "I am bringing to Europe, as yet unaware of it, the fruit of a new autumn, a new message of the Soul, the symphony of India. Vivekanand has serenely wedded the West and the East. He saw that his first duty was towards his first neighbour, his own people. His universal soul was rooted in its human soul and the smallest pang suffered by its inarticulate flesh sent a repercussion through the whole tree. His claim to greatness lies in the fact that he not only proved its

1. Swami Vivekanand on himself, page 129.
2. Swami Vivekanand on himself, page 334.

> unity by reason, but stamped it upon the heart of India in flashes of illumination. He had a genius for arresting words and burning phrases hammered out white hot in the forge of his soul so that they transpierced thousands. It may justly be said that India's destiny was changed by him, and that this teaching re-echoed throughout humanity.[1]"

The influence and relevance of Swami Vivekanand should be looked into the present scenario and ground realities keeping in view the communalism, casteism, corruption, poverty and inaction in the public and various limbs of the Government. The Indian vision of life is full of love, compassion, inter-dependence and co-existence. Ved and Upnishads see oneness in the whole of creation. Life is full of struggle, pain and miseries and calls for consistent effort by doing own duties and "Karm" to achieve the goal. The goal is peace and harmony in the society along with food, cloth and shelter for the peoples of the country. The illusory destination cannot bring us happiness. Peace and joy can only come through the shedding of desires and detachment to lusty life. The ancient Indian philosophy speaks of the pain of the life and that is why, it was received with open arms where it reached. The culture of "continence" was nurtured by knowledge and philosophy of life propagated from time to time, by Indian philosophers, saints and preachers in its thousands years of its civilization by noble souls born from time to time. Vivekanand is one of them.

According to Romain Rolland,[2] Swami Vivekanand was a pure soul chosen by Bhagwan Ram Krishna to enlight not only the Indians but the whole world and show the right path, in the era when the country was struggling for independence, peoples were depressed and fighting with not only the Britishers but also among themselves on the basis of caste, creed and religion. Majority of the population was poor and starving.

---

1. A colossus named Vivekanand (whose mission awaits completion) published in 1931, New revised edition, 2010, page 14.
2. *Ibid.*

Romain Rolland, while writing the biography of Swami Vivekanand, in 1927-28 further observed, to quote:

> "But the flame of that pyre is till alight today. From his ashes, like those of the Phoenix of old, had sprung anew the conscience of India—the magic bird—faith in her unity and in the Great Message, brooded over from Vedic times by the deaming spirit of his ancient race—the message for which it must render account to the rest of mankind.[1]"

Swami Vivekanand himself in a letter, written on 1-11-1896, observed that human society is in turn governed by the four castes—the priests, the soldiers, the traders, and the labourers. Each state has its glories as well as its defects. Swami Ji observed to quote:

> "If it is possible to form a state in which the knowledge of the priest period, the culture of the military, the distributive spirit of the commercial, and the ideal of equality of the last can all be kept intact, minus their evils, it will be an ideal state. But is it possible?[2]"

Meaning thereby, Swami Vivekanand was of the view that every Indian should be given opportunity with all facilities and training to develop in such a manner so that he or she may inculcate all the qualities of 'four-fold order'. Needless to say that in case the vision of Swami Vivekanand is implemented, there shall not be any hatred nor discrimination in the society on the basis of cast, creed or religion.

While writing another letter on 3-1-1896, Swami Vivekanand observed that the present caste is not the real Jati, but a hindrance to its progress. It really has prevented the free action of Jati, *i.e.*, caste or variation. According to Vivekanand, India fell because it failed to abolish caste, and adapt system based on Karm. Every phase of aristocracy or

---

1. A colossus named Vivekanand (whose mission awaits completion) published in 1931, New revised edition, 2010, page 14.
2. Letters of Swami Vivekanand.

privileged caste is a blow to caste and is out-caste. The second thrust of Swami Vivekanand is to educate India. According to Swami Ji, the Vedic doctrine of Karma is the same as in Judaism and all other religions, that is to say, the purification of the mind through sacrifices and such other external means—and Buddha was the first man who stood against it. But the inner essence of the ideas remained as of old look at that doctrine of mental exercises which he preached, and that mandate of his to believe in the Sutas instead of the Vedas. Caste also remained as of old (caste was not wholly obsolete at the time of Buddha), but it was not determined by personal qualification.[1]

Emphasis of Swami Vivekanand is for knowledge coupled with Karm which is the decisive factor to determine one's cast.

In a letter dated 24-4-1897, Swami Ji observed, to quote:

> "The only way to solve problem of India is to educate peoples. Swami Ji observed that the main cause of India's ruin has been the monopolising of the whole education and intelligence of land, by dint of pride and royal authority, among a handful of men. If we are to rise again, we shall have to do it in the same way, *i.e.*, by spreading education among the masses. A great fuss has been made for half a century about social reform."
>
> "Education, education, education alone! Travelling through many cities of Europe and observing in them the comforts and education of even the poor people, it was brought to my mind the state of our own poor people, and I used to shed tears. What made the difference? Education was the answer I got. Through education comes faith in one's own self, and through faith in one's own self the inherent Brahman is waking-up in them, while the Brahmin in us is gradually becoming dormant."

1. Swami Ji, Letter dated February, 1890.

I would say what Swami Ji means is, the real unpolluted education with a goal to make a man perfect not only in the literary field but also to fight with the odds of life for national development. It is unfortunate that the system we possess is not the same education which Swami Vivekanand professes. A lot of corruption and evil have crept in our education and governance. Whatever we possess, seem to be our faulty system and peoples in general are not discharging their obligations in just and fair manner.

Mahatma Gandhi as well as Dr. Radhakrishnan also in their lectures, opined that purpose of education is to check and control animal instinct but it appears that we are moving in reverse direction.

Swami Vivekanand said, to quote:

> "The Education that our boys receive is very negative. The schoolboy learns nothing, but has everything of his own broken down want of Shraddha (Faith) is the result. The Shraddha which emboldened nachiketa to face Yama and question him, through which Shraddha this world moved the annihilation of that Shraddha! अज्ञश्रवाश्रद्धानश्रवा संशयात्मा विनश्यति – "The ignorant, the man devoid of Shraddha, the doubting self runs to ruin." Therefore, are we so near destruction. The remedy now is, the spread of education. First of all, Self-knowledge. I do not mean thereby, matted hair, staff, Kamandalu, and mountain caves which the word suggest. What do I mean then? Cannot the knowledge, by which is attained even freedom from the bondage of worldly existence, bring ordinary material prosperity? Certainly it can. Freedom, dispassion, renunciation – all these are the very highest ideals, but स्पज्पूप्यस्य धर्मस्य त्रायते महतो भयात् – "Even a little of this Dharma saves one from the great fear (of birth and death)."[1]

1. Letter of Swami Ji, written on 24-4-1897.

While showing deep concern with regard to faulty education system, we possess, Swami Vivekanand said, to quote:

> "The education that you are getting now has some good points, but it has a tremendous disadvantage which is so great that the good things are all weighed down. In the first place it is not a man making education, it is merely and entirely a negative education. A negative education, or any training that is based on negation, is worse than death. The child is taken to school, and the first thing he learns is that his father is a fool, the second thing, that his grandfather is a lunatic, the third thing that all his teachers are hypocrites, the fourth, that all the sacred books are lies! By the time he is sixteen he is a mass of negation, lifeless and boneless. And the result is that fifty years of such education has not produced one original man in the three Presidencies. Even man of originality that has been produced has been educated elsewhere, and not in this country, or they have gone to the old universities once more to cleanse themselves of superstitions. Education is not the amount of information that is put into your brain and runs riot there, undigested, all your life. We must have life-building, man-making, character-making assimilation of ideas. If you have assimilated five ideas and made them your life and character, you have more education than any man who has got by heart a whole library. यथा खरश्चन्दनभारवाही भारयस्य वेत्ता न तु चन्दनस्य –"The ass carrying its load of sandalwood knows only the weight and not the value of the sandalwood." If education is identical with information, the libraries are the greatest sages in the world, and encyclopaedias are the Rishis. The ideal therefore is that we must have the

whole education of our country, spiritual and secular, in our own hands, and it must be on national lines, through national methods, as far as practicable.[1]"

Swami Vivekanand further while writing a letter dated 24-4-1897 to Sarala Ghoshal, deprecated the monopolization of education by one sects of the society. He was of the view that every citizen has got right of learning and education. No person should be deprived of education for any reason whatsoever. Swami Ji observed, to quote:

> "From the day when education and culture, etc., began to spread gradually from patricians to plebeians, grew the distinction between the modern civilization as of Western countries and the ancient civilization of India, Egypt, Rome, etc., I see it before my eyes, a nation is advanced in proportion as education and intelligence spread among the masses. The chief cause of India's ruin has been the monopolising of the whole education and intelligence of the land, by dint of pride and royal authority, among a handful of men. If we are to rise again, we shall have to do in the same way, *i.e.*, by spreading education among the masses."

Swami Ji was disturbed with the untouchability and communalism and said that it is a social evil and obstacle in the development of country. He says to quote:

> "What can you expect of a race which for hundreds of years has been busy in discussing such momentous problems as whether we should drink a glass of water with the right hand or the left? What more degradation can there be than that the greatest minds of a country have been discussing about the kitchen for several hundreds of years, discussing whether I may touch you or you touch me, and what is the penance for this touching! The themes of the Vedanta, the sublimest and the most glorious

1. *Selection from the Complete Works of Swami Vivekanand, pages 290-291.*

conceptions of God and soul ever preached on earth, were halflost, buried in the forest, preserved by a few Sannyasins, while the rest of the nation discussed the momentous questions of touching each other, and dress and food.[1]"

Swami Ji speaks to break all the existing barriers dividing the humanity on one or the other ground and said, to quote:

"A broader and more generous conception of life is before us; and although at first we have been deluded a little and wanted to narrow things down, we are finding out today that these generous impulses which are at work, these broader conceptions of life, are the logical interpretation of what is in our ancient books. They are the carrying out, to the rigorously logical effect of the primary conceptions of our own ancestors. To become broad, to go out, to amalgamate, to universalise, is the end of our aims. And all the time we have been making ourselves smaller and smaller, and dissociating ourselves, contrary to the plans laid down in our scriptures.[2]"

According to Swami Vivekanand, Advaitism is the last word of religion. Only by following Advaitism, one can look upon all religions and sects with love. It shall be religion of future "enlightened humanity". He speaks to harmonise the different religions to serve humanity. He was disturbed by the inner division of Hindu community. While writing a letter to one of his friends on 10.6.1898, Swami Vivekanand opined, to quote:

"My experience is that if ever any religion approached to this equality in an appreciable manner, it is Islam and Islam alone.

Therefore, I am firmly persuaded that without the help of practical Islam, theories of Vedantism, however fine and

1. *Selection from the Complete Works of Swami Vivekanand, page 2321.*
2. *Selection from the Complete Works of Swami Vivekanand, page 233.*

wonderful they may be, are entirely valuable to the vast mass of mankind. We want to lead mankind to the place where there is neither the Vedas, nor the Bible, nor the Koran; yet this has to be done by harmonizing the Vedas, the Bible, and the Koran. Mankind ought to be taught that religious are but the varied expressions of THE RELIGION, which is Oneness, so that each may choose the path that suits him best.

For our own motherland a junction of the two great systems, Hinduism and Islam—Vedanta brain and Islam body—is the only hope.[1]

Those who are involved in communalism, religious Jehad or religious favouritism and fanatism may be inspired by Swami Vivekanand's logical and constructive approach for social harmony and peace. Swami Ji on one hand, proclaimed religion at highest pedestal of human thought and life, on other hand, found religion as the main cause for creating hatred and conflict across the world.

According to Swami Ji, to quote:

> "Religion is the highest plane of human thought and life, and herein we find that the workings of these two forces have been most marked. The interest love that humanity has ever known has come from religion, and the most diabolical hatred that humanity has known has also come from religion. The noblest words of peace that the world has ever heard have come from men on the religious plane, and the bitterest denunciation that the world has ever known has been uttered by religious men. The higher the object of any religion and the finer its organisation, the more remarkable are its activities. No other human motive has deluged the world with blood so much as religion; at the same time, nothing has brought into existent so many hospitals and asylums for the poor; no other human influence has taken such care, not only of humanity, but also of the lowest of

1. *Letter dated 10-6-1898 of Swami Vivekanand from "Letters of Swami Vivekanand"*

animals, as religion has done. Nothing makes us so cruel as religion, and nothing makes us so tender as religion. This has been so in the past, and will also, in all probability, be so in the future. Yet out of the midst of this din and turmoil, this strife and struggle, this hatred and jealousy of religious and sects, there have arisen, from time to time, potent voices, drowning all this noise—making themselves heard from pole to pole, as it were—proclaiming peace and harmony. Will it ever come?[1]"

Swami Vivekanand found that ignorant people have used the religion to create conflict and disharmony in society. Religions have three ingredients *viz.*—philosophy, mythology and rituals. Religious fanatism is one of the most dangerous disease. Individually, it is hard to found any universal features in religions. Yet unity in variety is the plan of the universe. Each one is growing and developing according to own nature. A religion to satisfy largest portion of mankind must be able to supply food for various types of mind. Such religions can be attained by Yoga—*i.e.*, union. According to Swami Vivekanand, to quote:

> "And this religion is attained by what we, in India, call Yoga—union. To the worker, it is union between men and the whole of humanity; to the mystic, between his lower and Higher Self; to the lover, union between himself and the God of Love; and to the philosopher, it is the union of all existence. This is what is meant by Yoga. This is a Sanskrit term, and these four divisions of Yoga have in Sanskrit different names. The man who seeks after this kind of union is called a Yogi. The worker is called the Karma-Yogi. He who seeks the union through love is called the Bhakti-Yogi. He who seeks it through mysticism is called the Raja-Yogi. And he who seeks it through philosophy is called the Juana-Yogi. So this word Yogi comprises them all.[2]"

---

1. *Selection from the Complete Works of Swami Vivekanand, page 157-158.*
2. *Selection from the Complete Works of Swami Vivekanand, page 167-168.*

Swami Ji professes for implementation of Yogas in real life.

He said, to quote:

> "It is imperative that all these various Yogas should be carried out in practice; mere theories about them will not do any good. *First* we have to hear about them, then we have to think about them. We have to reason the thoughts out, impress them on our minds, and we have to meditate on them, realise them, until at last they become our whole life. No longer will religion remain a bundle of ideas or theories, nor an intellectual assent; it will enter into our very-self. By means of intellectual assent we may today subscribe to many foolish things, and change our minds altogether tomorrow. But true religion never changes. Religion is realisation; not talk, nor doctrine, nor theories, however beautiful they may be. It is being and becoming, not hearing or acknowledging; it is the whole soul becoming changed into what it believes. That is religion.[1]"

In spite of rich heritage and possessing wonderful intelligence, why India turned into pieces, is a question which stimulated Swami Vivekanand from time to time. He attributed it to the variety of causes. Religious orthodoxy is one of them. A religious orthodoxy, hypocrisy among Hindu priests and preachers found to be the part of such causes. While writing a letter to a brother Monk, Brahmananda in 1895, Swami Ji observed, to quote:

> "..The whole truth about austerities and spiritual exercises is, in a nutshell, that I am pure and all the rest are impure! A beastly, demoniac, hellish religion this! ...Monks and Sannyasins and Brahmins of a certain type have thrown the country into ruin. Intent all the while on theft and wickedness, these pose as preachers of religion! They will take gifts from the people and at the same time cry, 'Don't touch me!

1. *Selection from the Complete Works of Swami Vivekanand, page 173-174.*

And what great things they have been doing!—'If a potato happens to touch a brinjal, how long will the universe last before it is deluged?' 'If they do not apply earth a dozen times to clean their hands, will fourteen generations of ancestors go to hell, or twenty-four?'—For intricate problems like these they have been finding out scientific explanations for the last two thousand years—while one-fourth of the people are starving.

..A dreadful slough is in front of you— take care; many fall into it and die. The slough is this, that the present religion of the Hindus is not in the Vedas, nor in the Puranas, nor in Bhakti, nor in Mukti— religion has entered into the cooking pot. The present religion of the Hindus is neither the path of knowledge, nor that of reason—it is 'Don't-touchism', 'Don't touch me!', 'Don't touch me!'—that exhausts its description. See that you do not lose your lives in this dire irreligion of 'Don't-touchism'. Must the teaching *atmavat sarvabhuteshu* [in the original letter, in Sanskrit script] –'Looking upon all beings as you own-self—be confined to books about? How will they grant salvation who cannot feed a hungry mouth with a crumb of bread? How will those who become impure at the mere breath of others purify others? Don't-touchism is a form of mental disease. Beware!

...The poor, the downtrodden, the ignorant, let these be your God."[1]

Swami Vivekanand was critical of spending million of rupees on temples benefiting handful of persons. He said to quote:

"If you want any good to come, just throw your ceremonials overbroad and worship the Living God, the Man-God—every being that wears a human form—God in His universal as well as individual aspect. The universal aspect of God means this world,

1. *In a letter dated 28-12-1893 to Haripad Mitra.*

> and worshipping it means serving it—this indeed is work, not indulging in ceremonials. Neither is it work to cogitate as to whether the rice-plate should be placed in front of the God for ten minutes or for half an hour—that is called lunacy. Millions of rupees have been spent only that the temple-doors at Varanasi or Vrindaban may play at opening and shutting all day-long! Now the Lord is having his toilet, now He is taking His meals, now He is busy on something else we know nor what...And all this, while the Living God is dying for want of food, for want of education.!
>
> ...Spread ideas—go from village to village, from door to door—then only there will be real work.
>
> ...It is only by doing good to others that one attains to one's own good, and it is by leading others to Bhakti and Mukti that one attains them oneself. Take that up, forget your own-self for it, be mad over the idea. As Shri Ramakrishna used to love you, as I love you, come, love the world like that. Bring all together."[1]

Shri Ramkrishna while pointing out towards Swami Vivekanand, once said to quote:

> "He seems to be walking with an unsheathed sword in his hand."

The prophecy of Ramkrishna, proved to be true, when Swami Vivekanand started to fight with orthodoxy and hypocrisy in Hindu religion ignoring the cause of masses, downtrodden and weaker section of society.

At Chicago, taking note of concerns of widow remarriage on 24-1-1894, Swami Vivekanand wrote to his followers in Madras, to quote:

> "Remember that the nation lives in the cottage. But, *alas*! Nobody ever did anything for them. Our modern reformers are very busy about widow remarriage. Of course, I am a sympathizer in every

1. Letter dated 27-10-1894 to Alasinga Perumal.

reform, but the fate of a nation does not depend upon the number of husbands their widows get, but upon the *condition of the masses.* Can you raise them? Can you give them back their lost individually without making them lose their innate spiritual strength? Can you become an occidental of occidentals in your spirit of equality, freedom, work, and energy, and at the same time a Hindu to the very backbone in religious culture and instincts? This is to be done, and *we will do it.*"

While speaking for universal equality or Vasudhaiv Kutumbakam, the basic tenets of Hinduism, of early Indian society, Swami Ji has shown his deep concern, to the present state of affair, where peoples are divided between caste, creed and religion. Feeling pain and hurt in the letter dated 20-8-1893 to Alasinga Perumal, Swami Ji said, to quote:

> "No religion on earth preaches the dignity of humanity in such a lofty strain as Hinduism, and no religion on earth treads upon the necks of the poor and the low in such a fashion as Hinduism."

We have brains, but no hands. We have the doctrine of Vedanta, but we have not the power to reduce it into practice. In our books there is the doctrine of universal equality, but in work we make great distinctions. It was in India that unselfish and disinterested work of the most exalted type was preached, but in practice we are awfully cruel, awfully heartless—unable to think of anything besides our own mass-of-flesh bodies."

Thus, we find that Swami Vivekanand on the one hand spoke with regard to Indian inheritance with passion and praise in authoritative manner and on the other hand, he also deprecated the anomalies orthodoxy, hypocrisy and selfishness and sectional divisions gradually originated in Hindu or Indian masses in due course of time. He persuaded to follow the old ancient Indian culture rising above the personal vested interest based on cast, creed or religion. He said, to quote:

> "In religion lies the vitality of India, and so long as the Hindu race do not forget the great inheritance of their forefathers, there is no power on earth to destroy them.
>
> Nowadays everybody blames those who constantly look back to their past. It is said that so much looking back to the past is the cause of all India's woes. To me, on the contrary, it seems that the opposite is true. So long as they forgot the past, the Hindu nation remained in a state of stupor; and as soon as they have begun to look into their past, there is on every side a fresh manifestation of life. It is out of this past that the future has to be moulded, this past will become the future.
>
> The more, therefore, the Hindus study the past, the more glories will be their future, and whoever tries to bring the past to the door of every one is a great benefactor to his nation. The degeneration of India came nor because the laws and customs of the ancients were bad, but because they were not allowed to be carried to their legitimate conclusions."[1]

Thus, it is obvious that for Swami Vivekanand, religion means, knowledge, practice of a system to serve masses, poors and downtrodden, remove inequality from the society to ensure everyone achieves his or her goal in accordance to capacity, competence with equal opportunity in every walks of life. God exists in poor and downtrodden and not in the deities of temples. Any religion which cannot wipe the tears of poor and widow, shall not be a true religion. On 27-10-1894, Swami Vivekanand wrote to Alasinga Perumal, to quote:

> "I do not believe in a God or religion which cannot wipe the widow's tears or bring a piece of bread to the orphan's mouth. However sublime be the theories, however well-spun may be the

1. Reply to Raja Ajit Singh of Khatri, 1894.

> philosophy—I do not call it religion so long as it is confined to books and dogmas. The eye is in the forehead and not in the back. More onward and carry into practice that which you are very proud to call your religion, and God bless you!

Judiciary, bureaucracy and legislatures should take lessons from views of Swami Vivekanand while discharging their duties. Secularism and socialism are the part and parcel of philosophy of Swami Vivekanand which shall guide and enlight the mankind for ages to come.

Equality, of job and equal distribution of public resources, all seems to be the part and parcel of the philosophy of Swami Vivekanand. That is why, on 24-1-1894, he wrote from Chicago, to quote:

> "My whole ambition in life is to set in motion a machinery which will bring noble ideas to the door of everybody, and then let men and women settle their own fate. Let them know what our forefathers as well as other nations have thought on the most momentous questions of life. Let them see specially what others are doing now, and then decide. We are to put the chemicals together, the crystallization will be done by nature according to her laws."

Swami Ji was eager to organise the young generation in every city to train them to serve India bringing comfort, morality, religious education to the doors of most downtrodden with a zeal to do or die. Let us inculcate such zeal in our young generation and to serve the nation with same spirit which Swami Ji professed in his life time.

An article published in the newspaper, 'Hindu', on 18-1-2011, written by Sri R.K. Raghvan, Former Director of Central Bureau of Investigation under the title, "The losing battle against corruption", shows how people feel helpless themselves with the increasing trend of corruption in public life. 'Times of India', dated 20-1-2011 while publishing a comparative increasing trend of corruption in the country, reveals that according to report of Transparency

International, India was at the serial No. 71 in the year 2001 and now, in the year 2010, it has ranked at the serial No. 87 in the world with regard to corruption.

I recollect the scandals of 60s under Mundhra & PL 480 scams were in lacs or few crores. Now, it reached to Rs. 1,76,000 crores and odd. India has become heaven for corrupt people.

Billions of Indian rupees lie in Swiss and Foreign banks which shall be sufficient to meet the requirement of the country for decades to come. All the three wings of the Government are charged for indulgence in corrupt practice. The fourth state *i.e.,* media, is also charged for paid news. People seem to be helpless and so judiciary seems to be helpless to some extent. The corruption and casteism has crept in the blood of our system. The 35% of the population of the country is illiterate and according to reports, the earning of almost 20% peoples is less than Rs. 20 per day. It is a matter of deep concern, when free education and free medical treatment has almost been stopped. Now, the discussion is not of corrupt peoples but the peoples who are "most corrupt". Persons who are concerned with the system, speak with regard to peoples who are most corrupt and not the corrupt persons holding public offices. Who is to be blamed? What is the remedy? The solution lies in the philosophy of Swami Vivekanand who said, to quote:—

> "Hidden under the ashes of apparent death, the fire of our national life is yet smouldering and that the life of this nation is religion, its language religion, and its idea religion; and your politics, society, municipality, plague-prevention work, and famine-relief work—all these things will be done as they have been done all along here, *viz.* only through religion; otherwise all your frantic yelling and bewailing will end in nothing, my friend! (V. 461)
>
> In every country, the means is the same after all, that is, whatever only a handful of powerful men dictate becomes the *fait accompli,* the rest of the men only follow like a flock of sheep, that's all. I have seen

your Parliament, your Senate, your vote, majority, ballot; it is the same thing everywhere, my friend. ...Now the question is this, who are these men of power in India?—they who are giants in religion. It is they who lead our society; and it is they again who change our social laws and usages when necessity demands; and we listen to them silently and do what they command. (V. 461)

First of all, try to understand this: Does man makes laws, or do laws make man? Does man make money, or does money make man? Does man make name and fame, or name and fame make man? Be a man first, my friend, and you will see how all those things and the rest will follow of themselves after you. Give up that hateful malice, that dog-like bickering and barking at one another, and take your stand on good purpose, right means, righteous courage, and be brave. When you are born a man, leave some indelible mark behind you. (V. 462)

Let New India arise—out of the peasants' cottage grasping the plough; out of the huts of the fisherman, the cobbler, and the sweeper. Let her spring from the grocer's shop, from beside the oven of the fritterseller. Let her emanate from the factory, from marts, and from markets. Let her emerge from groves and forests, from hills and mountains. (V. 327)

I consider that the great national sin is the neglect of the masses, and that is one of the causes of our downfall. No amount of politics would be of any avail until the masses in India are once more well educated, well fed, and well cared for. They pay for our education, they build our temples, but in return they get kicks. They are practically our slaves. If we want to regenerate India, we must work form them. (V. 222-23)

While showing deep concern to the material based development of the country Swami Ji said, to quote:—

> "But mark you, if you give up that spirituality, leaving it aside to go after the materializing civilization of the West, the result will be that in three generations you will be as extinct race; because the backbone of the nation will be broken, the foundation upon which the national edifice has been built will be undermined, and the result will be annihilation all round. (III. 153)
>
> We now mostly need the ideal of a hero with the tremendous spirit of *rajas* thrilling through his veins from head to foot—the hero who will dare and die to know the Truth—the hero whose armour is renunciation, whose sword is wisdom.
>
> We want now the spirit of the brave warrior in the battlefield of life, and not of the wooing lover who looks upon life as a pleasure-garden! (V. 388)[1]"

The philosophy of Vedanta was transmitted to Bhagwan Ram Krishna by his Guru, a great saint and Vedanti Swami Tota Puri and Bhagwan Ram Krishna taught it to his most beloved disciple Swami Vivekanand. Hence it shall be necessary to speak few words about Vedant as envisaged or professed by Swami Vivekanand.

The philosophy of Vedanta virtually comprises of various sects existing in India. There have been various interpretation of Vedanta, which have been progressive beginning with the dualistic of Dvaita and ending with the non-dualistic or Advaita. The word, Advaita literally means the end of the Vedas—the Vedas being the scriptures of the Hindus. Vedanta system comprises of systems of Hindu philosophy having one common psychology *i.e.*, psychology of Sankhya system. Sankhya psychology is very much like the psychology of the Nyaya and Vaisheshika systems, differing only in minor particulars.

All the Vedantists agree on three points. They believe in God, in the Vedas as revealed, and in cycles. According to Sankhya philosophy, the reactive state of the mind called

---

1. *Vivekanand – His Call to the Nation.*

Buddhi or intellect is the outcome, the change, or a certain manifestation of the Mahat or Cosmic Mind. The Mahat becomes changed into vibrating thought; and that becomes in one part changed into the organs, and in the other part into the fine particles of matter. Out of the combination of all these, the whole of this universe is produced. However, Vedantists reject the Sankhya ideas of soul and nature. They claim that between them, there is huge gulf to be bridged over. On the one hand the Sankhya system comes to nature, and then, at once it has to jump over to the other side and come to the soul, which is entirely separate from nature. How can these different colours, as the Sankhya calls them, be able to act on that soul which by its nature is colourless? Every dualistic Vedantist admit that the Atman or God is not only the efficient cause of this universe, but also the material cause. But the Advait Vedantists *i.e.*, non-dualistics, reject the theory of soul and having nearly the whole range of Upnishads in their favour build their philosophy entirely upon them. Upnishad says, "Just as by the knowledge of one lump of clay we have the knowledge of all the clay in the universe, so what is that, knowing which we know everything in the universe? The ideas of the Vedantists is to generalise the whole universe into one—that something which is really the whole of this universe. And they claim that the whole universe is one, that it is one being manifesting itself in all these various forms. They admit that what the Sankhya calls nature, exists, but say that nature is God. It is this Being, the Sat, which has become converted into all this—the universe, man, soul, and everything that exists. Mind and Mahat are but the manifestations of that one Sat.

Ignorance or Maya, as it is called, is the cause of all this phenomenon—the Absolute, the Unchangeable, being taken as this manifested universe. This Maya is not absolute zero, nor non-existence. It is defined as neither existence nor non-existence. It is not existence, because that can be said only of the Absolute, the Unchangeable, and in this sense Maya is non-existence. Again, it cannot be said it is non-existence, for if it were, it would never produce the phenomenon.

Thus, in case we follow the Vedanta philosophy, there shall be oneness in the world without any differentiation of caste, creed or religion or sect. There will be no hatred, animosity and conflict.

Swami Vivekanand said, to quote:

> "Behind everything the same divinity is existing, and out of this comes the basis of morality. Do not injure another. Love every one as your own-self, because the whole universe is one. In injuring another, I am injuring myself; in loving another, I am loving myself. From this also springs that principle of Advaita morality which has been summed up in one word—self-abnegation. The Advaitist says, this little personalised self is the cause of all my misery. This individualised self, which makes me different from all other beings, brings hatred and jealousy and misery, struggles and all other evils. And when this idea has been got rid of, all struggle will cease, all misery vanish.
>
> So this is to be given up. We must always hold ourselves ready, even to give up our lives for the lowest beings. When a man has become ready even to give up his life for a little insect, he has reached the perfection which the Advaitist wants to attain; and as that moment when he has become thus ready, the veil of ignorance falls away from him, and he will feel his own nature. Even in this life, he will feel that he is one with the universe. For a time, as it were, the whole of this phenomenal world will disappear for him, and he will realise what he is. But so long as the Karma of this body remains, he will have to live. This state, when the veil has vanished and yet the body remains for some time, is what the Vedantists call the Jivanmukti, the living freedom."

In one word, the ideal of Vedanta is to know man as he really is and this is its message, that if you cannot worship your brother, man, the manifested God, how can you worship a God who is unmanifested?

Time has come, philosophy of Vedanta as propagated by Swami Vivekanand, should be included in the curriculum of schools and colleges to create peace and harmony in the society and to develop the country as professed by our forefathers, particularly Swami Vivekanand.

We may say how it shall be possible to follow the path of Vedanta. There should not be hesitation in mind to follow the right path. Once, we decide that there is oneness in whole universe and in case it is truth then as Advaitists say सत्यमेव जयते नानृतं। सत्येन पन्था विततो देवयान:—Truth alone triumphs, and not untruth. Through truth alone lies Devayana, the way to Gods."

Swami Ji said, good (people) live for others alone, the wise men should sacrifice himself for others. Swami Ji encouraged young generation saying तत् कुरु पौरुषम—(Manifest your manhood) to achieve destination. He said whole universe will lie to feet and it is the self alone the predominates and not matter. He said, Sri Ram Krishna's child does not look his personal good. They wish to do good to others even when at the point of death—उत्तिष्ठ जाग्रत्—Arise! Awake!

Country wants a Vivekanand of 21st Century with unsheathed sword in hand to serve the nation as the leader and to fulfill the vision of 19th Century's Vivekanand.

Really, Swami Vivekanand, is the soul of Indian masses and only way to solve the complex problem of not only the Indian society but the whole of the world is to follow Swami Vivekanand in personal as well as public life. Let us start and begin to live the way, Swami Vivekanand has shown to us.

Arise! Awake!, and stop not till the goal is reached.

Bibliography

Books Referred

1. *Word and Phrases, Permanent Edition, Vol. 39B*
2. *Espirit des Lois: Spirit of Laws, published in 1748*
3. *Religion, Caste and Politics in India by Christophe Jaffrelot*
4. *Parliamentary Sovereignty by Jeffrey Goldsworthy.*
5. *Pakistan a hard Country by Anatol Lievel*
6. *Human Development Report, 2011 prepared by Institute of Applied Manpower Research Planning Commission, Government of India, published by Oxford University*
7. *U.P. Human Development Report, 2003*
8. *Mahatma Gandhi Essays and Reflections by Sarvepalli Radha Krishnan*
9. *Service of the State, The IAS Reconsidered, autobiography by Bhaskar Ghose.*
10. *Inside story of Bibliography by IAS Officer Shri Radhey Shyam Agarwal*
11. *Bible*
12. *India from midnight to Millennium and Beyond by Shashi Tharoor*
13. *The Argumentative Indian by Amartya Sen*
14. *Brihad Aranyak Upnishad*
15. *Article 'India and the Constitution' delivered by Hon'ble Mr. Justice M. Katju, Judge of Hon'ble Supreme Court of India*
16. *Yajnawalkya Samhita.*
17. *Narad Samhita.*
18. *Mimansa Rule of Interpretation by Prof. K.L Sarkar*

19. *Legal and Constitutional History of India by Justice M. Rama Jois*
20. *India's legal System: Can it be saved? By Fali S. Nariman*
21. *Shatpath Brahman*
22. *Manu Samhita*
23. *Freedom as development by Amartya Sen*
24. *The Wonder that was India by A.L Basham*
25. *Rig Veda (Hyms)*
26. *Atharva Veda*
27. *Yajur Veda*
28. *Kautilya's Arthshastra*
29. *U.N. 2006 Development Report*
30. *The Discipline of Law by Lord Denning.*
31. *Geetanjali by Nobel Sri Ravindra Nath Tagore*
32. *Child Sexual Abuse and Exploitation in India by S.C. Singh*
33. *Women in India Trails and Triumphs by Shweta Prasad*
34. *Morality in Law by author of this book*
35. *Inside Terrorism by Bruce Hoffman*
36. *The Clash of Civilization and the remaking of world Order by Samuel P. Huntington*
37. *The Dhammapada*
38. *Hand Book of Global Research and Practice in Corruption edited by Adam Graycar and Russel G. Smith*
39. *Discipline of Law by Lord Denning*
40. *Wonder that was India by A.L. Basham*
41. *The Rediscovery of India by Meghnad Desai*
42. *Biography of Swami Vivekanand by Romain Rolland*
43. *Freedom at midnight by Dominique Lapierre and Larry Collins*
44. *Study on Child Abuse: India 2007 by Ministry of Women and Child Development, G.O.I.*
45. *Sane Sex Oder by Russian Laureate Pitirim Alaxendrovitch Soroken*

SUBJECT INDEX

W

•••